D1291966

# KNOWING
# THE UNKNOWN GOD

# KNOWING
# THE UNKNOWN GOD

*by*

WILLIAM J. HILL

*PHILOSOPHICAL LIBRARY*

*NEW YORK*

Printed in United States of America

# CONTENTS

# INTRODUCTION

"Rightly understood, the problem of God is not one problem among several others; it is the only problem there is."[1] The question is raised in entirely new terms today, and one significant way of posing it is to ask: what is the knowing act involved in seeking to approach God cognitively. Thus the God question quickly reduces itself to the epistemological consideration. Unavoidable in this question is the somewhat more precise one of the relationship prevailing between understanding itself and the ideas or concepts with which it is inseparably bound. Paul Tillich has put the same thing in a slightly distinct set of terms: "Historical forces determine the existence of the idea of God, not its essence; they determine its variable manifestations, not its invariable nature . . . the concept is dated, but not the fact that one is grasped by the idea."[2]

Neither does the event of revelation enable one to circumvent the difficulty, if anything it intensifies it, for revelation is not simply a message to be read but a meaning to be deciphered. The task is a hermeneutical one; revelation must needs be interpreted, which is to say one cannot avoid coming eventually to philosophical theology, and so to the epistemological problem.

The difficulty can be reduced to its simplest components as follows: all human knowledge is conceptual;[3] but a proper concept of God is an obvious impossibility;[4] therefore what value attaches to the ideas we do employ in speaking of God? If our ideas are creaturely, what meaning remains to them when they are transferred to the realm of the Divine? The question

i

is not what we intend to designate by these conceptions but rather what is the intelligibility within the objective content of these concepts; is there anything proper to God expressed in any way by the intelligible word? A careful consideration of St. Thomas' texts dealing with the phenomenon of naming God tends to suggest a larger dimension of "theological agnosticism" than has been acknowledged generally within the Catholic tradition;[5] the conviction grows that, even in the language of revelation and faith, God remains *conceptually* inapprehensible, and so ineffable. Confirming this is the plethora of notions by which historically God has been conceived: as Ideal Good (Plato); Unmoved First Mover (Aristotle); The One (Plotinus); Subsistent Being or Purely Actual Understanding (St. Thomas); Substance endowed with Thought and Extension (Spinoza); Absolute Spirit or Idea (Hegel); Ultimate Concern (Tillich); Process (Whitehead) — not to mention systems that deny validity to all such ideas (Kant); or that reject all human ideas of God as projections and illusions (Feuerbach).

Historically, the problem ranges from the "representational realism" that dominated Catholic thought from about two hundred years and fifty after St. Thomas, in which understanding is the very conceiving process itself (Chapter 1), to the "symbolic relativism" traditional within Protestantism and defended today with the use of Existential categories by Bultmann, Tillich, Ott, etc. (Chapter 2). The newer Catholic theologies have stressed an epistemological base that seeks to surmount the shortcomings of both; where these agree is perhaps only on the very general principle that whereas there need not be· a proper concept of every known object, still every reality available to man's intelligence, including God, can be known only in virtue of some concept, i.e., by way of the objective intelligible content of a concept. (Chapter 3). However, the conviction persists that an adequate solution demands a return to that perennial question of philosophy — the doctrine of analogy. What the following pages hope to build towards is a new, emerging understanding of analogy, inspired by contemporary interest in the phenomenon of language, but finding its roots in the work of St. Thomas; this will involve bypassing the quite distinct understanding of analogy within the so-called Thomistic tradition, dominated by the highly original work of Cajetan. (Chapter 4). There will remain then only an attempt to implement such a theory of knowing and naming God in certain fundamental conceptual areas (Chapters 5 and 6).

All of this will lend itself to an emphasis upon the developmental character of our knowing of God, which emphasis is the natural issue of a Critical Thomism. By the latter is meant a Thomism that recognizes the necessity of absorbing the critical problem introduced by Kant, if not his solution, and with it the focus upon subjectivity and temporality. This in turn sets the problem: to what extent can and should the categories of Existential and Analytical Philosophy be broadened out to include reference to God? Any effort at accomplishing this must avoid the serious misconstruing of God that can result from constricting him within a thought system that, for all its modernity, has limitations of its own — especially in the exclusive shift of focus to the plane of immanence. What is needed, and what the Christian theologian cannot neglect, is that negative yet wholly valid knowing of a God who remains unknown, whose transcendence eludes us and yet can be darkly surmised from within man's cognitive capabilities.

The task of the Christian thinker appears in Merleau-Ponty's wise observation that one must at once "remain faithful to what one has been (and) take up everything again from the beginning."[6] The leitmotif is continuity within a process of creative discovery. Hopefully, in the process, nothing will be lost, everything will be deepened. The renewed discovery of God for this age, then, may well begin with a deepened experience of God's inconceivability. And with this we may well find our way back from Heidegger's "Night (that) has fallen again on Reicheneau"; we may well begin to see again "the Light (that) has gone out of the West".[7]

# KNOWING

# THE UNKNOWN GOD

# CHAPTER ONE

## THEOLOGICAL CONCEPTUALISM I:
## REPRESENTATIONAL REALISM

### 1. Cajetan and the "Tradition"

What value attaches itself to the finite and human concepts we can alone employ in speaking of the Divine? Granting this simple problematic, a spontaneous starting place is the "Thomistic Tradition", so called, wherein an analytic probing into the process of conceptualization reached a high point of intricacy. At the threshold of that tradition, and dominating it throughout, is the figure of Cajetan (Thomas de Vio; 1468-1534). The two and a half centuries separating him from the death of St. Thomas were centuries during which the actual thought of the latter (as distinguished from the "tradition" of Thomism) struggled for recognition — first against the already established system of Peter Lombard, the new Augustinianism of people such as Durandus, the innovations of Scotus, and later, less successfully, against the gradual emergence of Nominalism. The most illustrious advocate of St. Thomas during this interval is Capreolus, and his efforts are directed towards an acceptance of St. Thomas, not an interpretation of his thought.

With Cajetan all of this changes, to some extent because of his own brilliance — his own resources of mind, especially in metaphysical considerations, very nearly matched those of St. Thomas himself. Also, he was foremost a commentator on

1

St. Thomas; this was the theological style from the Tridentine Era onward, giving way in time to theological compilations (e.g. that of Billuart), and gradually deteriorating into the manuals. The consequence was a shift in theological focus from the sources of Revelation to St. Thomas' own personal and unique synthesis. While this did amount to a displacement of theological endeavor — not nearly as radical as that of Scotus who, unlike Cajetan, does not initiate his theological work with Biblical commentaries — it explains to some degree the uniformity that marks Thomism from Cajetan's time down to the twentieth century; this is the period at least in which the "tradition" (as distinguished from the corpus of St. Thomas' own writing) becomes consolidated. For all its being a commentary, Cajetan's work was penetratingly original — unlike, say, that of Conrad of Cologne written at the same period. This raises the question as to what is of Thomas and what is of Cajetan. On the question of man's knowledge of God the crucial difference, if there is one, will appear most graphically in the doctrine on analogy. Procedurally, however, it will be simpler to consider: (1) the conceptual knowledge of God developed within the tradition dominated by Cajetan, then (2) the divergent position of those who see such awareness as fundamentally non-conceptual, and (3) finally to contrast them within the perspective of St. Thomas' explicit teaching on the focal question of analogy.

At least a fundamental identity has to be supposed between Cajetan's metaphysics of knowledge and that of St. Thomas. The noetics involved is basically a realism — willing to accept at face value the naïve and uncritical certitude man experiences of knowing *things*.[1] Obviously this presupposes a corresponding natural philosophy; one wherein man is a part of nature, a distinctly existing substance, an individual sharing an essence common to other men yet specifically distinct from and superior to that of other existent beings of nature. Individual existence is thus at once isolated yet in communion; the latter communion, however, while radicated in a common participation in being is actualized only in the exercise of those powers resident within the nature. Thus a basic subject-object dichotomy is accepted as given and irreducible. The self, in its distinctness, is capable of transcending its isolation by attaining to other realities *as objects*. This is possible only if other existents come to be in some fashion within the subject, first of all by way of cognition. On the intellective level this demands the "species", it being obviously impossible for the existent as such to enter the knower. Unavoidably, this poses a dilemma: whence does the species acquire any value of the real? Cajetan, following St. Thomas, opts at the very beginning for the insight that it must have such a value. Kant, nearly three centuries later, in an inverse option, contented himself with investigating the intelligibilities of such immanent objects in terms of the *a priori* constituting powers of the subject. Descartes, in separating body and spirit into parallel mechanisms, had begun the reversal; the severance of intellect from sense activity made it necessary to conclude that the object of the former was not reality but thought itself. The intellect's preoccupation then is with ideas, not things, and any extra-mental reality behind the phenomena can only be left unknown and merely postulated (Kant) or acknowledged on the basis of the Divine veracity (Descartes). It is highly significant that the scholasticism which might have had some influence on these two dominant figures in modern philosophy was one that had become highly essentialistic under the influence of Suarez, and more remotely, Scotus.[2] On the contemporary scene, Hüsserl, while avoiding any idealism as extreme as that of Descartes or Kant, is able to affirm the real object (as opposed to the ideal) only as it appears in consciousness, and must fall back upon his *epoché,* a suspension of judgment where the extra-mental as such is concerned.

This new and tempered emphasis upon subjectivity, upon inner structuring states of consciousness, is unquestionably the prevailing mood in contemporary philosophy and the directing influence in the new theological stances, Protestant and Catholic alike. For the latter, it is finding articulation (with obvious differences) in the writings of such theologians as Rahner, Schillebeeckx, and Lonergan. Where an admitted essentialism and conceptualism within Scholasticism is concerned, this is a welcome corrective. Nonetheless, it would be a disastrous oversimplification to neglect a more authentic Scholastic perspective. Its inspiration is Cajetan and it deserves a critical appraisal here. It does not merely reproduce St. Thomas' own teaching but goes beyond that as interpretative of it, yet it is *the* interpretation that consolidates itself into the "tradition". It avoids the extreme essentialism of the Suarezian School, yet Cajetan too was unavoidably a child of his own age. At the University of Padua, especially, he was engaged in polemic against an arising Averroism on one hand, represented by Pompanatius and Vernias, and the Scotism of Anthony Trombeta on the other. To what extent he was influenced by the truth-value of the very systems he reacted against and rejected remains an open question. Certainly, the position has its own inadequacies and leaves unanswered questions that are raised within the problematic that is now current; also the tradition has been subject to developments within itself, notably in recent times those of Maritain and Nicolas. In the question of man's conceptual grasp of God, however, it retains its identity as distinct from those new approaches inspired by the insights of Existential Phenomenology. The awareness of God delivered to man is different in the two approaches. Whether they be not merely alternatives but mutually opposed is a question whose solution can only arise out of a critical consideration of the merits of each.

## 2. The Process of Conceptualization

The approach to God in Thomistic epistemology begins not with any examination of the inner states of structuring consciousness, nor with a primal intuition of the self as consciousness — on the basis of which God can be affirmed. Rather, at the very outset of intellectual life the mind lays hold upon the real, thus eliminating the necessity for some sort of a farther projective act, one released from a prior state of cognitive immanence. Nonetheless since we are concerned with knowledge we are dealing with the existence of the real *within* the knower. This must not be construed as some sort of intuitionalism or the psycho-physicalism usually attributed to American Neo-Realism. Contemporary thought is indebted to E. Hüsserl for focusing attention on the *object* as distinct from the *thing*. The theory elaborated by Cajetan and others insists upon the basis for this distinction, scil., that the object is the limited dimension of intelligibility within the thing that the mind seizes upon and conceives within itself. This latter conception is the "intelligible species" which while *entitatively* itself a thing (i.e. a spiritual product of the intellect) is, in an entirely new order of being, i.e. *intentionally,* not a thing at all but is purely significative and expressive of some aspect of intelligibility within the original extra-mental thing.[3] The concept then cannot itself be directly known; only in attending reflexively to its own act of knowing does the mind discover the "species" as a component element in its awareness of the thing. In technical Scholastic terminology this is conveyed by the insistence that the species is a pure means or *quo* (i.e. as sign, it is not *instrumental* or known first of all in itself, but *formal* as a pure making known of the other) rather than a *quod*, i.e. an object. Implicit in this is an understanding of the distinction between the two kinds of species that go to make up the integral cognitive act — the *species impressa* and the *species expressa.* The impressed species or *species intelligibilis* belongs to the pre-conscious aspect of knowing; it is the product of the *intellectus agens,* an abstractive rather than cognitive power, despoiling the sense phantasm of its conditions of singularity, and rendering the nature involved intelligible rather than actually understood. Only with the expressed species does knowledge occur and it only then functions as a formal sign or a pure "quo". Cajetan makes a further revealing precision on the "expressed species", distinguishing between the *formal* and the *objective concept*.[4] It is the former that is purely representative, and so properly intentional; it is given birth to in the possible intellect and so is strictly designated the *concept*, or in more theological terms, the mental *word*. By contrast, the objective concept is that intelligibility within the real thing, which terminates the act of knowing; it is that which the formal concept represents and which it "intends". What is significant here is that the extra-mental *thing* and the known *object* (i.e. the objective concept) are not two distinct *quods;* they are one, but with a dual mode of existence, the object being the thing as it inexists the mind. By this is meant, of course, not the thing in its existential entirety — but that dimension of its being and intelligibility that the intellect seizes upon. This inexistence is, of course, "being" on an entirely new plane, intelligible rather than "real", intentional rather than entitative.[5]

The real significance of *esse intentionale* for the Scholastics lies in the fact that thereby intellection is seen not as action or operation but being. The known achieves another existence in the knower, which existence is that of the knower precisely as he has "become" intentionally (i.e., in intellective tendentiality) the thing. This is expressed in the insistence that intellection is not transient action ordered to the production of an effect, but immanent action whose *raison d'être* is rather the intrinsic perfecting of the subject; ultimately such knowledge is not reduced to the Aristotelian categories of action or passion, but that of quality. "To know" then is (in an order all its own) "to be"; to understand is to have as one's own the actuality of whatever is known. The correspondence then of understanding to intellect in act is that of *esse* to *ens in actu*. Obviously, this calls for some sort of form; and this is exactly the role of the "species". The intelligible species will place the intellect in first act; understanding itself then follows as the dynamic response of the possible intellect, vitally eliciting its second actuality; the consummation of the knowledge occurs in a final phase, a self-manifestive eruption or conception of the word or idea.

In this it can be seen that the production of the concept is not, formally speaking, the very understanding itself; the distinction between them is real, characterized by John of St. Thomas as of *res ad rem*.[6] Nevertheless the proferring of the latter does not occur in any action other than that of intellection itself. The expressing or conceiving is only a further modality, a spontaneous termination of the understanding. Ordinarily it is required, but even in cases where the particular knowledge is such as to render a word impossible, the intellect still tends inefficaciously toward such utterance.[7] As the normal term of the act of understanding, it achieves a "transformation" of the reality outside of the mind into a radically new state of actuality, so that the concept or mental word *is* that very thing *as known*. If in one sense the concept is a pure means of knowing, at the same time it is what is known, i.e. the very object. This view of knowledge is not then that of Lonergan and Schillebeeckx who (in different ways) tend to separate much more radically the process of conceptualization from that of understanding. Each of them, Lonergan more so than Schillebeeckx, pictures the emitting of the concept as more dependent upon subjective and inventive resources within the knower, a continual striving to express what one already "understands" preconceptually.[8]

### 3. Inadequacy of the Concept

In fairness to the traditional view of knowledge, the deficiency of the concept must be constantly kept in mind. Its perfection lies in its being manifestive of all that the knower seizes upon in the object. This is by no means to see it as expressive of all the intelligibilities inherent in the real existent. Thus, far from rendering the mind static, it orientates it toward the endlessly knowable real. It is this dynamic "tending" (from *intendens, intentionale*) process that initiates judgment and ratiocination as a further penetration into reality; it also explains the commonly experienced phenomenon of ideas that are surpassed and thus lost in the process of refinement, as well as illusory ideas and the occurrence of error.[9] Were the concepts exhaustive of what they signify, there would, of course, be no sciences as we now have them. The real retains a certain infinity of intelligibility (ultimately concealed in the mystery of existence), and so there is no question in authentic Scholasticism of a naïve essentialism that would suppose a kind of transfer of an essence, whole and entire, to within the knower. The concept is, in terminal act, only one of the inexhaustible intelligible determinations of the real.

Then, too, it needs to be borne in mind that for the most part the Scholastics were concerned with a description of the conceptual process at its initial and lowest level. Man's continuing encounter with reality proceeds out of a background of innumerable concepts already determining our cognitive life. These notions pre-determine the angle of intelligibility in proceeding to new concepts, so that every advance in understanding is necessarily partial, and possibly misleading. This is explainable in terms of the close inter-connectedness of concept and judgment, wherein the latter is not the mechanical putting together of two concepts but the spontaneous and vital consummation of every conceptual act. It is to this area that the work of Lonergan has so richly contributed — i.e. to the further building up cognitively of our vastly complex concepts.

### 4. The Concept as Possessing Value of the Real

The point, however, is that for Cajetan the concept, no matter in how deficient a way, was still significative and ex-

8

pressive of the real. This is to say that contrary to the position today of D. DePetter and E. Schillebeeckx,[10] he saw no problem in allowing to the concept in and of itself a value of the real. There was no need to appeal to a non-conceptual element, distinct from but paralleling the conceptual in knowledge. Clearly, this is going to raise a major question in our knowing of God, especially as mediated in Revelation and affirmed in faith.

The one major objection to this conceptual realism is the obviously abstract and universal character of the concept. Yet ultimately it is the very abstractive process as exercised upon the data of sensation that guarantees the realness of the cognition. Then, too, what is in question here is what Cajetan characterizes as a *formal* as opposed to a *total* abstraction;[11] it is an attempt to penetrate into what is most real, into the most intimate formality of a being rather than a separation of a common nature from its individual instances. J. H. Nicolas draws attention to a general tendency to confuse abstract knowledge with knowledge of the abstract, i.e. knowledge by way of a universal with knowledge of the universal.[12]

This emphasis upon the conceptual does nonetheless run the risk of a certain essentialism — a serious and not always unwarranted charge against Scholasticism and one moreover that is frequently brought of late against Cajetan himself.[13] The basis for this is the implication that what the intellect lays hold upon is only an essence, without any of the real determinations that are rooted in actual existence. As so isolated, the essence is of the ideal order, and it is this abstract quiddity alone that comes to expression in the concept, since real existence clearly eludes conceptualization.

It does seem true that an "essentialistic" metaphysics, owing its inspiration to Scotus and finding later expression in the system of Suarez, came into gradual ascendancy within Scholasticism,[14] but this is radically different from anything to be found in the more authentic Thomism of Cajetan and the tradition he dominates. Scotus was inclined to look upon being primarily in terms of essence. There was a tendency, while acknowledging existence as really distinct from essence, (as in Scotus' unique actual and formal distinction *"a parte rei"* — which was more than a conceptual distinction even with a foundation in reality and less than a real distinction of thing from thing) to actually conceive of it after the fashion of a form, and so as transposed into an "essence". The practical consequence of this was an ignoring of actual existence; especially since (among forms) it was deemed the least perfect of all perfections. Suarez goes so far as to give to created secondary causes the power of causing existence, and by contrast gives to essences the characteristics of eternity and immutability. The implication of this for epistemological theory is far-reaching, especially in exaggerating the intelligible content of the concept, rendering it initially all-sufficing, and thereby leaving little room for a view of knowledge as dynamic and ever progressive. Even more to the point here is the suggestion that the intellect's power of conceptualization is a mere reflection of abstract intelligibility that cannot as such encompass real existence. This is a far cry from Cajetan's explicit teaching that the distinctness of existence from essence is genuinely real (and not merely formal "a parte rei"); that *esse* is the greatest of all perfections, simply considered; and that God alone is its cause *per se primo,* i.e. in an absolutely exclusive sense.[15] He does, it is true, cast some doubt on his inclusion among those who acknowledge the primacy of existence by his adoption of the bewildering distinction between *esse essentiae* and *esse existentiae.*[16] Especially does this give pause if one interprets his favorite designation of existence as *"ultimate* actuality," as inferring that there is another *prior* source of actuality. Bañez took rather uncompromising exception to this, and insisted against Cajetan upon the contrary, scil., that existence was *first* actuality.[17] Some see in this a divisive moment in the Thomistic tradition, but a more benign interpretation of Cajetan is possible,[18] especially in the context of his entire thought, and against the background of such an explicit statement of St. Thomas as: "essence without existence is nothing" (*De Pot.*, q. 3, a. 5, ad 2$^{um}$) with which he was surely familiar. This is not to deny that Bañez may have seen more lucidly the mysterious and ineluctable character of existence and nuanced with greater precision his thought and language. What Cajetan means to emphasize is that no further actuality can possibly convene to a thing beyond that which renders it "outside its causes and outside nothing." He speaks of essence as having its own actuality somewhat like, inversely, he occasionally refers to existence as form; i.e. the essence *as existing* has its own determined grade of intelligibility, somewhat as *esse* when it actualizes an essence enjoys a causality that is reductively formal — in both cases the speech is analogical and (it would appear) only by an extrinsic attribution. Essence is not, in other words, pure potency but bespeaks an order to real existence whence all of its actuality (but not the determined limitation thereof) derives; only in virtue of this order can quidditative being be called "being" at all.

Cajetan further removes himself from an essentialistic position when he makes clear that the "being" which is enclosed in our *concept* is *esse ut significata* not *esse ut exercita*. Neither can be confused with essence, but especially the latter which eludes even the very mode in which the mind can conceptualize. This very truth, however, poses all over again the question as to how then the concept achieves any value of the real. Two solutions to this problem have emerged from within the tradition: (1) a primal intuitive grasp of being at the very origin of intellection, (2) a later explanation of this intuition in terms of the judgment.

### 5. The Intuition of Being as Primum Cognitum

Thomism, in its very origins, is a realism; i.e. its point of departure is at once an option for the reality of things and for the realism of knowledge. Two ontological presuppositions to knowledge are engaged here: 1) truth is a transcendental passion of being, which is to say that something is intelligible only on the

11

assumption that it "is," 2) every finite cognitive power necessarily proceeds from potency to act which means its initial object is the least determined, and itself the starting point for more perfect knowing. On these two premises rests the assumption that the first object delivered to the illuminative power of the intellect is being itself, in such fashion that it functions as the objective principle of all further cognitive progress. This is no denial of the fact that the notion of being is also the ultimate term of the intellect's dynamic orientation — the lucid, metaphysical penetration into the mystery of being in all its analogical comprehension and amplitude. For the Christian, man is destined to an inexhaustive vision of Him who is limitless Being. The primal encounter, however, is with being as utterly undifferentiated yet concealing within itself all the richness that is to come. This occurrence has to be in an act of the intellect that is totally simple and irreducible; as such it obviously precedes the more refined process of complex and intricate elaboration and construction that builds up the edifice of knowledge. Granting that the roots of intellection lie in the prior activity of sense, this demands that the original act has to possess the character of concreteness. The problem then is how this is possible for a faculty that cannot function other than abstractively and whose object is the universal. Cajetan himself cuts quickly to the core of the solution by insisting that the "being" in question is "being embodied in an essence able to be sensed,"[19] which John of St. Thomas further describes as being "entering into the very composition of the thing."[20] The being thus yielded is, then, concrete and actual; it is not yet explicitly recognized as transcendental or universal. There is a genuine abstractive process involved and the product is being as such (there is no question then of a mere awareness of the individual, with a consequent necessity of going from one singular to another). But the abstraction indigenous to the mind at this point is negative in kind, lacking the positiveness on the basis of which subsequent abstractions can be differentiated into formal and total.[21] All that is known, and in the vaguest possible way, is "something there" or "something existing" in an aware-

12

ness that expresses nothing more than simple opposition to nothingness. The child touching the hot stove not only senses a singular instance of heat from which it instinctively recoils, it also gains (at the very moment intelligence is engaged) a *concept* of "hotness" in which it is simultaneously made aware (through the "is-ness" of the heat which radicates its very knowability) of actual and concrete being; it now knows existence in its contrast to non-existence. Only later, and in a new act reflexively turning back to sensorial activity, is it known explicitly that this singular hot thing exists; as only much later is it possible to precise the actuality of *esse* from the quiddity or essence that it renders actual.

This phenomenon, which is nothing other than the very dawn of intelligence, answers to all the requirements for genuine intuition. Obviously its intuitional character is not to be confused with that proper to sensation where the sensible quality acts directly upon the receptive sense organ. What occurs here is possible only within the intellect's own vitally elicited inmanence. Sense intuition is in fact far less perfect since it attains only to an isolated formality — such as color or sound — and undergoes thereby a sort of extractive "abstraction" of its own. By contrast, the intellect's abstractive activity (which here is not a knowledge of the abstract but rather an abstractive knowledge of the concrete)[22] means that it avoids the limiting aspect in knowing only the singular; what it intuits is being itself of which the individual is but one restricted instance. Neither can this intuition be construed in a Kantian sense as an envisionment not of reality itself but of the intelligibilities inherent in immanent objects structured within consciousness. The intuitive character of this act then rests in its being an *immediate* grasp of what is *concretely actual*; it is an utterly simple and irreducible act anteceding all inferential or discursive activity. The Phenomenological reductions of E. Hüsserl are a very subtle investigation into the character of intellectual intuition; the insistence upon "a return to the real" coupled with an awareness of the primacy of the object (as opposed to the thing) offers much promise. It marks, none-

13

theless, an apparent point of departure from the Thomistic intuition of being in two noticeable respects: 1) *all* intellection is seen as intuitional and not merely the intellect's primal act, 2) the emphasis, by way of the *epoché*, is upon the pure object; i.e. the intelligible manifestations of the real within consciousness rather than the real itself now existing intelligibly within the mind. It is in this latter point, especially, that the two theories of cognition draw immeasurably closer at a new depth level, and that some *rapprochement* is at least not out of the question.

## 6. The Role of the Judgment

The above explanation is not, however, exhaustive — especially for the demands of philosophies that grow more and more critical in spirit. The reason is that this explanation contents itself with an analysis on the level of the first operation of the mind alone, the simple apprehension, which avowedly has only a preliminary function in the state of total cognitive awareness. Intellection is spontaneously consummated itself in the judgment, the cognitive act par excellence. This is St. Thomas' clear understanding,[23] and it seems to follow that the third act of the mind (ratiocination or the reasoning process) also is ordered to the judgment, in so far as it itself culminates in a further, more complex judgment. Cajetan and the other classical writers do not pursue the matter where the primitive intuition of being is concerned; it has rather been the contribution of modern thinkers within the perspective of the Thomistic tradition, notably J. Maritain[24] and J. H. Nicolas,[25] and in a distinct way, E. Gilson,[26] to explore the existential implications of the judgment. The point here, it should be noted, is not the clear precision of the formality of existence from that of the nature which exists, of *esse* or *actus essendi* from essence, which occurs within the science of metaphysics in the very refined elaboration of its own subject. St. Thomas designates the activity of the mind at this point as a "separation," whereas he reserves the simple term "abstraction" for what occurs in the first and second degrees of abstraction (proper to philosophy of nature and to mathematics);[27] and this is ground enough for perceiving that the abstraction proper to the metaphysician is a judgmental one. Long before the technical achievements proper to science, however, is the primordial intuition of being that stands at the very origin of every man's intellectual life; and the question of whether and how this involves the judgment.

An initial difficulty is that the judgment necessarily involves at least two concepts. Because of this, judgment is seemingly a posterior function, ordinarily after multiple acts of apprehension. But this is to picture the most perfect cognitive act as a sort of mechanistic juxtaposition of isolated elements, and is to fail to recognize the unity that characterizes the intellect in its various functions. In this initial intuition the apprehension and the judgment are closely intertwined in one integral vitality; the first spontaneously elongates itself into the second; the same spiritual energy released in the perception consummates itself in the judgment. The initial perception of an existent (sensorially but then intellectually) of itself awakens the judgmental process; in the latter there is affirmed the "being" that is first given implicitly in the prior, imperfect beginning of intellectual awareness. The reason is that the intellect in "becoming" something other than itself has to ratify for itself (within the depths of its own consciousness — though in a pre-conscious way) what has rendered this phenomenon possible, namely objective being. The intellect first awakens in a seizure from sense experience (which already recognizes in its own "blind" fashion the existence in the singular) of the quiddity which it perceives as "something" rather than nothing, i.e. implicitly and vaguely as having "being".

The illuminative power of the intellect, however, is such that it recognizes that the specific quiddity is not its very "is-ness", that the latter is a further dimension of intelligibility which, since it is not an essence, cannot be enclosed in a concept and so is rather affirmed in an existential judgment: something is or exists.[28] Every judgment is thus an affirmation of existence, expressed through the use of the copula "is" (or its denial in the proposition "is not"). Obedient to its own laws, the intellect must differentiate, at least notionally, between what constitutes the subject and predicate of the affirmation. In this primal act, the predicate "is" enjoys a quasi-formal role apropos of the subject, i.e., it expresses the actuality of the latter; its spontaneity as the normal complement of the apprehension is such as to preserve its intuitional character.

It is somewhat misleading, and does away with the intuitional aspect of this initial judgment, to describe it as is sometimes done as a process of "replacing" essences in real existence. Neither should it be confused with the reflexive judgment that comes later, wherein the intellect considers its own act of knowing and critically attempts to evaluate its own correspondence with reality. There is a kind of reflection involved here too, but it is one that is entirely spontaneous which, without demanding any new concept, merely affirms that the extra-mental order is indeed as it knows it to be.[29]

What one should not fail to grasp here is the implication of the intellect's spirituality in making this judgment; it is not "conceiving" of existence, but is "becoming" or entering into the order of real existence in its own vital and immanent way. It is in other words "laying hold" of existence *in actu exercito*; only subsequently will it render this into the concept "being", which Cajetan explains is expressive of existence only *in actu signato*.[30] In this it is evident how the judgment terminates in the mental word, expressive of the subject as having the predicate. Also since the faculty involved here transcends sense, being is not just recognized as a mere empirical fact but is encountered, implicitly, in all its analogical amplitude as an irreducible source of understanding of which every other idea is a variant. Because of this, intellect never relinquishes its root involvement in the real and existent order. The Scholastics saw no need for an appeal to an extra-cognitive principle which would project man out onto the real order.

What fundamentally characterizes this noetic then is that it originates with an intuitive contact with the real. So much so,

16

that the knower can gain awareness of himself only subsequent to a grasp of the real, and by turning his own knowing activity itself into a secondary, reflex object of cognition. It is precisely here, by a sort of Copernican revolution, that contemporary epistemologies inverse the process. Schillebeeckx, taking over a basic phenomenological insight that knowledge is "being, present to itself" and understanding in this light St. Thomas' teaching that the human soul is naturally present to itself,[31] founds his system upon an initial intuition of the self.[32] Lonergan, to take but one more example at random, is rather disposed to explain that man is originally aware of himself not reflexively and as an object, but precisely as a subject.[33]

## 7. The Concept of God

Basic to this traditional noetic is the primacy of the concept; the contention in effect that all human intellection is conceptual and not merely in the sense that other possible, non-conceptual modes of thought are always accompanied by a concept. Even the primal intuition of being as judgmental means a judgment that lives within a conceptualizing process; one that simultaneously is born from and terminates in the *verbum mentale*. The knowledge of God, whether natural or supernatural, is no exception to this; in the latter case, God can address us only in and through those realities which make up the human world we inhabit. Since the beginnings of our contact with the Divine are cognitive, this cannot occur otherwise than through the medium of concepts that directly represent the creaturely. Obviously, this cannot be without a major re-working and a vast extenuation of such ideas; the key to which the Scholastics discovered in the doctrine of analogy. The question (which continues to re-address itself) is what is the value, objectively considered, of these concepts so transformed — especially in light of the fact that it is man himself who so alters them. Granting the undeniable distinction between the Divine Reality in itself and in man's knowledge, it still has

17

to be asked whether the latter be in any sense a formal likeness of God, or only a symbolic designation of him. The question is deepened somewhat when God is seen within a Christian context, i.e. within the perspective of the mystery of a God who, remaining transcendent and ineffable, is at the same time a self-disclosing God.

Within the "tradition" (Thomistic as opposed to Thomist —to borrow a distinction of Lonergan's)[34] perhaps no single work has had the influence enjoyed by Cajetan's magisterial study on analogy, *De Nominum Analogia*.[35] The searching studies of such moderns as S. Ramirez[36] and T. L. Penido,[37] who stand within that tradition, are only explorations in depth of the implications of what Cajetan achieved, and serve to illustrate the enduring vitality of his work. There remains the underlying question, of course, as to how authentically Cajetan interprets St. Thomas' own mind; there have always been those whose interpretation differs, and it would not seem an exaggeration to say that most contemporary Thomists have made a radical break with the school of Cajetan on this problem of analogy. A definitive answer to this question is simply unattainable at present, and any attempt to so resolve it would be an under-estimation of the speculative task involved. Still, there has to be an answer — and a tentative exploration that does not pretend to close the question off can further somewhat the groping towards it. This will call for a consideration of the two apparently conflicting solutions on their own merits, and then (if any progress is to be attempted) the making of an option — which may well be less an outright rejection of one answer than the striking of a position somewhere on the spectrum that joins as well as separates the two available solutions.

Cajetan's position, put very briefly, is that the relationship between God and the world he has created is such that there are certain perfections discernible in the latter which, being known, deliver to the mind an authentic knowledge of what God is. The perfections in question are only those convertible with being itself (unity, truth, goodness, etc.) or with the higher modes of being

18

(life, intelligence etc.) which are never found as actually existing in the finite world save as immersed in imperfection. Nonetheless, the mind can, in its abstractive powers, liberate the pure concept which, so denuded of all sources of limitation, actually serves to signify the Divine Being. The signifying (and naming) here is not merely *negative* (as when it is denied of God that He is imperfection) nor merely *relative* (when he is acknowledged as the cause of creaturely perfections). This is an instance of designating God in his very substance (*substantialiter*) and not in a merely metaphorical way either; the pure perfections in question are in God intrinsically and in a way that retains a resemblance with the finite order that is formal, though only analogically so.[38] This is Cajetan's well known analogy of proper proportionality — allowing that certain proportions within finite being are themselves proportionate to proportions within God (for example, the finite relation of knowledge to love mirrors an analogous relation between divine knowledge and love realized on a totally different level of being).[39]

It would be a complete misunderstanding of what Cajetan means to suppose that the Divine Reality is enclosed within a finite concept; that man is capable of a knowledge here that is at once proper and quidditative. This, quite simply, would be beatifying vision, inaccessible to man prior to that eschatological state which will be his final supernatural destiny. Such vision, moreover, is completely outside of the kind of knowledge that is mediated by a concept. The force of one of Cajetan's arguments here is revealing: the objective concept is the known reality (not as a thing but as an object) with an intentional existence within the knower; but the identity of essence and existence in God is such as to render any duality of existence (i.e. entitative and intentional) incomprehensible; thus a quidditative conception of God is an utter impossibility.[40] Man's conceptual endowment is such that he can know the very quiddity of God (in one way by reason, in a higher fashion by faith) but not quidditatively.[41] Even so, these concepts remain always defective; the intelligible values they express are truly in God and formally so, thus they give authentic knowledge but they cannot express the divine mode (or better the absence of all modality) that such perfections exercise as Divine. The use of analogy includes an awareness that God is this perfection, but *eminently* so. Cajetan explicitly cautions against failing to see that this eminence cannot be objectively enclosed within the analogical concept.[42] Occasionally, dismissals of this traditional teaching as "essentialistic" betray an unconcern for the necessary nuances, and the impression is given that it implicitly allows for finite concepts that represent the Divine perfections in themselves.[43] But whereas this is overly facile, it does call attention to the deep, underlying problem. There are not a few theological writers basing themselves on Cajetan who do not so easily escape this charge; a lack of accuracy in language and balanced presentation does oftentimes betray a perhaps unwitting rationalism.[44] But even when the correctives are supplied the genuine difficulty remains: do these concepts actually convey to the human intelligence what God is formally? Granting that the knowledge they give is true and authentic, is it then enough to say that they are inadequate and deficient? Or is the "otherness" of God so total that the most that the intellect gains is a sort of perspective on God that leaves him as an unknown and ineffable term of such cognitive tending?

The enduring merit of the Scholastic noetic is that it safeguarded the authenticity of conceptual knowing; the objective value of the concept saved knowledge from deteriorating into something merely functional and pragmatic. Where God was concerned this meant no floundering on the shoals of agnosticism; it meant that the Christian experience of faith in historical Revelation did not dissolve into subjectivism. But the over-all effect was a lessening of the sense of mystery; a tendency to project, in overly direct fashion, the contents of human conceptions upon the Divine Reality. The deficiency was the negative one of forgetting the disproportion between the uncreated and the participated perfection discoverable in the created transcendentals. What Cajetan understood was that the analogical concept

20

(i.e. properly speaking or in the instance of proper proportionality) was *one;* it included actually even if confusedly, all of its differences. The unity was then only proportionate, but this meant it could be applied in one way (predicamentally) to all creatures and in another way (transcendentally) to Divine Being. The unity is only analogical, *not univocal,* obviously, and so there is no question of an abstract, essential perfection predicated of God and creatures in ways that only differ in degree. The Scholasticism that remained faithful to the inspiration of St. Thomas cannot be accused of the kind of "essentialism" that developed within the Scotist school. For Cajetan's followers, the analogical concept remained bound to the finite order in a way that the Scotistic transcendental did not; they did not entertain the possibility of transcendental ideas possessing unity in virtue of abstracting *perfectly* from actual conditions of finitude and infinity and applicable equally to creature and God, with the one difference of the attribution being finite in the first instance and infinite in the second. Rather, the transcendentality in Cajetan's concept resulted from an imperfect abstractive process that enabled the idea to embrace qualitative differences expressive of the various gradations within *created* being. Cajetan never says that such a concept contains the "difference", so to speak, of God.[45] Rather, because the concept is not limited to any one of its finite realizations it has an intrinsic expandability that justifies its *application* to God, where it expressly bespeaks the *ratio* of perfection involved and implies but leaves unexpressed the Divine mode (or modelessness) of that perfection. What renders this possible is the mind's capacity to distinguish the *ratio significata* from the *modus significandi;* the latter is always finite and creaturely and never carried over in predicating the *ipsa perfectio* of God. But in what sense, then, is this pure, unlimited perfection that remains expressive of the Divine? The manner in which God is, e.g. wisdom, is nowise within the ambit of human knowing; when he is said to be such infinitely — this is not a difference of degree but of kind. Is there any sense then in which the perfection objectified in

21

the concept can be said to be "of God" or is it merely expressive of the entire range of finite realizations of that perfection which thus can be "projected" onto the Divine order to give a purely functional (but not thereby untrue) orientation to knowledge? In short, does the analogical concept represent only created perfection but in abstraction from any particular condition of limitation, or does it also represent somehow the infinite perfection of God? If the divine *modus essendi* can nowise be represented within the concept, where then does the formal correspondence between idea and Divine Reality lie? At the very least, surely, in a certain directedness in the concept's playing at least a referential role. But the Scholastic tradition does seem to say more than this; it does appear to establish a conceptualist climate that estimates overly much the objective contents of the concept. Cajetan's own language tends to overstress the formal correspondence of the concept with the extramental quiddity in its entire intelligibility.[46] And it can be honestly asked if an essentialistic viewpoint has been entirely avoided in the extrapolation of a divine perfection from a creaturely *ratio significata* simply separated from its *modus significandi*. There is at least reason for caution in the procedure that seeks the objective intelligibility of the Divine prerogatives in isolation from their actuality as Divine, this suggests a tendency to forget that perfections in God *are* their very actuality, and that the incomprehensibility of the latter redounds on the former.

## 8.  Some Theological Instances

The acknowledgement of God's existence, for example, can easily be made to affirm more than is possible. In the statement "God is" (whether demonstrated by reason or acknowledged in faith) more is intended surely than the logical correctness of the proposition. The "is" is not the grammatical copula alone, but expresses the attribution to God of real being. But the only being that the mind can conceive of is created existence, and this must be its starting point, its sole principle of cognitive reference. Otherwise one is saying that the finite concept contains within itself (representationally), no matter how imperfectly, the Divine Being. The better Scholastic writers were aware of the impropriety of this, and continually remind themselves of the perspective of *via negationis* and have frequent recourse to such qualifying phrases as *eminenter*. One is left with the impression that the epistemological system within which they work lacks the tools to express positively what is surmised negatively. Thus it is a question of making positive statements and then adding the qualifying phrase. It is understandable that in lesser hands the latter are oftentimes not sufficiently attended to, with the eventual consequence of misapprehension especially in the non-academic sphere.

Another case in point is the synthesizing of the various attributes of God by recourse to the Divine Simplicity. It is said that God is truth, goodness, wisdom, justice, mercy, etc., and that these are one because of God's simplicity and yet remain *virtually* distinct. But it is fair to ask if this is not, in effect, to unwittingly introduce into infinite being something proper to finite being. These formalities are *really* distinct in man's world; this distinction in turn founds a purely formal or conceptual distinction in man's knowing of these. But the distinction remains one between concepts. It continues to characterize our *knowing* of God, but the projection of such distinctions onto God himself even as merely virtual appears somewhat misleading. The foundation for the mind's distinguishing is only in the created order, and to find intrinsic grounds for the distinction in the Divine eminence might well be to attempt what in fact lies beyond the powers of the intellect. To insist that the distinction is only virtual is not enough to avoid the suggestion that the complex inter-relationships between one formality and another is also verifiable in God.[47] The question is: does this amount to projecting a limitation of human knowing onto the Divine Reality?

But it is the effort to render into concept the mystery of God as Three-Personal that most graphically testifies to the limits of the analogical concept. If St. Thomas' efforts here were the most successful of all, even they do not escape the disadvantage of separating the treatment of the Trinity from that of the One God, with a noticeable shift in methodological emphasis and the implication that God merely "happens to be" Triune, thus necessitating an extrinsic imposition of *"De Deo Trino"* upon the mystery of *"De Deo Uno."* The inadequacy here is less a failure of St. Thomas' synthesis than an indication of the depths to the mystery itself, but it illustrates the unavoidable shortcomings of any conceptual system.[48] In the lesser hands of a disciple — John of St. Thomas — this conceptual framework lends itself to making no mention whatsoever of the specifically Trinitarian dimension to God's creative activity.[49] The magnitude of the task is exemplified in Karl Rahner's attempt to study at once the Trinity as encountered within the economy of salvation and the Trinity in Itself; a bold and much needed theological achievement but not one without inherent difficulties of its own.[50] The older approach began with a clear assertion of God's Oneness as certain and real and then "superimposed" mutual relations of real opposition which while articulating logically the mystery of the Trinity did not quite do justice to the import of seeing the Subsistent Relations as Personalities. Once again there was no denial of the latter; on the contrary, there was never lacking a verbal and conceptual affirmation of it. The question is whether it was possible to adequately affirm this in an exclusively conceptual fashion or whether recourse is not demanded to a level other than that proper to concepts. Of late, there have been instances of a reversal of this perspective, i.e. the distinction of Persons which is conceptually represented as real but merely relative has so stressed the former truth that it is not at all clear that the unity and simplicity of God remain intact.[51] A reflection of the above divisiveness is had in the continuing controversies over the Indwelling of the Trinity within man: the former approach does not always clearly indicate how its explanations go beyond mere "appropriation"; the latter suffers the contrary defect of not adequately safeguarding God's inviolate Oneness.[52] Allied closely with this is the companion problem of viewing sanctifying grace too exclusively in its created aspect as an infused quality or in its uncreated aspect as an experience (less conceptualizable obviously) of God as present.

Another instance of a possible corrective in Trinitarian theology is pointed out by Martelet[53] in his attempt to justify the contention of Greillmeier and Rahner that *only* the Second Person of the Trinity could have become Incarnate. The Scholastic approach dealing with the *concept* of Divine Person argued for the possibility of each or all Persons so assuming human nature.[54] But the historical Incarnation seems to convey a further truth, not necessarily included in the developed concept of Subsistent Relation, that only the Verbum, by a hypostatic characteristic proper to himself, could be the enfleshed Revealer. If this be granted, the question is not of the need for a dialectical movement from a highly abstract concept to one grounded more concretely in events of salvation history (this can be readily admitted) but of recourse to a knowing that is itself non-conceptual, or is at least the extra conceptual use of concepts.

## 9. Re-focus of the Question and Summary

There is a possibility that the above observations may have displaced somewhat the exact problematic here. Its scope is actually very narrow and not to be confused with allied questions whose investigation would be far more ambitious — such as resolving the tension between a knowledge by way of faith and the reflective knowledge of theology; or within the latter context, between a purely formal knowledge proper to science — speculative, abstract and systematic in kind, and a concrete experiential knowledge with overtones that are personalistic and historical. What is in focus here is a difficulty that lies beneath the conflicting claims of a personalist-essentialist approach in theology; it is not precisely the problem between directly seeking God in himself as he transcends the world or turning rather to the *oikonomia* and discovering the self-disclosing God immanent to the world.[55] All of the above are varied ways of posing a problem in theological methodology — that of the tension between an intellectualist *system* on one hand and an experiential salvation-history concern on the other. In both cases, however, concepts are involved — though in the latter the inadequacy of such ideas is more strongly felt. The more modest effort here focuses precisely on these concepts, and asks what is the objective cognitive value of these in light of the fact that they do not express the Divine *modus essendi* and yet are said to express what God is formally. Do such concepts which, as analogical (in a mode of proper proportionality) are proportionately one, contain and express a proportion to God or not?

What the above reflections yield is an appreciation of the achievement represented by what is best in the Thomistic tradition. Its rejection out of hand, and the attempt to theologize seriously without dependence upon it is overly facile and undeserved. Its positive values lie in an insistence upon the realistic character to human knowing, a quality not lost when the mind turns itself towards God. The basis for this is the intentionality or tendential aspect to intellection; an "intending" moreover that is cognitive and thus objective in kind, avoiding thereby any need to fall back upon projective acts of a noncognitive character. The basis for all this is the concept, and in dependence upon it, the judgment; i.e., the spiritual power of the intellect to conceive within itself what is less a replica of reality than reality itself as rendered intelligible (not in potency only but now *in actu*).[56] Because Revelation, whose very possibility lies in the above understanding of man's intellectuality, is humanly orientated, man's grasp of it is conceptual, i.e. he encounters God in and through his own finite ideas even when the latter are occasioned by faith. The experiential immediacy of this Revelation, occurring as it does only within history, is no bypassing of the need for the concept. Nor can man, in the in-

26

terests of truth, violate the *objective* perspective upon the Divine delivered to him in his own immanent objects of knowing.

This is not to say, indeed it is to deny, that man has a concept of any Divine perfection as it is in itself; here the tradition is faithful to St. Thomas' insistence that God is known only *mediately* through a concept that immediately represents what is creaturely.[57] As a consequence, the affirmation of faith terminates not at the proposition but at the Divine Reality.[58] However God himself terminates the intellect's belief *only through the conceptual elements* which make up the enunciation; anything more than this is vision.[59]

In this, there is no explicit teaching that knowledge is *merely* conceptual, only that it is never without a conceptual aspect. Nonetheless, there is no development of other possible non-conceptual dimensions to knowing, with the one exception of the influence of affectivity, understood as a knowing by way of connaturality, but for the most part limited to mystical knowledge under the operation of the Gifts of the Holy Spirit. To this extent, in the over-valuing of the concept and the neglect of other factors, the teaching of the tradition can be categorized as a "limited conceptualism." Epistemologically, one of its profoundest insights was the identity of object, i.e. the oneness of the intelligible real and the objective concept (as distinguished from both the extra-mental thing and the concept as entitatively an accidental product of the intellect). But this unavoidably gave rise to the tendency to forget, at least in practice, the partial and negative character of such conceptions. The two moments of *intelligere* (actual understanding) and *dicere* (issuance into mental word) were so brought together that nothing was given to the former that did not find expression in the latter. In an age that had not yet been brought to an awareness of the historicity of man, the result was a neglect of the experiential and the empirical (not in the narrow sense of directly involving the sensorial order); of what was contingent and non-necessary, with an almost exclusive emphasis upon the formal and the notional in cognition. This was especially so in the further synthesizing activity of intellect, emphasizing the scientific and logical structuring at some cost to the complex, varied, and dynamic processes involved.

Where God is concerned, the Scholastic endeavor after St. Thomas located itself too exclusively within the perspective arising from the objective contents of concepts. The loftier concepts (i.e. those expressing perfections of the transcendental order) while not encompassing the Divine *modus essendi* were nonetheless looked upon as representing, however deficiently, formalities proper to God — these Divine intelligibilities were expressed *in the very concept,* only proportionately it is true, yet properly and not merely metaphorically so.

The question is whether this does not bestow upon the concept an intelligible content where God is concerned, that it cannot have. There is surely some concept of God — He cannot be humanly known otherwise. But does that concept "represent" Him (in virtue of proportions intrinsic to the concept) or does it merely "designate" Him in a totally referential manner? The inconveniences inherent in choosing the prior solution have already been touched upon; they are hardly to be wondered at in the face of a question that will always elude full human solution. The alternative, representing one of the more creative efforts in contemporary Catholic thought, brings to the fore a whole different set of objections. The resolution may lie beyond the concept itself in a further knowing act that retains an analogical character; a dynamic of analogy that goes beyond the imperfect abstractive act. The Thomistic tradition should however be judged by what is best in it; of upmost importance will be the balancing and shading of judgment required. What remains of enduring value in the tradition is its insistence upon taking the very signification of the concept seriously, so that any employment of analogy as a projective act cannot be seen as reducing the concept to a mere symbol or as only functional and of subjective value. Rather the cognitive value of analogy is one deriving from the objective contents of the concept. J. B. Metz has suggested in a provocative essay [60] that the Christian

28

truth which escaped the Hellenic mind was the revelation that God was nowise to be discovered within the context of nature. This seemingly could reduce analogy to man's creativity as symbol-maker, to what Cajetan meant by analogy of *improper* proportionality, i.e. metaphor. The question this leaves us with is whether it then be possible to bridge, even with Divine Revelation, the hiatus between the realm of human concepts and that inaccessible realm which God inhabits.

# CHAPTER TWO

## THEOLOGICAL CONCEPTUALISM II:
## SYMBOLIC RELATIVISM

On the whole, the modern religious mind seems inclined to take pause before the conceptual clarity and explicitness that the Medievals sought in their cognitive approach to God. The stress upon the empirical origins of all man's knowledge gives rise to the tendency to see God's transcendence of the world in a reverential way that lends itself to greater hesitancy. The consequence in religious history, by and large, is a predominance of a sort of "religious agnosticism" before the mystery of God — an instinct that prefers to leave the Divine in a veil of mystery, in a "cloud of unknowing." The more constant tendency has been to at least mitigate if not negate the cognitive value of the human concept in the approach to God. In fact, the theological project of the Middle Ages was developed somewhat in counterbalance to this "agnostic" spirit, not only within Christianity but even outside of it, as e.g., in the thought of the Moslem Avicenna and the Jewish Rabbi Moses Maimonides. Within Christianity the difference appears sharpest in the disinclination of Reformational theology to concede to the finite concept anything like the representational power that Scholastic analogy had allowed. Contemporary Protestantism has not only remained faithful to this original instinct but has made strong attempts to refine and consolidate that epistemological stance.

31

# 1. Moses Maimonides

In Maimonides,[1] it is the negative character of man's knowing that is stressed, to the extent that he represents less a *theologia negativa* than a *theologia negationis*. God inhabits regions so remote from anything that man has access to that all the latter can do is to continuously deny to God the limitations of the creaturely. He, too, was a man of his times; an age in which anthropomorphic notions of God had gained an alarming currency; among some Jewish writers this had gone as far as picturing God as corporeal.[2] Against this, Maimonides extols the negating power of human speech about God; our knowing is an acknowledged unknowing.[3] He did affirm the causal nexus between God and world, but this could not be used to think that God bore any similitude or formal correspondence to the perfections he caused, even those that could be ideally freed of all limitation. The causal relationship merely rendered man aware of his origin from and total dependence upon Him who remained unknown. The assertions of the prophets, gathered together in the Jewish religious literature, occasioned only a minor qualification of this negativity. There, God lent his approval to man's historical conduct as this exemplified, not God himself but God's *activity* within the world of man. What was revealed and grasped in human imagery and language were created effects of God's providence. When he intervened into human history, God's effects bore some resemblance to e.g., those of the man who was wise and good.[4] This is similar to what Cajetan understood as metaphorical predication, which he categorized as analogy of *improper* proportionality.[5] But this is the only point at which Maimonides' teaching will allow anything other than merely negative assertions. Underlying this agnostic approach is a basic univocity. If the concept has only a univocal manner of signifying, it obviously cannot designate the Divine in any positive way, except as used metaphorically. The language of Revelation abounds with such poetic imagery, and it is possessed of a religious efficacy uniquely its own. What it calls

32

into play is a human creativity rooted in the imagination as the latter subserves the intelligence. It delivers to the mind sudden (and usually astonishing) illumination about God as He occupies a zone of darkness above the contents of those concepts which will not admit of being employed in this symbolic role. Implicit in this awareness, is the realization that God is indeed not what the image represents at all; it is the very disproportion that occasions the mind's delight. The perspective on mystery that is achieved is entirely from a human vantage-point, one that is graphic because originating from the sensed order. The clue to identity here constantly eludes one, and releases a curiosity that impels towards the unknown; it becomes an intuitive groping from the image towards what one subconsciously recognizes as beyond objectification. The Scholastic tradition, of course, made room for this, but insisted at the same time, against Maimonides, on another category of concepts whose significative power was proper rather than metaphorical, intellective and rational rather than imaginative.

The epistemological stance assumed by Maimonides could only culminate in a form of nominalism, in an ultimate refusal to acknowledge the real existence in God of any attributes whatsoever. After all, if the contents of our conceptions cannot be transferred to God, then he cannot be understood as really possessing (even in the mode of simplicity) the multiple aspects of intelligibility represented within such human ideas. Assertions about God were thus in final analysis assertions about the Unknown. Theological discourse then, for all its variety and complexity, is only a vast system of tautological statements.[6]

## 2.  A. D. Sertillanges

It is a long span, both chronologically and intellectually, from the Twelfth Century rabbi to a Twentieth Century French Dominican priest. Nevertheless, this is what was achieved in the thought of the influential and highly esteemed Father Sertillanges, who was not at all hesitant to expressly identify his own thinking with that of Maimonides and Avicenna.[7] The occurrence is vivid testimony to the enduring attractiveness of Christian "agnosticism". Sertillanges' position did provoke a positive and rather devastating criticism within Thomistic circles;[8] and his contention that he was reflecting the mind of St. Thomas himself is not at all credible. It has been pointed out in a recent study that a chronological reading of St. Thomas indicates a gradual tendency to judge the position of Avicenna and Maimonides with greater and greater severity.[9] Making much of St. Thomas' remark about God remaining *quasi ignoto*,[10] Sertillanges limits the sphere of human intelligence to the Aristotelian predicaments, so that man attains God merely as the Cause of that order. Parallel with this initial limitation is an understanding of the mind's abstractive and/or synthesizing power as achieving what is, in effect, a concept of being as a genus with the corresponding univocity this implies. From here, there is no alternative but to insist that God is nowise reducible to that category, save as transcendent Cause, neither knowable nor nameable from that category. What we do know, then, is not Divine "Being" itself but the network of relationships we bear towards him.[11] To what extremes this leads, he himself declares: "We do not know God *in any way, in any thing, in any degree*".[12] Even in the basic affirmation that "God is", the predicate is nowise to be understood as referring to real being; it is only the "copula", and can with quite as much truthfulness be said of that which we know does not have actual existence.[13]

### 3. Modernism

Perhaps the high-water mark within Catholicism of the tendency to distrust and devalue the conceptual side to the act of belief was reached in the early twentieth century during what came to be known as the Modernist Crisis.[14] This controversy, which in both France and Britain threatened to eliminate entirely the objective character of belief, was resolved only with papal intervention and the condemnations of the Decree *Lamentabile* and the Encyclical *Pascendi* in 1907.[15] The ferment was such that disciplinary action was probably unavoidable, though the intemperate language of the condemnations was lamentable and did impede any intellectual clarification of the underlying problem and thus defer theological progress. Alfred Loisy[16] (1857-1940) and George Tyrrell[17] (1861-1909), the two major advocates of the movement, represented rather distinct approaches — the former historical and exegetical, the latter more in terms of a philosophy of subjectivism. The focus of the controversy was now less narrowly epistemological and conducted in the broader, less scientific perspective of the entire faith-experience of the Christian, especially concerning Divine Revelation. Generally speaking, the scientific spirit of the Enlightenment and the Nineteenth Century, with a prevailing philosophic rationalism had occasioned some Christian discontent with dogmatic formulae. In Germany, a Protestant solution had emerged in the Pietism of Schleiermacher (1768-1834) and Ritschl (1822-1889), and eventually with Harnack (1850-1930) in the Liberal movement. The Catholic situation offered a parallel to this, at least in sharing a basic anti-metaphysical attitude and in giving new emphasis to the human, the emotive, the subjectively-experienced, the relative. Thus at the very beginning, a separation was made between the faith-experience itself and the subsequent attempts to render that life-phenomenon into mental construct. Once the conceptualizing process was divorced from the "prophetic" experience of Revelation, it was not at all difficult to give to the former only a relative value: the hiatus between the two was such that the explanatory function of the concept was never adequate to the inexpressible experience within religious consciousness. Loisy, logically enough, extended this to the Scriptural language and imagery, and focused the act of faith not on the truth-statements of such literature but on

35

an inner intuition of one's personal relationship with God which then issued into whatever words were at hand to serve such subjective impulses of the heart. Dogmatic statements are thus culturally conditioned to the point where they can be no more than transitory. The perdurance of the Scriptures is understandable because of the normative role played by the primitive experience and its lingual expression in the case of the New Testament due to the privileged character of that experience arising from personal association with Christ. What is *not* involved here is any noetic value to the concepts and propositions themselves; they are merely variable expressions, whose objective element is limited and largely directional, of a non-communicable impression.[18] Tyrrell described them as ultimately barren and dispensable. As totally human in origin such conceptions could not lay claim to any Divine confirmation; and as playing a purely interpretative role there was no possible objective verification of them, no non-subjective realities against which they could be measured. Such a non-intellective notion of faith obviously demanded dogmatic evolution, not in belief itself but in all its intellectual expressions, as superstructures that overlay faith. The development was thus heterogeneous with only the barest minimum of objective, cognitive directedness. The identity of God in this system necessarily pales; He is a presence mysteriously experienced, but what He is eludes any human capacity; He is felt but not known. The concepts and words we do fall back upon for the sake of human communication are so fallible and tentative that there is always the danger of a sort of speculative "idolatry". Images and metaphors were far more congenial to the Modernist temper, insofar as their use implicitly acknowledged the subjectivism and relativism indigenous to that outlook.

#### 4.  Karl Barth

It is from within the Reformational tradition, however, that this devaluation of the concepts of faith — that is, the capacity of such concepts to give a *proper* knowledge of God by way of their objective significative power — has been most effectively refined in positive and original ways. In fact, the whole Modernist venture appears somewhat pale and unsubstantial against the liberal currents within Protestantism that precede it in point of time. This merely indicates how indigenous it is to the Protestant spirit to distrust the abstract, speculative, formal aspect to man's noetic groping towards the Divine. There has been little compromise with the reaction against Scholasticism that attended the birth of Protestantism; at the same time the necessity to ground the noetic aspect of faith in some philosophic outlook, if not system, has led to theological ventures first within a Kantian or Hegelian perspective and now since Kierkegaard's time in the congenial climate of Existentialism. Karl Barth's clear and vehement disavowal of any philosophic substructure is only the refusal to accept the limitations of a *closed system;* his own monumental achievement testifies in its coherence and consistency to certain initial and dominant intellectual options, especially concerning the nature of man, that are implicitly philosophical. Rudolf Bultmann, on the other hand, who is generally considered to have won the battle for the German universities against Barth, is undeniably indebted to the *Sein und Zeit* phase of Heidegger, his former associate at the University of Marburg.[19]

Barth rejects the *analogia entis* out of hand,[20] substituting in its stead what he calls the *analogia gratiae,* something radically different from analogy in any of its traditional meanings. His every effort is directed towards safeguarding the total transcendence of God; to this end he insists upon an absolute inaccessibility of God from any human or created point of departure. The horizons of man's cognitive life do not reach beyond what is this-worldly and within the ambit of human existence.[21] His noetic representations are not of God, either properly or improperly, thus there is simply no possibility of expanding or transforming even our loftiest conceptions to where they make contact with the divine realm, for the latter breaks continuity with the creaturely. Tillich's religious symbol is then purely a human invention, and if it serves some human need, it does not give man access to God. In his well-known dismissal of analogy and "natural theology" (in strong terms, yet from a perspective that is quite narrow).[22] Barth readily allows the validity of the whole process *in its own order*. He grants that the term of such knowing may even be designated "God" and "Creator". What is unthinkable is that this mental construct should in any sense be confused with the living God who is as totally other from this "abstraction" as from any other idea.[23] This unqualified rejection of analogy is only possible if the analogical concept be understood as somehow properly representative of both God and creature, i.e., that God be somehow circumscribed within the concept; and this is exactly Barth's misunderstanding of classical analogy.[24]

So stressed is the hiatus, qualitatively infinite, between God and world, that the question arises as to whether or not language of any sort be possible where God is concerned. Barth's solution is direct and simple. It rests upon the coping stone of his thought as a theology of the Word of God, a theology focused upon Revelation as dialectical. If man cannot speak of the invisible God, God can nonetheless speak of himself.[25] This divine revelatory speech, moreover, is in man's own words, but God gives to those words a meaning they cannot have in themselves, a meaning that continues to remain inaccessible to man even after the occurrence of Revelation, one that can not be approached humanly even from inspired Scripture itself. Revelation occurs only in the existential moment of belief as a divine initiative. In his Revelation act, God "requisitions", as it were, human language, but the meaning now is a transforming, even a contesting one.[26] Only the former or proper meaning of the words is open to man and he cannot bridge his way from them to what God means. The concepts of faith are adequate expressions but only for God; man in utilizing these is not designating God at all, not even symbolically, not even when such conceptions and images are derived from the

Bible; he is merely representing realities proportionate to his own creatureliness. It is quite other with God's "requisition" of this speech; at this moment God discloses himself in ways that are not only proper but adequate. Thus it comes about that what man looks upon as mere metaphors are not such at all in God's employment of them! The meaning in faith of saying that God has "face, eyes, mouth, ears, nose, back," etc., that He undergoes "wrath, pain, pleasure, remembrance, forgetting," etc.; these are no more to be taken figuratively or as similes than is God's appropriation of Fatherhood and Sonship.[27] This explains why Barth can urge a continuing proclamation of the literal contents of the Bible, against Tillich who expressly discourages this endeavor — not because the objective contents of such preaching is directly significant of divine mysteries, but only because such preaching may afford the occasion of God's breaking through in Revelation. In Catholic circles, at least, this has understandably led to the charge of "theological occasionalism".[28]

What Barth envisions here at any rate, is a replacement of, or perhaps better, an assumption of, the *analogia entis* by his *analogia fidei* or *analogia gratiae;* every word of man dissolves before the Word of God.[29] But it is difficult to see how this is not an instance of pure equivocation, wherein a single set of words has totally unrelated meanings; when Barth acknowledges that the *analogia gratiae* calls for a partial correspondence (otherwise we would be denying the gift of God) he means a correspondence that is total on one side (God's) and nonexistent on the other (man's).[30] In Revelation, our words and God's are then identical; outside Revelation our words can only falsify the Divine.

The insuperable problem here is the break in the circuit; the dichotomy between the Word of God and any human language, including that of the believer. "In the *analogia fidei* God knows us, but we do not know God".[31] Man's very faith-response seems voided of all intellectual or objectively cognitive elements.[32] In John MacQuarrie's words "something is missing".[33] The leap does occur but there is no reasonable explanation offered. Frederick Ferré, by way of characterizing the theological stance of T.F. Torrance — a position indebted to and markedly similar to Barth's — writes of a "logic of obedience",[34] and this may well be the most that Barth can offer. It is a fair question to ask whether or not this be theologically satisfactory; whether or not it be too depreciatory in a Calvinist spirit of the powers of man's intelligence as the image of God; whether or not it be a retreat from the real theological challenge into a sort of "fideism", for the sake of a much needed caution about neglecting the alterity of God.


## 5. Emil Brunner

Emil Brunner is generally looked upon as carrying the discussion a step closer to its situation in Catholic theology, which makes a word on him appropriate at this point. His distinctiveness among Protestant theologians lies in his willingness to grant something to the analogy of being. This enables him to look upon creation as a primal revelation. Paradoxically, however, this analogical structure to real being cannot play a cognitive role; analogy is not an instrument of human knowing and speaking about the Divine and so Brunner is quite as irrevocably set against natural theology as any of his coreligionists.[35] At the bottom of this radical differentiation between the analogous character of being on one hand, and any resultant accessibility to man of an analogical knowledge of God on the other, is the sinful corruption of man. A basic intellectual pride or autonomy of reason blinds man to both Revelations of God — the primal revelation in creation, and the redemptive Revelation in Christ. The believer, who is unable to take the first step towards God, can surrender to God's initiative undertaken in Christ and thereby undergo a justifying *metanoia*. Then and only then is he able to open himself to the primal revelation inherent in the structures of the world.

Without the conversion in faith man retains only a radical possibility of knowing God naturally, which "does not actually take effect".[36] The temptation to use reason in this autonomous way, apart from faith, is nothing less than idolatrous. At the very beginning Brunner posits an irreconcilable separation (suggestive of Pascal) between the Judaic-Christian God of Abraham, Isaac, and Jacob and the so-called God of reason. The latter is not an imperfect knowledge of the one true God but an insurmountable obstacle to any contact with the living God of Revelation.[37] It is the fruit of speculation, which is the enemy of faith; it is an absolute and abstract idea, Platonic rather than Christian, which at the very most is "only the shadow of the Reality of God cast onto rational thought."[38] What has to be noted here is Brunner's very narrow understanding of the arena in which "autonomous" reason can function. Its powerlessness resides finally in the fact that it refuses the initiative to God and takes things entirely into its own hands. Brunner denies that the *logos* structure of finite reality can in actual fact mediate God to man, and that the endowment of man with reason is God's making possible such an inchoative revelation. When he defends this denial in saying that sin has rendered it *de facto* impossible — the question might then arise as to how one is to know that what appears to be a natural knowing is not indeed actually accomplished under grace. But Brunner's understanding of revelation is in fact limited to the explicit occurrence of Christian Revelation, and thus he can avoid the question. He does not see rational speculation as an approach to the true God; the only possibility for the latter is Revelation. This does not mean, however, any literalist interpretation of Biblical literature.[39] Rather, Revelation, though its source is not man's reason, actually occurs within man's reason as its subject,[40] so that, *under faith,* a knowledge by way of analogy does come into play. Brunner thus makes room for at least a qualified intellectual dimension to faith; as illuminating the intelligence of man it enables reason to grasp the intelligibilities inherent in the finite order from God. He does not

41

deny the reasonableness of faith but only insists upon a one-directedness, the movement is always *from* faith *to* insight into creation. The question then is: how does analogy function under Revelation? Not in reaching from creation to God: "the *logos* of reason is not the Verbum Dei."[41]

Brunner makes much of a distinction between the nature of God and his attributes; the former is God in himself, the latter is the nature of God "as it works itself out and is made known to us in view of the world which has been created by him."[42] Thus the Revelation of God puts us in possession of two sets of ideas signifying him. The first, designating him in himself, are largely negative in content; he is "Wholly Other", free from and nowise conditioned by the world, wholly self-sufficient. The second conveys a more positive knowledge, but of God only as he relates himself to this world — both by way of grace and by way of nature. In effect then, these latter concepts represent directly the worldly order, an order whose relationship to the Godly order is fundamentally one of incommensurability. God himself cannot be conceptualized or grasped in logical categories. Reason is only a tool for mastery of the world; its concepts represent objects of that world. It is also true that reason is receiver of the Word, and under that Word can then make further use of its concepts once God has taken the initiative, thus here is some radical continuity between God and the world. But that continuity is totally subsidiary to a predominating discontinuity. Thus the occurrence of Revelation does not so much assume the ideas of rational man into its higher expression of truth as it violates or contradicts them. Since Revelation is neither verbal nor conceptual, the human or worldly expression of it must use a language that is impersonal, whether objective or subjective, rather than personal.[43] Thus all speech about God is necessarily paradoxical; its dialectical character means the posing of the contradiction.[44] The affirmation that God is the author of law means at the same time that, in his mercy, he is the destroyer of law — thus the dialectic of law and Gospel.[45] He is known, in this "analogical" way, as holiness (which Brunner understands to mean wrath), but that is also to say that he is love — the contradiction of holiness. His eternity means that He is not temporal, i.e., nowise dependent upon created time, and simultaneously that he freely enters into the context of our time.[46] In short, Brunner's insistence that there is not a conflict between reason and faith is achieved only at the cost of a devaluation of reason in its service to faih. The contents of the concepts of which the believer makes analogical use, merely signify what is objective and worldly, what is not God. They "point" towards God only in negating and contradicting what objective cognitive value they contain. Brunner's contribution beyond Barth is to allow that some vestige of man's having been the image of God previous to sin remains within human reason. What remains of that image, however, is only its structural form; its contents have been emptied out and are now supplied solely from faith.

## 6. Dietrich Bonhoeffer

Some approximation to Barth and Brunner comes to the surface out of a distinct Protestant tradition in the work of Dietrich Bonhoeffer. At first sight, this is surprising in light of the latter's "religionless Christianity" which, in locating God and his Revelation within the structures of the secular, appears to stand over against Barth's uncompromising insistence upon Transcendence. But this is to forget Bonhoeffer's early tutelage under Barth, and especially his crucial commitment to the latter's theology of Revelation, a decision which effected Bonhoeffer's definite break with the older liberal and modernist theologians at Berlin — especially H. Holl, R. Seeberg, E. Troeltsch, and A. von Harnack.[47] At any rate, he unquestionably shares with Barth, an anti-philosophical and anti-metaphysical attitude that puts him somewhat at a remove from such Protestant thinkers as Tillich, Brunner, Bultmann, and Heinrich Ott. As with Barth, there is clear evidence on one hand of a distrust of the abstract, of the formal constructs of the conceptualizing intelligence; and on the other hand, an acceptance of Biblical language and imagery, and even of the Conciliar language with which the primitive Church sought to express its belief.

At least two original elements appear in Bonhoeffer's thinking here. The first is his own emphasis upon a self-negating power to the concepts used in faith. The words and ideas of religious speech tend indigenously to cancel each other out. The clue lies in the only question which Bonhoeffer will allow to be raised, scil., *"who is* God and Christ?"* What the religious spirit seeks is a personal identity which will not admit of being rendered into categories. *"What"* or *"how"* they (God and Christ) are, is not answerable because of the objectifying categories that the question seeks, and which are not available. There is a normal inclination to seek for concepts as vehicles of expression, and this is valid as long as one keeps uppermost in mind the falsity of such notions if carried beyond their negating power. What Bonhoeffer means here is most clearly illustrated in his early Christological theology: a statement about Christ is allowable "only if it is qualified and supported by its contradictory opposite."[48] This he sees as the achievement of the Chalcedonian definition which acknowledges that "Christ is God" only if that statement be limited and cancelled out by its opposite "Christ is man". In effect, this is to say that the definition of Chalcedon, expressing the mystery who is Christ in terms of a duality of natures within a unity of person, carries no *positive* intelligibility; it rather says that Christ is *not* whatever he is literally represented as being in such formulae.[49] The Council makes use of such concepts for the very reason of showing their unsuitableness. It is misleading to conceive of Christ as if he were simply God, and quite as untoward to consider him as merely man. Bonhoeffer's own distaste for logical subtlety has here played him false, precluding any metaphysical penetration into the deeper implications of "hypostasis," and causing him to interpret as contradiction

44

what Chalcedon intended as only the distinctness prevailing between the two natures in Christ.

Secondly, Bonhoeffer stresses a non-cognitive element in the encounter with God in Christ. This encounter occurs above all on the boundary-situations of human existence, or as Bonhoeffer prefers to say in the very center of life, where ultimate questions are forced upon him.[50] It is here above all that a breakup of the natural order of things takes place, including the habitual context of man's acquired and thus objectified thinking. If an Existential inspiration be denied here, at least Bonhoeffer's Lutheran heritage comes to the fore.

It is in the paradoxical experience of a God humiliated and hidden in Christ that one is enabled in faith to surpass conceptual truth. The unknowableness of God is carried further for he comes to us *incognito,* in the guise of humanity which conceals more than it sacramentalizes. In this way, God "takes hold" of our lives in ways that are personal and non-objective; it is not the *Deus in se* that concerns Bonhoeffer but the *Deus pro nobis,* i.e., not so much the Christ who presents to us the human face of God as the Christ who is "the man for others".

It has been pointed out in a recent exhaustive study of Bonhoeffer that the focus and fundamental interpretative principle of his entire theology is Christological.[51] This emphasis, however, is against the background of an absent God. It is Christ, as the "presence in absence, or absence in presence" of God,[52] that allows us to "drive God out of life"; it is He who gives us to understand that "we must live as men who manage our lives without God".[53] For Bonhoeffer, unlike the American "God is Dead" theologians, this is not a rejection of the reality of God but rather of the ideas of God that have prevailed until now. Seen in this perspective, Bonhoeffer's "non-religious interpretation of Biblical concepts" takes him far from Karl Barth, but betrays a shared point of departure with the latter. What needs to be asked is whether it be possible to develop a "this-worldly Transcendence", in any meaningful theological fashion, without recourse to objective, conceptual categories.

If it be impossible to speak of divine attributes in analogical concepts (even symbolically), and if the reality of Christ contradicts all our human categories in their analogical reach, what is left apart from an incommunicable mystical experience or a nebulous fideism?

## 7. Rudolf Bultmann

Rudolf Bultmann, of course, deserves a word here, most of all because his theological system readily acknowledges, in contrast to Barth especially, the need for philosophical concepts in the attempt to decipher the message of Revelation.[54] At the same time, his theology, in common with that of the other Protestant thinkers reflected on above, is one that gives dominant place to a non-verbal Revelation, a Revelation that is so strongly nuanced as a personal, non-objective disclosure of God in Christ that it leaves little room for an intellectually elaborated faith. Bultmann's problem is a hermeneutical one, and his starting point is a critical evaluation of human language about God, i.e., the Biblical language in which the primitive experience of God acting in Christ is expressed. The mythical character of this demands as the first task the process (for which Bultmann is best known) of demythologization. It is perhaps more perspicacious to see that his original contribution here is not so much demythologization (which has a long previous history in various modes) as the Existential re-interpretation of the message concealed within the myth. The precise character of myth is a bit elusive, and a penetrating understanding of what Bultmann is about probably demands two rather distinct notions of myth. First is the use of figurative language proper to folk fables to convey truth about the mysterious, as e.g., in the *Genesis* account of creation. Such language is no longer meaningful to contemporary scientific and technological man, and what signals the necessity for demythologization is the need for communication. This has led Barth to accuse Bultmann of "accommodationism"; of adapting the Biblical texts to the temper of modern man, rather than an unqualified fidelity to the text itself.[55]

The second mythological element is the identification of the faith-event with actual concrete happenings of history (i.e., *Historie* as opposed to *Geschichte*), and the conceptual representation of the faith-experience in objective language. The results of this are no mere failure in communication but a falsification of the *Kerygma*. Myth in this latter sense is any mode of language that objectifies what is experienced in faith, any speech that renders God as an object of thought.[56] This is improper because faith is, in a Kierkegaardian sense, only subjective. The contact with God is by Existential encounter alone, a contact marked by its *presentiality*[57] and delivering to the spirit of man not knowledge about God in himself or his attributes but rather an awareness of God's meaningfulness for self.[58] Bultmann is insisting then that the *Kerygma* cannot be re-interpreted in the language and concepts of any classical philosophical system. This would be but to substitute another "mythological" language. Thus the only concepts he allows to serve faith are those of Existentialism which alone do not objectify or "mythologize" God. This he sees not as a personal and arbitrary preference, but something that the New Testament, especially the *Gospel of St. John,* itself impels. More precisely, the Existentialist thought operative here is that of the earlier Heidegger, the Heidegger of *Sein und Zeit,* of the phenomenological analysis of *Dasein,* prior to the so-called "reversal" and the transition to what is less a phenomenology of *"Existenz"* and more an ontology of existence.[59] Tillich's indebtedness to Heidegger extends to the later phases of his thought as does that of Heinrich Ott, and marks their theologies off from that of Bultmann who did not follow Heidegger into his further speculations.

Since existential encounter with God occurs within human existence, it issues in a self-understanding, which is the human dimension to Revelation. And this is what the believer articulates in his conceptual knowledge. The notional knowledge operative here is not expressive of God but of the self in its meaningful

47

relationship to God. Its existential momentariness means that it is subject to a process of constant alteration and that its validity cannot be measured against any past concrete events or enduring concepts. It is rather, in a way indigenous to Existentialism, self-validating.

Bultmann, then, starting out at the opposite shore from Barth, rejects the latter's Biblical language (as requisitioned by God in Revelation) and also the non-Biblical symbolic language of Tillich;[60] he retains only the language of human existence. The basic problem then is how the transition can be made noetically from self understanding in religious encounter to the God who allows himself to be so encountered. Surely God himself cannot be explained in terms of human existence, in terms of *our* authentic being, creativity, freedom, concern, etc. John MacQuarrie has lamented that Bultmann's approach "while it undoubtedly illuminates many things, comes to a halt at the crucial point where we want to extend it to God."[61] Bultmann himself has noted the shortcoming and seeks a solution by saying that existential language can refer *analogically* to God.[62] But *only* existential language! Which means that the self-understanding delivered to us by demythologizing the myths of Revelation can in its turn supply us with some clue to understanding God as subject acting *in relation to us*.[63] Analogy remains an awareness arising out of personal encounter and resisting all objectification in human noetic categories. Unquestionably, there is in mystical experience a reach into the transluminous darkness that leaves the normal processes of understanding and reasoning behind, but some objective reference point serves as the starting point and guide for this. Faith as the context of Bultmann's encounter is without content; its focus upon the act of God can lead only to a subjective awareness of limits being put to my existence, of demands being made upon me, without any clues as to the identity of the One who acts, the nature of his acting (e.g., its historical character), or what it is determinately that is being asked of or promised to me. The sharp opposition he draws between the subjectivity of faith and the objectivity of reason means that there is no possibility of speaking about God or his actions *in them-selves*, and thus dogmatic formulations lose even a derived significance. His characteristic insistence that God's self-revelation is simultaneously a concealment does not mean simply that events of history are revelatory only to faith but that such events themselves (e.g., the earthly deeds of the historical Jesus) cannot be understood as an objective embodiment or sacramental disclosure in a human mode of the face of God.

Where Bultmann's thought is somewhat unsatisfactory is in its inability to explain how self-understanding can lead to a surmising of God *apart from* some objective, cognitive directedness supplied by our concepts. The resultant religious language might well bear meaning within the faith community, but there would be no way to justify it without; and even within the community of believers it would have to be considered as self-authenticating (which is perhaps the impasse to which much of Existential Theology has come). At the base of Bultmann's considerable contribution lies a Kantian spirit, developed Existentially, which strictures his achievement rather narrowly. The question it poses is whether this context be not pre-ontological and itself demand a more definite ontological setting if full justice is to be done God's revelation of himself. The work of Paul Tillich is at least a tentative probing of that question.

## 8. Paul Tillich

The theology of Paul Tillich,[64] while developed basically within an existential framework, does draw richly from other sources and is perhaps the most direct and venturesome confrontation of the faith-concept problem. For him every statement arising from religious faith is by an intrinsic necessity *symbolic*. This becomes transparent in theological elaborations of faith, but subconsciously characterizes unreflective faith also. Symbol is thus the key to any cognitive approach to God, and this is radicated in a capacity of the human spirit; man's openness to the Divine lies in his symbol-making creativity. The *symbol* must not be confused with what is a mere *sign.* The latter is purely functional and only points to something other than itself. The symbol on the contrary has participational powers;[65] it itself enters into the meaning of what it manifests, and so involves man the symbol-maker in the realm of being that it symbolizes. Conversely, the world of the symbolized is introduced effectively onto that level where the symbol originates, i.e., the reality symbolized transforms the raw materials out of which man has constructed the symbol in the first place. In this sense, the symbol belongs to a "theonomous" realm.[66] The notion of "fatherhood," to take his own concrete example, originates from a familial experience and signifies in a non-symbolic way the unique relationships that characterize the head of a household. Man's creativity can however endow this concept with the qualities of symbol which then becomes the focal point of a participation (humanly achieved, and human in mode, but bespeaking commitments proper to faith) in that realm of being which is the Fatherhood of God. Mutually involved in this is a spontaneous process which gives a new depth-dimension to the original idea or image.

How the symbol participates in the reality it symbolizes remains mysterious and at this crucial point Tillich's explanation grows somewhat nebulous. The term itself "participation" is intended as an ontological category usually contrasted with individualization. It denotes that structure of human existence whereby the individual enters upon various relations with the world in common with other individuals. Thus "the knower participates in the known; the lover participates in the beloved; the existent participates in the essences which make it what it is, under the conditions of existence. . ."[67] Seemingly then, the symbol comes to birth spontaneously as expressive of this prior structure to reality. As originating out of human consciousness, it unveils dimensions of the spirit in its primordial unity with all of being. Because reality corresponds to consciousness, certain depths of the real are thereby opened up to which we do not otherwise have access.

This reveals a second characteristic of symbols; they are not conventional or arbitrary: "As different from signs, symbols are born and die. Signs are consciously invented and removed."[68] Their ontological or existential character means that every transformation of a symbol bespeaks a prior alteration of the relation between the symbol-maker and the symbolized.[69]

It is clear from this that Tillich's use of symbol should not be confused with mere figurative or metaphorical speech (though metaphor, too, can be used symbolically), or with what Cajetan called analogy of improper proportionality. Still, it does seem to manifest a hidden analogical power, i.e., Tillich appears to endow it with something of what the Scholastics gave to their analogical concept. For the latter, every concept "participates" in the reality it makes known by expressing that aspect of its intelligibility seized upon in the cognitive act, and when the concept is analogical the transferral of meaning to the secondary analogates is never literal but always *simpliciter* diverse. Both Tillich's symbol and analogy involve a designation of the Divine from the creaturely in virtue of an elusive affinity between them. They differ in Tillich's attempt to combine into one mode of symbolic signifying what the Scholastics felt obligated to distinguish into two modes of signifying — the metaphorical and the properly analogical. What Tillich's symbol points to always negates any proper meaning of the concept used. By way of illustration, "eternal life" as a symbol means "that the joy of today has a dimension which gives it trans-temporal meaning."[70] The Scholastics preferred to signify improperly by metaphor, wherein a term retained its proper meaning and was only transferred improperly by a process implicitly recognized as an extrinsic denomination in terms of "likeness"—e.g., eternity was called "endless time" which they knew it literally was not. And then, dialectically, this was rectified with a proper concept, analogical in kind, expressing the proportion of experienced temporal life to non-experienced, atemporal life — e.g., eternity was immutable, non-successive vital existence. The intent in both cases is the same: to harmonize the unknowability of what is designated (life in its eternal mode) with a meaningful relationship to what is experienced (temporal life), founded on participation.

Ultimately, Tillich speaks in a way that is more than metaphorical yet guards against any untoward literalism by an appeal to symbol. The major difference in his Existential understanding of analogy is that its basis is not ontic being with its causal relationships as a consequent category for knowing God (thus his repudiation of what he calls "a questionable natural theology"),[71] but the *logos* structure to the whole finite order coming from the fact that God is its ground. Thus analogy is taken up onto an entirely new level, one to which the way has been opened by Heidegger's "ontological difference." On this level Tillich synthesizes into the symbol by a creative and constructive act of projecting consciousness what Scholastic theology differentiated into the various modes of analogy.

What underlies this is an Existential understanding of man whose humanness gives him a unique mode of being which because of its self-transcending powers alone deserves to be called "existence" (*Ek-sistenz*). There is a *logos* structure to all of reality but only in man does this emerge into consciousness; within man the world assumes explicit "meaning." This means that man's being is seen as his very understanding; these are not two dimensions to human life (as in the two orders, entitative and intentional, of Scholasticism) but ultimately one and the same. Conscious knowing is not the operation of a faculty of nature but human existence itself. This demands some previous proportion of man to world whose explanation lies in their common involvement in being; man already participates or communicates in a pre-conscious way in the totality of the real.[72] The finite real, in its turn, participates in God; He is the ground of being of the latter. Once again this is not the traditional notion of being as a state outside of nothingness and outside of one's causes (this would implicate Tillich in the Scholastic categories of causality and creation, which he explicitly rejects)[73] but "existential" being. Man participates in the Divine — first in a fundamental, ontological, and pre-conscious[74] way and secondly in conscious religious experience which involves the use of symbol —because in both of these ways God is his ultimate concern. This enables Tillich to make clear that the symbolic is not to be thought of as the unreal; such a confusion is possible only if the real be truncated to the sphere of things and empirical events.[75]

The dynamism of the symbol in its own realm of meaning is clarified somewhat by Tillich's explanation that the symbolized enriches, through the very use of the symbol, that segment of finite reality from which the latter is drawn in the first place. The affirmation of God's Fatherhood is at the same time a deepening of the intelligibility of human paternity. And this is not a mere transferral or attribution of new conceptual contents; rather God who is symbolized himself participates in the finite order which is the vehicle of the symbolizing activity. God is thus the "absolute participant."[76] Interpreted ontologically, i.e., in an ontology other than that of Existentialism, this would seemingly not escape the charge of Pantheism. This is not, however, what is meant; it is to be taken "not categorically but symbolically," and means (in a phrase suggestive of Heidegger's *Mit-Sein*) "the being-with of that which is neither here nor there."[77]

The symbol is then universally characteristic of religious language, (with the possible exception of the admission that God is Being-itself). Godhead, Spirit (the most perfect symbol for Divine life), *Logos*, creation, life, person, the Fall, sin, wrath, condemnation, the Cross, Resurrection, etc. are all religious symbols. They point to something beyond themselves which *negates* their own proper meaning and at the same time confirms them as symbols.[78] Far from being limited to the order of transcendental perfections they are more often concrete and imaginative in kind, as Biblical language illustrates. The abstract consideration of the concrete symbol is an interpretative function of theology as distinct from the function of religion in engendering the symbol. Somewhat surprisingly, Tillich allows that such symbols are "adequate"; this is so even when they are anthropomorphic.[79] This is seemingly so because the symbol, as a cognitive element, is neither true nor false; It is rather authentic or inauthentic, adequate or inadequate — and this in terms of its expressive power, which can gain in intensity or become self-contradictory.[80] Tillich's over-riding intent is unmistakable, namely to preclude the tendency towards a "literalism" that would analyze conceptual contents on this basis and then conclude to the absurdity of projecting them as such onto the Divine.

How successful, theologically, this venture is; to what extent it marks genuine theological advancement — all this is not easily answered. While it appears to reduce conceptual contents to a functional role, it insists that only by means of them can the human intelligence reach towards God. Their significance is in their "pointing power." The question that remains concerns the origin of this transcending capacity, i.e, how one is to explain the power of the human mind to so elevate its ideas into symbols of the Divine. The symbolizing act seems to demand roots in a prior awareness that is non-symbolic. But is there for Tillich any non-symbolic order of knowing and speaking in which the symbolic can be grounded and authenticated? He does translate religious statements into philosophical or ontological ones: "God is omnipotent" e.g., can be rendered as referring to "the power of being which resists nonbeing in all its expressions and which is manifest in the creative process in all its forms."[81] Further, he does explicitly say that the statement "God is Being-itself" is a non-symbolic one, the only such statement that can be made of God.[82] But Being-itself is quite as ineffable as is God, fully as resistant to literal analysis; all statements about it are symbolic in their own order. Ontological statements about God then are merely translations from one sphere of symbol to another. The identification of God with Being-itself would then appear to be tautological, or perhaps it would be better to say with William Rowe that both terms are irreducible symbols about which further symbolic statements can be made in their respective orders.[83] This being the case, Tillich obviously does not intend that the statements in ontological language be taken as authentications of religious discourse; at the most they can serve as elucidations of the latter. John MacQuarrie would appear to be close to the mark when he suggests that Tillich merely intends to give an arbitrary definition to the term "God" as a starting point for his theological task.[84]

But we are left with the problem of authentication. Either the statement "God is Being-itself" is not symbolic but an ontological, *a priori* assumption, or perhaps intuition comparable to Heidegger's irreducible insight into the "ontological difference," in which case Tillich's project should reasonably lead into an analysis of the proper concepts that lie beyond or undergird the symbols.[85] Or it is symbolic, and then Tillich is unable to ground man's symbolizing power in anything beyond itself. The latter alternative does not deny that his symbols possess and convey *meaning,* but it does cast suspicion on their efficacy in respect to *truth.* How is one to know if there is any transsubjective referent to which they correspond? How, in short, can they be authenticated apart from a faith act? Or even interpreted, if every explanation is itself symbolic?

❀　❀　❀

The Reformation, marking a definitive break with the past (after a brief period of Protestant Scholasticism), set the tone for the modern religious spirit. The subsequent deculturization process fostered the new theological stance that emerged fully in the Nineteenth Century theology of Schleiermacher and Harnack. The Twentieth Century protest of Neo-Orthodoxy against Protestant Liberalism devolved eventually into the Dialectical Theology of the Barth-Bultmann axis with its strong insistence on the negative and relative character of human knowing as objectivized and conceptual thinking. Similar inroads were made at the same time within Catholic thought, notably the Modernist Movement at the turn of the century, the so-called *Nouvelle Théologie* of the Forties, and the new theological epistemologies of Post Vatican II. Of late, Dialectical Theology has found a natural issue in the Eschatological Theologies most popularly represented by Jürgen Moltmann and Wolfhart Pannenberg.

In all of this, God-language has grown increasingly vague and problematic; the referent to such language tends to be anthropological rather than *theo*-logical, with theology collapsing more and more into Christology and threatening a final collapse into Humanism. What is sought is existential self-understanding rather than any noetic intentionality towards the Divine (Bultmann). Non-cognitive elements in the faith experience of God have been emphasized, with primacy given to the prereflective, lived world of feeling and spontaneous symbolization (Eliade[86] and Ricoeur[87]). It has become commonplace to defer any attempt at thematic articulation, on the reflective level, of the Transcendent; such conceptual groping towards a human identification of God is positively avoided. The yield of this within the realm of ideas has been a focus upon God, not in himself, but as one whose promises portend man's own future; the future thus becomes the paradigm of transcendence (Moltmann,[88] and in a Catholic vein—Schillebeeckx [89]), with a corresponding theology of political endeavor directed towards secularity and the building of the human world (Metz[90]). The concepts predicted of God are now problematic not in terms of objective referent, nor even of verification, but of the very possibility of any trans-empirical *meaning* attaching to the words. Recent attempts to recover such possible meaning "bracket" the further question of truth and look for meaning not on the ontological level but on the prior level of ontic experience (Gilkey[91]).

The attempt to "conceive" God can all too readily be misconstrued into an ideological idolatry. Moreover, the intentionality of such activity demands a continual surpassing and surmounting of each objective point of reference reached. Likewise, understanding and reasoning cannot be isolated from the prior, preconceptual world of human consciousness in which they are rooted and nourished and to which they must return as a touchstone of their authenticity. With this there can be no dispute; the question rather is whether this latter by itself does full justice to the integral range of human religious capabilities. Does not man have to come eventually to the ontological question;[92] does not the question of truth and falsity have to be met on the level of concept, judgment, and logical discourse; can the Christian era preceding the Modern be dismissed as thousands of years of passionate yet empty debate? To choose a central concrete example: must not the Christian eventually ask himself "is Christ indeed God or not?" Mere formal analysis would be seriously misguiding here, but the question is ontological and tentative answers must venture metaphysical language of some sort whatever its inadequacies, or run the risk of superficiality.

The ineffability of what is deepest in religious experience may well demand silence at specific points; it is only the Transcendent itself, after all, that makes any absolute claims on us and not any of its cultural expressions. But there is an indigenous movement of religious language in general (including that of silence) into theological language. The very experience itself forbids dismissing the effort to form ideas which will convey at least some limited perspective onto the Divine Reality; to dismiss it in fact is to truncate that experience in its full humanness. Isaiah's words "to whom then will you liken God or what likeness compare with him" surely inspire the theological endeavors of the authors reflected on above. But they do not mean that the believer's reflections must be restricted to a *via negativa* or to the language of metaphor or paradox. There must be some *locus* in the world inhabited by man, accessible to experience and thought, where the encounter with God can occur, some juncture for the insertion of God's Word (both of creation and of revelation).[93] What the authors considered above do not allow is any affinity between reality so experienced and the God who discloses himself there, which can serve as the basis for thought and language about God beyond the figurative or paradoxical; though the participative symbol of Paul Tillich does open up some possibilities beyond this.

Any language that claims to go beyond this must, of course, establish its own credentials; this will be the burden of the pages to follow: first, in an examination of the epistemological assumptions of the various "systems" presently at work within Catholicism (Chapter 3); secondly, in offering an alternative in a somewhat new interpretation of St. Thomas' analogy (Chapter 4); thirdly, in authenticating religious symbols and concepts in their origin and evolution (Chapter 5). It will then remain to enter upon the actual restructuring of some of the central concepts which offer to man an authentic though inadequate perspective onto the *Deus Absconditus* (Chapter 6).

Three cautions to such a project need to be borne in mind: 1) any proper concept of God, one presuming to represent him as he is in himself, is an utter impossibility;[94] 2) every conceptual vantage point reached merely opens up the horizon of new possibilities in the intentional dynamism of knowledge; 3) in every epoch there are specific areas of darkness wherein God does not yield up his identity and before which the theologian must stand in silence.[95]

# CHAPTER THREE

# THEOLOGICAL INTUITIONALISM:
## BEYOND CONCEPTS

## 1. Joseph Maréchal: Subjective Dynamism of Spirit

More than any other Catholic thinker, perhaps, it is Joseph Maréchal who has influenced the direction that the question of man's cognitive groping for God has taken in contemporary times, and his influence is a continuing one. At least more profoundly than others, he set himself the task of facing up to the dilemma into which the critical studies of Kant had thrown the traditional epistemology derived from Scholasticism. The achievement of St. Thomas ushered in a brief phase of equilibrium on the epistemological question, but there was a surprisingly sudden disintegration due to the dominance of Nominalism on one hand, and the Scotistic option for an essentialist theory of knowledge on the other. In time, the former opened the way to empiricism while the latter lent itself rather to a sort of dogmatic ontologism. Descartes, in his own way, perpetuated the latter line of development, but empiricism came rapidly to the fore and by the dawn of the Nineteenth Century, the prevalent theories of knowledge reflect a strange liaison between the two currents of thoughts. This can best be described as an exaggerated object-ivity, polarized into a naïve physicalism or phenomenalism on the one hand — where the external appearances of reality give themselves to consciousness; or an uncritical rationalism on the other — in which the extramental world was understood as

59

coinciding rather exactly with the involuted constructs of abstract reason. The knowing subject was depicted as a mere passive receptor, receiving knowledge that streamed to him from the external world, or an ego-subject granted direct access to the meta-sensory order of substances. At least before Kant, the complex contributions of the knower to his own knowledge situation (beyond an abstractive process frequently presented in a mechanical way) were considerably neglected. The Kantian *Critiques*, however, had to be taken seriously and it is against this precise background that Maréchal attempted to reintroduce the whole epistemological problem. The fifth *Cahier* of his major work[1] is subtitled *Le Thomisme devant la philosophie critique*, indicating that it is less an historical exposition of St. Thomas than a reinterpretation of the basic Thomistic insights in the light of the Kantian crisis.

Acknowledging that human intellection must either be dependent upon sensation and so not intuitive, or intuitive in some fashion or other and so not dependent upon the senses, Maréchal definitively opts for the former.[2] The nature of the intellect, however, is such that it has a natural, spontaneous agency (*intellectus agens*) in the face of sensible receptivity, which issues inwardly in an abstract essence. This latter is a pure *representation*, immanent to the knower, so that from it there cannot be inferred the extramental reality or existence of what is represented. The representation, then, is totally phenomenal in kind, and possesses of itself no value of the real. Already there is the suggestion that what man is first of all cognitively aware of is his own concepts, not realities themselves. The mould of subjectivity is broken by recourse to an activity other than this primal one of "representing" in mental constructs. This is *affirmation*, wherein the human spirit "drives through" the concept, as it were, to make contact with the noumenal order. Unlike Blondel (to whom Maréchal's thought is somewhat indebted) this activity is not that of the human will; it is not simply the need for action in a world external and real that necessitates man's affirming the objective reality of his mental constructs. Maréchal explicitly identifies affirmation as an activity of the intellect,[3] consisting actually in the judgment, seen however not as the mere composition or disjunction of terms but as a "substitut dynamique de l'intuition intellectuelle."[4] In this sense it is not mere synthetic activity, but objectifying; something midway between an exclusively synthetic activity reaching only to the formal aspect of being and an intellectual intuition knowing *being* in full.[5] If the judgment involves a concretive synthesis that is static and categorical, its full role is to achieve an objective synthesis that is dynamic and trans-categorical.[6] The *representations* immanent to our thought have no value of object apart from an implicit *affirmation,*[7] which, in the largest sense of the word, is the active reference of a conceptual content to the reality (*ad rem*).[8] The discursive intelligence thus works by a process that "imitates intuition," achieving in affirmation a virtual prolongation of its own movement beyond the frontiers of the subject, to the thing.[9]

While the concept as such "does not yet contain for consciousness the elements of immanent opposition of subject to object,"[10] there is in judicative affirmation a reflective intuition which "presents implicitly the elements of such an opposition and thus constitutes the object as object in consciousness, and attaches it to the ontological order."[11] What the knower comes to discern is the innate tendency of his intelligence through and beyond the contents of his concept to a trans-subjective order of being outside the knower. This is the intentionality of intellection, based on this that one comes "to know oneself, implicitly or explicitly, as really distinct from an objective end."[12] The word "end" in the above phrase is significant, indicating that it is the indigenous drive or appetition of spirit towards termination at real being beyond the phenomenal being of consciousness that founds the affirming judgment. Thus, Maréchal explains the dynamism of a cognitive faculty towards its own proper object as something radicated in the natural and antecedent finality of the integral subject possessing the noetic power.

One final step remains: the projection of the contents of an intentional representation onto the entitative order demands at the same time the affirmation of absolute and infinite Being.[13] The dynamism of the intelligence is then towards the Absolute, indeed it is precisely this tendency that founds all other "affirmations" or judgments of reality.[14] Though not intuitive, the working of the human intellect is synthetic and so constructive; modeling itself on the unity of its phenomenal similitude, it is able to reconstruct a noumenal unity that is the analogical and universal unity of being, which in its turn is founded on the Absolute Unity. Finite objects are incapable of quieting the intellect's quest for Being, but to the extent that such objects participate in the Infinite, it does find therein partial terminations to its tending; on this basis it affirms them in the judgment of reality. But this is simply to say that the affirmation of finite being is actually the positing of existents in the extra-mental real world at some relative point on the ontological scale with a necessary reference of greater or lesser remotion (in excellence) from Absolute Being. Thus the judgment of reality preserves an analogical character, one wherein the prime analogue is always present and measuring the being affirmed of lesser realities.[15]

This solution of Maréchal's to the epistemological problem was decidedly new, and marked some basic departures from the traditional theory surviving from St. Thomas. At bottom is its Cartesian starting point — seeking to find in unquestioned immanent consciousness a validation for the objectivity of knowledge. This meant supposing that man's first awareness was of his own subjective mental representations or constructs rather than a prior awareness of the externally real through such conceptions; a reversal of the classic introduction of the problem.[16] Where then can the bridge to the trans-subjective world be found? Not in any further activity that is rational in kind. Thus Maréchal is forced to appeal to an activity within the knower that is itself non-cognitive. He achieves this by recourse to a *subjective* dynamism of the knowing subject, whose explanation

62

lies in the natural finality of intelligence (or better, spirit) itself, in its intrinsic and necessary orientation towards the real.[17] In actual fact, Maréchal is denying the capacity of purely rational knowledge to attain the real because the affirmation which does achieve this, though it is called judgment, is not a cognitive act at all; it is rather a "projective" act or a "positing" by the subject — somewhat akin to Kant's postulates of the practical reason. The judgmental affirmation is thus not intuitional but a "substitute for intuition." He does not mean by this an activity of the will, at least in the sense of the *elicited rational* appetite ("volonté élicite"); what he does maintain however is the identification of this tendency with the internal *natural* appetite of the rational being, designated (on the basis of an appeal to St. Thomas) as a "volonté naturelle."[18] What he fails to detect, and this is a basic defect underlying Maréchal's whole position, is the subtle transposition from the cognitive order to the appetitive or conative. When he states that affirmation is an act of the intellect, he understands here an affirmation entirely determined by an antecedent finality extrinsic to cognition as such. The innate tendency or dynamism, which imperates the objectifying affirmation, is indeed *of* the intelligence but is not a "knowing" activity; it is not assimilative but rather conative. Through "desiring" the real order, man's intelligence is led to "affirm" it, without however "knowing" it. This is the foundation for the charge that Maréchal's intellectual dynamism is in fact non-intellectual and non-cognitive.[19]

Complicating the problem somewhat further is the relation between the objective contents of our notions and the existential world "affirmed." If concepts do not from the very beginning and of themselves somehow or other possess an ontological character, then what I affirm by means of them as really existing would seem to be something beyond and quite other than what those concepts objectively express. Why then do not the notions used in the affirmation of being — such as "cause," "end," "participation," etc. — actually designate something existentially other than what is embodied in those ideas? At the very least, there is a nebulous area here in Maréchal's theory of knowledge, and one that challenges it in its basic postulates.

The question, however, is whether or not *in spite of this* Maréchal's original re-thinking of the problem has not opened up possibilities and given a new direction to the larger question of God's knowability for man. At the very least, his position is a strong reaction to the supposition that conceptual contents can be simply transferred to God, with only an "analogical" expansion. The basic Maréchalian stance is one wherein the affirmation of God is a quasi-intuition of Absolute Being, involved in every specifically human activity — thus something necessary and universal, if only implicit. Such acknowledgment, then, is not the term of a demonstration; the latter being reduced to the consequent formulation in logical categories of the metaphysical principle of causality already grasped in the prior intuitive seizure of the analogous character of being. The novelty of this is above all its non-intellectual character. The attainment of Absolute Being is not through an activity of the intellect distinctly its own and engaging its own proper object; the "forms" immanent to intelligence are mere occasions for the spontaneous eruption of a dynamic impulse toward the goal of the human spirit. What is affirmed is something quite other than what is represented in the objective contents of our concepts.[20] This is as true in the order of faith as in that of reason; in the former, the supernatural *assensus* is only the correlative of the rational *affirmatio;* whether the representation be directly abstracted naturally from the physical world or formed more complexly in the experiential response to historical Revelation is incidental to knowing as such. What is affirmed then remains radically unknowable and ineffable beyond its being Transcendent and Absolute, the Unlimited Fulfillment of human spiritual aspirations. This is to say that we do not know God conceptually at all; deficient creaturely concepts merely enable us to tend dynamically towards him as a super-exceeding Unknown. In objectifying its "forms," the intellect surpasses them.

Here Maréchal can appeal to St. Thomas: the names we assign to God (apart from those which are only negative or relative) do indeed *signify* Him but do not *represent* Him;[21] in the analogical transposition the *"significatio nominis"* is freed of its *"modus significandi."*[22] There is then a Thomistic basis for distinguishing the object of representation from the object of affirmation. Affirmation reaches to the *"modus rei in essendo"* while representation remains bound to the *"modus intelligentis in intelligendo."*[23] The difference lies in Maréchal's exaggerated separation of the two activities. Are there then no objective concepts of the divine attributes? Maréchal's acknowledgment that there are such is largely verbal in the light of his qualifications. There are, of course, mental representations of some kind, but these are creaturely and are not *as such* projected onto God. Any prolongation of them God-ward is possible only by way of a "correction,"[24] which is not an alteration of the conception at all but an *impulse* from the latter's contingency towards its necessary correlative — the All Perfect and Necessary. "Here is what in effect we arrive at: we know creatures as relative to an Absolute Principle, as contingent, and by that — by that alone — we know God."[25] The accompanying illustrative image is revealing: we know God from creatures somewhat as we know the target towards which the arrow flies from knowing its projecting arch from the bow.

It remains true that Maréchal at least places God within the perspective of "being" and thus implicitly its transcendental properties, unlike some moderns who seek a non-metaphysical context for the idea of God.[26] But this is not the perspective of the *concept* of being, it is rather being realized in a non-cognitive, non-conceptual way, in a lived dynamism of the human spirit. Even so, what concepts there are (even if only expressing the formal perfections of being, in a phenomenal way) at least give a clue to the direction or orientation in which man tends dynamically towards the unknown Absolute.

In terms of a developing knowledge of God, Maréchal's theory would seem to preclude any possibilities in terms of re-working and creatively expanding the concepts we now have, or of acquiring new ones. Development would appear to be only in the direction of a continuing penetration in non-objective and non-articulated ways into the mystery of the Absolute; an intensification if not a clarification. Needless to say the question of dogmatic evolution — in the precise form the question takes today — had not arisen in his time. Others — notably Henri Bouillard — have attempted some such application of the representation — affirmation distinction, maintaining in effect that only the affirmation of faith attains to an immutable object while conceptual representations are of themselves always variable.[27] Conceptual progress is thus possible, indeed necessary, without any alteration in what is really affirmed "across" (as it were) such conceptions. But the solution is an overly simple one. Dogmatic formulations, i.e., authoritative ones, would not then fall within the ambit of belief even as secondary objects. The act of faith itself would appear devoid of any intelligible content. In spite of such failure at providing an adequate solution, Maréchal's reaction to an overly facile and empirical conceptualism opened up an approach to the problem of dogmatic development, in its underlying epistemological dimensions, that nearly every contemporary attempt has pursued.

## 2. Karl Rahner: Spirit in Matter

It is well nigh impossible to over-estimate the implications for philosophic thought of the epistemological problematic posed by Kant's *Critique of Pure Reason*. The transcendental method definitively established the "Copernican Revolution" inaugurated by Descartes, and confirmed modern thought as radically different from the classical thought of antiquity and of the Middle Ages. After an initial resistant negativism, Scholasticism faced up to the challenge of critically grounding the validity of knowledge with the work of Joseph Maréchal (and such associates as Pierre Rousselot). Maréchal's attempted *entente* with Transcendental Philosophy has survived as a distinct orientation within Thomistic thought; André Marc, Bernard Lonergan, Johannes B. Lotz, Emerich Coreth, and Karl Rahner are, in their various ways, contemporary expositors of Maréchal's version of the transcendental method, much as Hüsserl and Heidegger are the heirs of Kant. In the forefront of these, at least in the field of theology, is Rahner; Lonergan, it is true, has made similar applications to theology but his focus upon insight as the all important noetic factor appears to give greater place to the receptive character of knowledge whereas Rahner's concern with the *a priori* conditions of the possibility of knowledge stresses the positing character of knowledge and is thereby more markedly Maréchalian.

At the outset, Rahner insists that theology today can only be theological anthropology; at the same time his dominant anthropological presuppositions are those of Existential Philosophy (reflecting in part an intellectual dialogue with Heidegger begun while he was a student at Freiburg) acknowledging in man a mode of being (*Existenz*) whereby he transcends a universe of things. *Geist in Welt,* retreating from earlier emphases upon man as a product of nature, defines him not as a rational animal but as incarnate spirit. The ramifications of this as a starting point in philosophy, and somewhat differently in theology, are immense. It means that being as object of metaphysics is not reached through the process of abstraction or judgmental separation but by a transcendental reflection upon the activity of understanding itself.[28] This return to the knowing subject constitutes what has come to be known as the "transcendental turn." The method is Kant's but the integral theory of knowledge to which it concludes is not; thus Rahner with others can contend that a transcendentally grounded metaphysics is in essentials not at odds with the Aristotelian - Thomistic synthesis. In contrast to Hüsserl, Rahner denies the possibility of any *epoché* concerning the real existence of extramental objects and believes that a phenomenological analysis of the act of understanding "discloses" (thus it is neither a demonstration nor a strict intuition) its noumenal object-relatedness. Starting with the phenomenal object, i.e., the content of consciousness, the direction of the method is back to the activity of understanding which manifests its own *a priori* structure, which is the condition for the very possibility of knowledge, as a prehension (*Vorgriff*) or pre-knowledge (*Vorwissen*) of being. Metaphysics then is not the discovery of what was previously unknown but the development in terms of concepts and thematic knowledge of this preconceptual and unthematic grasp of being. This indeed is man's prerogative as a spirit, which is nothing but a total openness to the horizon of being; the latter understood by Rahner not merely as a field of consciousness implicitly grasped in the knowledge of concrete objects but as a genuine *a priori* projection of a totality allowing for the experience of the concrete object known precisely in its character as being.

The act of knowing quite apart from its content, reveals man as a dynamism orientated towards being as a "horizon" that man already "intends" or anticipates (*vorgreift*). This very activity itself mediates the things that form the concrete contents of consciousness, it endows the latter beings with their Being. While this horizon of being is itself unlimited and unconditioned, man's openness onto it is limited for he is not pure spirit but finite spirit or *Geist in Welt*, (thus there is no possibility of an intuition of being, properly speaking). This gives rise to a dialectical tension between an unlimited *desire* to know what is inexhaustibly knowable and a limited power to know. As such, spirit is a continuous dynamic orientation towards unrestricted being.

At this point, two vastly significant features of Rahner's thought come to the fore. One is that man's preconscious global anticipation of being is radicated in spirit as conative, i.e., it is a drive or impulse (in Lotz's phrase: a striving), an innate reaching out through the known towards the unknown. While Rahner does speak of this primal foreknowledge in terms of the *lumen intellectus agentis,* as the active illuminative power of finite human intelligence,[29] it is at bottom something deeper than man's cognitive faculty. It is spirit itself which while bespeaking a noetic or cognitive dimension is not structured exclusively within that sphere.[30] Place is obviously being made here for a volitional element that reveals how closely Rahner shares the deepest intuitions of Maréchal, and it will find a parallel in his teaching, apropos of explicit, reflective knowledge, on how personal decision affects and contributes to the act of understanding.

Secondly, man's openness to the horizon of being as something unlimited means an orientation towards the infinite and the absolute, in short a transcendence towards God. His integral being (existence) as incarnate spirit is an indigenous but free movement towards Pure Spirit whence he originates and towards which he is in ontological recoil. The knowledge of particular beings (*das Seiende*) is possible only as the clarification of a previous knowledge of being itself (*Sein*), which latter as the implicit horizon of all man's knowing is unconditioned and unrestricted. Though there is no confusing being itself with God, still human knowledge is a dynamic orientation towards God. The affirmation of real existence as limited and finite demands as its condition not only an unrestricted horizon of being but also the reality of the Absolute as the ground of being. Our experience of being is thus a presence of the Absolute even when not recognized as such. Indeed, Rahner's "proof" for God (required since the *a priori* awareness is entirely non-objective) is simply the phenomenological explication of our experience of being as excluding, in its ground, all finiteness.[31] Apart from Absolute Being or Pure Spirit all finite being would be unintelligible, and thus thinking an impossibility.

The metaphysical crux of Rahner's thought, it would seem, lies in subtle identity of being and knowing; there is a point at which the two coincide. Echoing Heidegger's *Dasein* as the "There-of-Being," the place where *Sein* comes to pass, Rahner construes being existentially as characteristic of man insofar as he is finite transcendence. Being thus comes to consciousness or knows itself in the act of thinking; being is "knowing and being known," it is ultimately "the being-present-to-itself of being, or the luminosity of being to itself as 'subjectivity'." [32] This Rahner sees as paraphrasing St. Thomas' *"reditio subjecti in seipsum,"* for knowledge is not a "moving outwards towards the multiplicity of knowable things," but a "coming to oneself" so that "anything is known in the measure in which it demonstrates itself to be ontologically identical with the knowing subject." [33]

Of itself this gives rise to the further problem of the differentiation of the known object from the knower himself. This is achieved on the level of conceptual thinking as a process of thematizing or objectifying what is already pre-known or anticipated in the implicit prehension of the horizon of being, and involves the empirical process of sensation and abstraction. The illumination of the *species* by the *intellectus agens* is a projection of it onto the horizon of being. To ask if that horizon is merely subjective is itself sufficient to establish that it is not; it is precisely the intentionality towards the real and the unrestricted that enables one to recognize the possibility of limitation to the subjective and so to pose the very question. This illustrates Rahner's understanding of man as a questioning being, the very possibility of posing a question betraying the fact that the questioner already anticipates an answer which he now seeks to clarify in a thematic way. To ask what "is" something, betrays a prior knowledge of "is-ness" and of the truth that this object in some fashion belongs to that order.

It is the "species" then that makes possible the location of a given object upon the horizon of being, but for Rahner this "species" is not first of all a gnoseological reality, but an ontological one, i.e., it is an entitative rather than an intentional determination of the knower. The reason for this is that "knowledge is not an 'intentional' stretching out of the knower to an object, it is not 'objectivity' in the sense of the going forth of the knower out of himself to something other . . . (but) the being-present-to-itself (*Beisichsein*) of an entity, the inner illuminatedness of an entity for itself . . . " [34] Only because the "species" is also the effect of an object distinct from the knower does it follow that "the being-present-to-its-own-self (*Beisichselbersein*) of the knower as an entity determined by the 'species' becomes also the knowledge of the object itself. . . ."[35] Rahner is here putting considerable stress on the immanence of knowledge and the basis for this is clearly his identification of being and knowing. What remains problematic is whether he has not eliminated the distinction between *esse entitative* and *esse intentionale* which marks the creaturely knower as set over against divine knowing.

At any rate, because the horizon of being is unlimited it cannot be thematically exhausted; there is no cessation point to the thrust of spirit towards the not yet fully known. Thus knowledge is a dynamism ever developing into deeper and more extensive comprehension through new and fresh conceptualizations. There are Hegelian undertones to this but Rahner qualifies them considerably by insisting that the dialectical movement is not bilaterally conceptual but between pre-conceptual and conceptual knowledge.

The basic hesitancy one feels before Rahner's metaphysics of knowledge revolves around the question as to whether or not his break through the wall of Kantian immanentism is indeed more than verbal. Gilson, Maritain, and M. Casula among others have suspected that this is not the case with Transcendental Thomism in general.[36] Otto Muck, however, has neutralized that objection by insisting that what Transcendentalism attempts is not an *intentional* analysis of the act of understanding but an *a priori transcendental* analysis, i.e., there is no attempt to dissemble the elements that become expressly conscious in the mysterious occurrence of knowing but only to analyze the *a priori* conditions for the possibility of knowing the real.[37] Thus Transcendentalists feel no need for a "bridge" back to the real order. Nevertheless, this does not entirely do away with the suspicion that Rahner's being is nothing other than "the unrestricted illuminating power of intellect," an objection incisively lodged by James B. Reichmann (against Coreth especially).[38] If the insight be a valid one then Rahner's being is mere potency. Should it be regarded as more than this, a further ambiguity remains because being still seems to designate something other than the actual exercise of be-ing by concrete existents.[39] The "transcendental turn" too, i.e., the comparison of the phenomenal object to the subject rather than to the extra-mental referent, offers difficulties. Does it not isolate the knowing subject from a world of intelligible objects at the very outset, from a world in which the subject already participates through common being (in the traditional sense) and through matter or corporeity? In this last respect, the thought of Merleau-Ponty appears to represent an advance over that of Heidegger in insisting upon bodiliness as an essential limitation to human transcendence; with Rahner the impression remains that engagement with the physical universe through *conversio ad phantasmata* while indispensable is somehow only *per accidens* to the knowing capacities of human spirit. It is this very mind-body problem that accounts for the bipolar character of human intelligence, i.e., the explanation of intellection in terms of an agent and a passive intellect — a distinction classic to philosophy since Aristotle's time and one preserved by all Maréchalians. The epistemological question then is how the illuminative power of intellect as agent can be known except in its very exercise upon its object, including being itself, which would thus appear to be something that intellect receives rather than projects or anticipates even implicitly.[40] Does Rahner, in effect, dismiss too readily the possibility of knowledge developing through a greater and greater comprehension of existents on the basis of man's empirical activity? Possibly the bedrock of all these gnoseological options is Rahner's recourse to the dominant Maréchalian insight on spirit, wherein conative drive or thrust logically precedes and accounts for the cognitive orientation.

This Rahnerian gnoseology, at any rate, transfers itself readily and with consistency to the realm of faith-knowledge. If all human knowledge takes place against an horizon of being that is itself unrestricted, then all human knowing is, in a further implicit way, an encounter with God as the Absolute, i.e., as the Ground of this very being.[41] The recognition of finite being, is, indeed, intelligible only on the assumption of some prior awareness of the infinite, since the finite is acknowledged precisely as a limitation of the Unlimited. God is affirmed then as the Unconditioned who is the condition for the possibility of finite being. The only alternative of man as finite spirit is the admission of total unintelligibility. As so encountered, however, God cannot be structured within human categories;[42] He is affirmed as the Absolute who is "intelligibly present without being objectively seen,"[43] and "even when known He remains unknown."[44]

Nonetheless, man's awareness of God is precisely by way of a consciousness of his own contingency which he recognizes as "a free deliberate act of delimitation"[45] by God, which is to say that man acknowledges his own contingency as the free gift of the Absolute. Man thus stands open before the *Deus Absconditus* not as before the mere absolute being of God but as before "a free autonomous powerful person," as open to "the possibility of the free action of God upon him, thus before the God of a possible material revelation."[46] So it is by a necessity of his nature that man is a "hearer of the Word" (*Hörer des Wortes*) for even if God chooses not to speak, man then hears God's very silence.

The actual occurrence of Revelation is conditioned by that openness to being which is the very structure of man, his receptive spirituality to which God's word is addressed. This is the *locus* outside of grace which explains the possibility of Revelation; it is the juncture in nature where grace can be inserted. From this it follows that the very conditions which determine man's affirmation of God prevail in his reception of revelation: the former is objectified through a knowledge of finite things with which man is engaged due to the necessity of *conversio ad phantasmata;* the latter through the events of history because, in his temporality, contingency, and freedom, man is open to a future to which he contributes. Consequently, Revelation is a dialogic event in which man stands before God as one free person before another who discloses himself; it occurs only within the parameters of history where man by his free response to the summoning word makes ultimate disposition of his life before God. In the broad sense Revelation is necessary and so addressed to men universally; it is, however, personal, non-objective, and non-verbal in kind.[47] Revelation in the more commonly accepted sense is the objectification and articulation of the above within particular cultural contexts, culminating in the unique and privileged objectification which is the Christ-Event as definitive Revelation that is never to be surpassed. The closing of Revelation with the death of the last Apostle, then, is not to be understood as any cessation of God's personal address to believers here and now; what it means is that the Apostolic articulation of God's word must be normative for all future articulations and that it is itself an implicit plenitude of all that later becomes explicit.

In Rahner's perspective, faith-knowledge is obviously and necessarily developmental by a process of ever greater concep-tualization of an original all-encompassing, preconceptual "hear-ing" in faith of God's free self disclosure. This progresses not solely within the confines of theological science, but of faith and dogma itself, which latter bind in conscience; indeed, the New Testament itself is an instance of development wherein God's word unavoidably submits to a theologizing reflection on the part of its various authors. It is on the propositional level that doctrinal evolution recognizably occurs even if the preconceptual experience is the matrix of such. And here Rahner is clear that, in spite of an inter-connection of truths on the deeper, precons-cious level, development cannot come about apart from some sort of explication of the contents of concepts and propositions. From the very beginning, then, we are dealing with the human objectification, necessarily historically and culturally conditioned, of God's word, and this must always be inadequate to the realities it serves to convey. This inadequacy at the same time is no denial of its truth value, nor any reduction of that truth value to the subjective or relative order. Earlier dogmatic pronounce-ments are never abrogated; on the contrary they perdure as authentic objectifications of the revealed word, but what is important at this moment of history is the *meaning* of such propositions and this, as the present address of God, can only be grasped in the light of the concrete historical situation of men who are here and now addressed. This entails the continual reformulation of those statements in which God's word is originally couched, otherwise these become no longer vehicles of Revelation but merely records of past Revelation. What emerges from this are genuinely new truths, not mere verbal modifications or paraphrases of past enunciations, but new truths exhibiting some conceptual continuity with authentic ones of the past which are not repudiated in the adoption of newer views or perspectives.

Rahner's determination of the concrete ways in which such evolution on the doctrinal level does occur is well known and has been amply exposed.[48] The expansion of knowledge indigenous to man on the natural level takes place against the background of the *a priori* horizon of being; where faith-knowledge is concerned the background is rather that of the light of faith, i.e., man's actual openness to a God of free self-disclosure. The major difference is that the "given" in the former case is that of an unrestricted potentiality whereas in the latter it is the actuality of God's self-communication. To deny this difference is to degrade faith to the level of an element of self-understanding. Revelation in Jesus Christ "implies the real, eschatological self-communication of God by incarnation, and by grace as glory already begun, to the created spirit . . . we now have not only the utterance, but the thing itself: God's self-communication to the spirit in his own proper reality . . . " (which) . . . "really takes place in the human word and not merely on the occasion of it . . . (so that) . . . we cannot — like the modernists — set up a wordless state of experience with regard to what is meant in faith. . . . Behind the verbal testimony of God in human concepts we cannot go, to reach a wordless possession and experience of the divine reality itself."[49]

The most obvious growth area in the human objectification of God's word is the *logical* explication of the contents of

75

concepts, but to this must be added the *lived* explication by believing Christians of the realities which such faith language renders present and operative. In both ways there can be an expansion of what is in the original deposit *formally and implicitly* or what is there only *virtually and implicitly*. Whereas the prior of these is merely a clarification, or application, or fresh nuancing of an original truth, the latter is a genuinely new truth somehow inferred (either logically or really) from an original which is its source in a germinal way. Nevertheless, Rahner sees the new articulation in this second case as able to be one of faith, i.e., expressly proposed by the Church as revealed. His explanation is that God is *formally communicating* (*mit-geteilt*) a truth that he does not *formally state;* it is virtually contained and really communicated in another truth that is formally stated.[50] His illustration of this is in terms of the human lover who "reads" in the utterances of the beloved dimensions of meaning actually intended but not literally said, due to the depth of what is being conveyed, something that will not easily yield to articulation.

The Spanish Dominican Marin-Sola evolved a somewhat parallel solution to the problem of doctrinal development in the early twentieth century but almost totally within an intellectualist context. Rahner is here having characteristic recourse to volitional and conative elements, i.e, seeing love as a factor of knowledge itself. This is one of the connotations of "spirit" as he employs the term to designate man, and it bears parallels to St. Thomas' use of the Augustinian term *mens.*[51] Significantly, the various reflective attempts at articulating a profound love experience themselves redound to intensify one's capacities for the continuing experience itself. The general directedness in all of this is progressive, in spite of accidental moments of retrogression occasioned by factors such as sin, because the thrust of spirit remains towards unknown Pure Spirit.

Rahner's theological presentation of God, then, is in terms of human categories with which the believer strives to objectify and thematize the reality of God as he discloses himself to human spirit in a free divine initiative whose human correlate is man's openness in faith to the anonymous Absolute Thou. The very inadequacy of such categories is itself the course of an ever-continuing process of reconceptualization. Still, all authentic religious ideas are true, due partly to God's providence as a guarantee given to the believing community that articulates its faith, and ultimately to the origin of the whole conceptualizing process with the divine revelatory act. Quite understandably, Rahner's notion of God—i.e., his analysis of that concept which the Christian community possesses at this moment of its faith-consciousness — is highly nuanced and still emerging into further intelligibility. In comparison with ideas of God but recently in vogue he feels compelled towards a healthy agnosticism, since the greatest mistake of all would be to endow any created idea with an absolute and terminal intelligibility. which would be to anthropomorphize God: "Even as known, God remains unknown." There is apt to be something misleading in putting too much store in analogical concepts of transcendental per-fections to convey understanding of the divine attributes. What the New Testament unveils to us of God are less his perfections than his attitudes towards man. Revelation is primarily by way of action and God discloses himself as "One who acts", and freely so, towards men. Divine love is experienced as an event, rather than known as an attribute, and one that frequently enough inverts human values. These divine "attributes," then, are existential and the experience of them bear us towards God as towards the Uncreated Ground of Freedom, with all the Spontaneity and Creativity therein connoted.[52]

Radicated in this emphasis upon a dynamic and existential character to God's self-disclosure in a free revelatory act is a second nuance to the emerging concept with which we strive to objectify his mysterious presence. Something of the perfection we experience in historicality and temporality is glimpsed as characterizing God himself. At the same time, this must be affirmed without any denial of God's Eternity and Immutability, and leads Rahner to the ambivalent formula that God is "immutable in Himself but mutable in us" to explain God's loving involvement in man's history.[53]

Consistent with this is a clear understanding of man's future as open, i.e., not pre-determined by any eternal decrees of God, with consequently a considerable transformation of what is understood as God's Providence. God remains the Lord of history, of course, but in the perspective of man as a personal existent (*Dasein*) whose free decisions shape in a genuinely free and non-predetermined way his essence as it arises out of the core of his being, his person, and who thus disposes of himself as a whole before God. This seemingly envisions the created freedom of finite spirit as imaging the uncreated freedom of Absolute Spirit even in its very autonomy, and poses in radically different terms the problem, and so the answer, to the mysterious reconciliation of the two. Successful or not, Rahner is attempting to surmount the theological context in which solutions were sought during the Sixteenth Century controversies on grace and free will.

Underlying Rahner's entire endeavor in this area is his conviction that ὁ Θεός of the New Testament writers is not a mere homogeneous expansion of Old Testament notions of *Yahweh;* rather, something conceptually new and distinctive is conveyed in this further phase of Revelation. The substance of this is, of course, the Trinitarian mystery, but the full impact of this disclosure to faith is not preserved if ὁ Θεός be taken as designating the Godhead which happens to be Triune in Personality. His painstaking hermeneutic of the New Testament seeks to establish that this is not how the sacred writers themselves understood the Revelation they were seeking to communicate. The God of the New Testament is not the Deity, even taken simultaneously as Father, Son, and Spirit, but the First Person of that Trinity; He is the Unoriginate God engendering an eternal Son who becomes incarnate in human history, and breathing forth an Uncreated Spirit. Clearly enough, Rahner will employ a new metaphysics here in his conception of the person-nature relationship to elaborate theologically this revealed datum, one not entirely foreign to the Scholastic tradition but not to be confused with it either. Concretely, the distinction of Persons within the Trinity is hereby given a decidedly new conceptual emphasis, with the practical result that the ideas used to objectify the so-called Immanent Trinity are closer in their intelligible content to ideas expressing the Trinity of the Economy of Salvation. There are further implications in our understanding of the processes of justification and sanctification by way of the grace of Christ; paramount among these are Rahner's suggestions of each of the three Divine Persons having its own proper relationship to the justified man,[54] and of the Word of God as *alone* the Divine Person who can begin a human history, i.e., *only* He can become incarnate.[55] At the same time, such an approach must safeguard itself against any suggestions of a crypto-Subordinationism. The significance of all this is that those who follow Rahner in his theological explorations do find themselves in possession of a concept of God — the primal idea in all of theology — that is subtly but meaningfully distinct from other viable concepts thereof within Christian tradition at its present moment of conscious articulation.

### 3. Bernard Lonergan: The Moving Point of View

Bernard Lonergan's master work *Insight*[56] is an illuminating instance of the phenomenological method in operation, basing itself on an examination of inner structures of consciousness, without presuppositions or reliance upon any classical texts or traditions. Nonetheless, the soil out of which it emerges is that of classical Scholasticism — but with a decidedly Maréchalian influence and evidencing an obvious parallel to Newman's theory of "implicit reasoning" with its distinction between notional and real assent.[57] These characteristics of innovativeness and continuity mark his work as original in the best sense of the term. This work has consisted largely in the development of cognitional theory and only subsequently in the attempt to flesh out such theory in the areas of science, metaphysics, and theology. Accordingly, what will engage our interest here is first, his epistemological theory and then the consequences this has had in any attempt to reconceptualize God. In addition to *Insight*, this will involve drawing upon various studies, notably the *Verbum* and *Gratia* articles, the Latin studies of the Trinity, and the volume *Collection* (see note No. 56).

Lonergan locates human knowledge in a very complex and variegated perspective, seeing it as a constant eruptive process and as maintaining a "moving point of view." This dynamism — sometimes polar ("from ignorance to empirical awareness, from confusion to understanding, from uncertainty to self-commitment")[58] and sometimes circular (experience, insight, inquiry, hypothesis, position, counter position, higher insights, etc.) — makes of the human knower a questioner.

Lonergan allows that the bodiliness of man enables his basic cognitive experiences, those of sensation, to be truly intuitive. Thought, however, is of an entirely other order; the intellect, having a prior dependence upon sense and forced to function abstractly, is not radically intuitional.[59] Above all it is not a passive receptor; its immanent "forms" cannot be the exact replicas of universal natures as they exist outside the mind. Only a theory of knowledge that sees the functions of intelligence as quasi-mechanical can justify such "representational realism."[60] Meaning, the proper concern of intellect, has rather a *partially* subjective origin;[61] without being able to depart entirely from an objective norm man is to some degree a constitutor of meaning. This quest for meaning is pursued on two levels: *direct understanding* terminating in the concept, and *reflective understanding* terminating in the judgment.[62] On each level there is a dual activity, an *intelligere* and a *dicere*, both of which are emanations within thought. The former is a *processio operationis*, the latter a *processio operati*. What needs to be borne in mind most of all is that not only does reflection precede judgment but that *understanding precedes conceptualization.*[63]

80

This very stress — upon the distinctiveness of conception from understanding — while not unique to Lonergan receives from him an emphatic statement, highlighting an emphasis that he wishes to throw upon the immanent nature of thought.

In conceptualization the knower strives to "express" to himself in a conscious and rational way his own inner state of being already aware of something. The concepts proceed from the intellect already understanding, i.e., from that which is both intelligent and intelligible in act. They are grounded in a conscious grasp of understanding and proceed as the rational utterance of the contents so understood, and precisely because they are understood. Secondly, even the understanding itself, because it is "insight" into the phantasm (involving an act of objective abstraction by the agent intellect and of apprehensive abstraction by the possible intellect, with respectively a *species qua* and a *species quae*) is something immanent, not only as act but even in terms of its object.[64] The object of thought is preconceptual, a reality of thinking itself, and not as in Conceptualism a more or less static similitude of the extra-mental reality passively impressed upon intelligence prior to thought.[65] As such it is a "moving" rather than terminal object, one setting in motion a dynamism in which new elements of intelligibility are constantly being grasped in a spontaneous eruption of "insight."[66] In all this, intelligence is laboring to understand itself in its own acts; what is misleading from the very beginning is to suppose that knowledge is a "looking" rather than an intelligible emanation;[67] to fail to grasp it as a *processio operationis* in understanding and a *processio operati* in conception. The object in understanding then is not something presupposed but something constituted by thought itself. This is the *species quae* — which is the quiddity of the material thing; not however as it is in itself (the singular *res*), nor as conceived (the *species in qua*), but precisely as understood.[68]

This emphasis upon intellection as immanent activity, as (unlike sensation) a matter of inner conditions, leads Lonergan into making the transcendental turn and seeing knowledge as providing immediate access to the subject. His investigations then bear directly not on what is thought but on the thinking activity itself. It is the invariant structure to all such activity that introduces us to the structures of finite reality itself, because the two — knowing and being — exactly parallel one another. Metaphysics is then grounded in a penetrating knowledge of the subject as knower. The phenomenon of knowing is mysteriously heuristic and intentional; i.e., it is a spontaneous process of posing questions and in the act of so doing of anticipating the answers in some obscure fashion; of intending what is not yet known. What this means to say is that the answer sought in posing the question can be anticipated by considering the kind of knowing act that will be necessarily engaged in striving for the unknown. The ground or root of this is a Maréchalian *desire* to know (operative in man apart from any conscious cognition of it) whose unrestricted character betrays that what we desire to know is being in all its amplitude. Without any limitations whatsoever, this in effect endows human consciousness with a proleptic "possession" of being that Lonergan designates a *notion;* it is not a concept but something presupposed, an *a priori* condition of understanding, out of which concepts are differentiated.

On the higher level of the second act of the mind, where understanding is now reflective and the terminal object is a judgment, a similar process is exhibited except that now entirely new factors are involved. First of all, it is here that the knower breaks through the confines of his own immanent activity to the extra-subjective order. It is utterly impossible that this be accomplished by merely comparing inner forms to extra-mental realities, for the very reason that the latter are unattainable except in ways arising out of the knower's own immanence.[69] Lonergan will not allow any primal intuition of the order of real being occurring at the onset of intellection.[70] Rather this is attained in the judgment which then is no mere synthesis of elements but an "affirmation;" what is affirmed is the union of quiddity and existence. Sufficient reflection allows for the emergence of evidence on the basis of which the judgment gains truth value, and thus affirms the real and trans-subjective order. Put most simply, this is just another mode of insight — a dialectical process of hypotheses, positions, and counter-positions leads first to the positing of a truth as virtually conditioned, and then, after awareness that such conditions are in fact fulfilled, to the positing of the virtually unconditioned, i.e., to the affirming of the true and the real. This process is most frequently described as "heuristic anticipation."

A second point is all important: every affirmation is at the same time a self-affirmation; what is affirmed being not simply the realness of the cognitive contents but also the reality of oneself as a knower of the real. Originally this is merely an empirical experience of the self precisely as a *subject;* such experience, however, leads to a grasp of the intelligibility of the self whereby it is turned into an object that finds representation in a concept; finally is the affirmation of the self as existent. The ego is thus grasped: a) empirically, in experience b) objectively, in conception c) really, in affirmation. It is experienced as a subject, understood as an object, and affirmed as existent.[71] In this last reflective phase, there is discerned the adequation of the intelligent-self to all being.[72] Such awareness (that the intellect can become intentionally all that is actual) is a grasp of the entire multi-dimensional universe. At this point, the object of intellect has become transcendental — all reality grasped implicitly as analogical in character.

A penultimate phase leads to the affirmation of God as Absolute Being, Understanding and Truth. This is necessary because without it the order of proportionate being by itself would be unintelligible, which for Lonergan is convertible with non-being. This constitutes Lonergan's "proof" for God: His existence is affirmed first in a heuristic anticipation as virtually conditioned; the conditions are discovered in reflection as actually fulfilled; then that God exists is posited as a virtually unconditioned judgment. Lonergan expresses this syllogistically as follows: "If the real is completely intelligible, God exists. But the real is completely intelligible. Therefore God exists." [73] Self-affirmation underlies this as the basic affirmation of reality, and by a spontaneous procedure of the mind this is expanded to the universe of proportionate being, and then extrapolated to the Source of being. The process is one that identifies: a) what is real and existent with being, b) being with complete intelligibility, and c) "complete intelligibility with the unrestricted act of understanding that possesses the properties of God and accounts for everything else." [74]

What is virtually unconditioned here is simply the judgment that God is; prior to this is the understanding (by way of a transcendental analysis) of God himself as signified in the idea of the formally unconditioned, i.e., as the transcendent ground for the very possibility of proportionate being. The judgment that the formally unconditioned is or is real comes later, and is verified not in experience, not in any demonstrative process (whether *a priori* or *a posteriori*), but in the critical activity of grasping a truth as virtually unconditioned.

Penetration into the self as knower is obviously then a focal point of Lonergan's gnoseological doctrine. The emphasis upon subjectivity and immanence is very marked, without however any suggestion that the external world lacks all objective meaning apart from man's constituting activity. On the contrary, Lonergan is concerned with safeguarding objectivity in acknowledging reality as an absolute norm in man's distinctive act of bestowing meaning. The kind of objectivity that he does not allow is that of a naïve realism that views the object as simply out there, able to be grasped as it is in itself by some sort of contact with it. Rather, the subject's critical analysis and judgments of virtual unconditionedness enables the knower to possess in his own intentionality the thing in its genuine conditions of objectivity.

He acknowledges no primal all-encompassing implicit intuition (as does, for example, Schillebeeckx); the closest approximation to such being the empirical experience of the bare fact that one is a subject-self. Such experience poses questions for intelligence and the very nature of the latter is to enter upon the dialectical interplay of heuristic anticipation, of tentative solution, etc., that is insight, a spontaneous seizure of intelligibility in an implicit preconceptual "reasoning" common to all minds. Consciousness underlies all this because knowing is not mere response to stimuli but becoming aware; becoming aware not simply of something but of the fact that one is a knower of something. The process of questioning is hardly intelligible apart from a basic awareness of the unity of the one who questions and a rudimentary grasp of his innate structure as a poser of questions. Only in awareness of one's own understanding is there found the way to the understanding of all else.

All that remains to consummate human knowing is belief or "special transcendent knowledge," which evinces a similar process of heuristic anticipation culminating in the affirmation of a proposition as believable and believed. The major difference is that " . . . while judgment results with rational necessity from reflective grasp of the unconditioned, the assent of belief results with natural necessity from a free and responsible decision to believe."[75] When such belief is supernatural, i.e., religious faith, the link between the conditioned and its conditions is reached "because of the initiating and preserving truthfulness of God."[76] The questioning and questing process indigenous to insight operating on this level is focused by Lonergan on the problem of evil; i.e., he sees man's faith in God as at bottom a believing in the truthfulness of those solutions that God offers to man's problem of evil. Such solutions are, for faith, completely supernatural since they meet not only human need but in fact one beyond human comprehension, and because "their sole ground and measure is the divine nature itself."[77]

What then does Lonergan's theory allow to the human intelligence in its knowledge of God? Such knowledge is clearly developmental. First of all, in its cultural expression, i.e., in the words, languages, formulation, definitions, etc., that serve as the vehicles of communication. Though closely bound up with knowledge itself, the actual expression of knowledge is sufficiently distinct therefrom to allow for a constant process of clarification in the very attempt at communication. What is involved here is largely the work of explanation or theological hermeneutics. Beneath this, however, is a constant revision of conceptual contents themselves, an ongoing *dynamis* of greater refinement, further nuancing, gradual clarification, and occasional increment. Thirdly, underlying even this is a prior and more radical development in knowledge itself, i.e., it is understanding itself that progresses and not only the subsequent conceptualizing process in which understanding comes to inner expression. In short, any attempt to understand Revelation (and to believe is spontaneously to seek to understand) sets in motion the preconceptual dynamic of insight. As potency in the realm of intelligence, man even in his knowing of God is subject to that process innate to all human knowing: the tripartite process of experiencing, understanding, and affirming. Even in faith, the organic process begins not with the understood (God himself) but with the dynamic structure of human knowing.

Lonergan identifies the sphere where all of this occurs as that of theology.[78] The reason being that theology as distinct from faith concerns itself with the question *quid sit* rather than the subsequent question *an sit;* its basic act in other words is understanding not assent.[79] The import of this is that the goal of theological thinking is not *truth,* which is found only in the judgment, but rather the *adequacy* of the understanding and the concepts wherewith it strives to grasp intelligibility. Thus, a certain cognitive progression is indigenous to theological reflection. The development that occurs here becomes a development of faith itself only when the Church assumes such change into her own doctrine by her authoritative judgment. In this sense, dogmatic development is derivative to that of theology.

The evolution in theological understanding works itself out on two distinct levels: the horizontal and the vertical. On the former, the historical context is uppermost; here there occurs a succession of distinct cultural perspectives, each of them relative, as e.g., when the *Lebenswelt* of Biblical man gives way to that of the Fathers inhabiting a world of Hellenism, and then to the university environment of the Medieval *magistri* and *doctores*. By contrast, on the vertical plane the development is one of deepening understanding in a more homogeneous line, differing, for example, on the basis of approaching a problem analytically or synthetically.[80] An integral theology will take cognizance of both these lines of growth: Lonergan himself instances the historical development in our understanding of the Christological mystery — through the primitive insights of Tertullian, to the more complex but imprecise ones of Origen, and then to the grasp of the intelligibility of *homooúsios* by St. Anthanasius, defined at Nicaea.[81]

Finally, Lonergan mentions a necessary reservation on any theory of development, namely that behind all semantic and conceptual differences, and behind the differences in developing understanding itself is doctrinal identity.[82] In this sense the *homooúsios* of Nicaea was not a new truth but both a new understanding of an original truth of Revelation and a new unified conceptual articulation of it. This ultimately stable element is the doctrine itself, understood as ontological truth rather than formal truth of knowledge. It shows itself even in a certain conceptual constant behind all conceptual variation, at least in the sense of a continuity of defined doctrine on which basis later definitions are not revocations of earlier ones.

In retrospect, Lonergan's theory is one that opens out onto broad horizons and yet is stated by its author in moderate and qualified tones. The continuing revision of our notion of God remains within classical perspectives. It is true that "the theologian is under no necessity of reducing to the metaphysical elements which suffice for an account of this world, such supernatural realities as the Incarnation, the Indwelling of the Holy Spirit, and the Beatific Vision."[83] Still, God is knowable only as Being; He is most perfectly conceptualized as *Ipsum Intelligere;* analogy yields authentic truth in penetrating into the mysteries of the Trinity (the analogy of human knowing and loving) and Grace (the analogy of created cause and effect); we cannot say that *Ipsum Intelligere* is analogous to nothing we know, for what is unknown cannot be meant or even named. In ultimate analysis the theologian has to have recourse to metaphysics to explain revealed mysteries and Lonergan is convinced of the unicity of metaphysics.[84] A clue to the balanced nature of Lonergan's thought is his conviction that in the gnoseological doctrine of St. Thomas, properly understood, there is to be found at least the tools for a theory on development of theological (and by inference) doctrinal understanding.[85]

By way of summary, Lonergan's contention is: we know what our ideas of God signify; we know that the judgments we make by means of them are true; yet we do not know what God is in himself.

## 4. Edward Schillebeeckx: Objective Dynamism of Intellect

If Joseph Maréchal charted the course that Catholic epistemologies were to follow (a movement brought to more contemporary fulfillment in the work of Rahner, Lonergan, and others), Edward Schillebeeckx[86] has pursued the same orientation in an independent way that actually marks a very radical departure from the Maréchalian approach. Both "schools" are expositors of St. Thomas; both, it must be admitted, bring to their reading of the Thomistic corpus a dominant intuition which imperates the resulting synthetic interpretation, a presupposition amounting in each instance to some form of intellectual dynamism. The parting of the ways occurs with Schillebeeckx's insistence that such dynamism is an objective one, whereas those faithful to the insight of Maréchal see it rather as subjective, as the knower's own transcendentally reflective act. Schillebeeckx's thoughts also have been developed more exclusively in an explicitly theological context, approaching then

88

the problem of man's knowledge of God more directly in the perspective of Revelation and Faith. Nonetheless, both approaches emphasize the continuity between natural and supernatural knowledge.

Schillebeeckx's underlying cognitional theory is more radically intuitional than either that of Rahner or Lonergan, in the sense that it is less an immanentist explanation of intellective knowing and allows for a direct rather than vicarious contact by the knower of the real in its extra-mental status. The intuition involved, however, is only *implicit* in the abstraction of the concept from the sense phantasm. That is to say, the very act of mentally representing the universal nature (the concept) takes place against the background of a simultaneous seizure of real existence which is non-conceptual. Thus all intellection is conceptual, but the conceptualizing is only one aspect of integral understanding and not to be equated with understanding itself as such. The explanation that came to be uppermost in the Thomistic School gave a value of the real to the concept itself; the mind knew the existent order precisely in its universal idea (which was thus a *species in qua*).[87] The Maréchalian objection to this denied existential value to the concept and was thus necessitated to seek a way back to existence through a projecting power of judgment — as e.g., in Lonergan's judgment of virtual unconditionedness. In the thought Schillebeeckx has taken over from Dominic De Petter,[88] it is the non-conceptual and pre-judgmental contact with reality that enables the subject to realize that none of his concepts are exhaustive of or even adequately representative of what simply cannot yield itself up to objectification. At the same time, every concept is noetically tendential in a way that is authentic, and *objectively* so. Thus the dynamism here is intellectual rather than conative; the act is precisely a noetic one of intellect rather than, more broadly, a striving of human spirit.

What the mind intuits, though merely in this implicit fashion, is being itself, but *real* being in all its amplitude, in its unity and analogical variety.[89] From this comes the conceptual construct which is a further attempt at explicating this awareness objectively as the *idea* of proportionate being. Subsequent reflection on being through this concept (thus conceptual and non-conceptual awareness interact one upon the other)[90] brings us to realize that the immediate but implicit intuition of finite being is at the same time an implicit though mediate acknowledgment of Absolute and Infinite Being. Thus, implicit in all our knowing, in however remote and unrecognized a way, is a "knowing" of God. The reason for this is simply that finite being *exists* (and to intuit something is to know it as it is) only as a participation of Pure Being. The intuition of the former is precisely a grasp of it as real, and so as intelligible, in terms of the former. Thus, there is no demonstration of or reasoning to God but rather what amounts to a unique "intuition" of him which then is articulated in logical categories as objective explanation and as a verification process. This is Schillebeeckx's explanation of what St. Thomas attempts to do with his *Quinque Viae*: to suppose otherwise is to confuse the psychological processes of intelligence with its logical ones.

Elsewhere, Schillebeeckx employs a distinct starting point in an attempt to explain this same theory. Here, he views all knowledge as initially a self-awareness, an intuition of one's own human existence as it opens out upon all other existents, above all, other humans.[91] Such awareness is of being-in-a-world, a world that is human or at least humanized. Man's bodiliness demands that this discovery of self be indirect, arising out of a prior sensation of material existents. At the same time, man becomes intellectually aware not only of a thing whose phenomena he has sensed but of his own constitution as a knower, and the peculiar quality of his existence that renders this possible. This primal experience is totally pre-reflexive and unthematic; it is a "being present to oneself," and nothing other than what St. Thomas understood in speaking of the soul as "naturally present to itself."[92] Its basic yield is a revelation of one's own human existence as mystery, as bounded by a dimension of unknowability. Implicit in this is the transcendence of self, in the drive towards fuller self-understanding, through intuiting the reality of the trans-subjective order and submerging oneself therein to be enriched by union with it. Being thus becomes a sort of "horizon" within which one apprehends all subsequent objects of knowledge. But that horizon itself demands and "points to" the Absolute as its own ground; the very relatedness of the self and of being in their contingency and limitedness guarantees the reality of the Absolute. This spontaneous and necessarily vague "experience" of the Absolute is pre-reflective and merely implicit, and so it leaves the Absolute unknown, i.e., unrendered into thematic knowledge.

Schillebeeckx's theory thus allows for an intuitional or pre-conceptual and pre-judgmental grasp of being originating in an intuition of one's own human existence as relational to others and ultimately to an Absolute. This relationality is in fact something transcendental, though differently so than "being" as object of the science of metaphysics (*ens in commune*). Moreover, there is no explicit awareness of the analogous character of being except in subsequent knowledge that is reflective and conceptual. But this primal experience, which is nothing other than human consciousness itself, is not yet human knowledge in a proper or integral sense. Of itself it is only the implicit horizon of explicit knowledge; it remains below the threshold of spontaneous reflection and objectification that renders communication possible. Man's experience of concrete existents (in a coalescence of sensation and agent intellection) issues in the process of imaging, conceiving, propositionalizing, etc. By and of themselves, these "intentional forms" are purely *representational;* they possess no value of the real of *themselves.* That contact with the existing order is de facto achieved by way of them is due rather to the non-conceptual aspect of all such knowledge.[93] All human knowledge is thus conceptual, but the concept is only "the limited expression of an implicit and pre-conceptual consciousness of reality unexpressed in itself."[94] At this point, through the conceptual representation, man "rejoins," so to speak, the ontic order but precisely *by way of the objective contents of those concepts.*

Here, Schillebeeckx's departure from the position espoused by Rahner and Lonergan is clearly decisive in the emphasis upon elements that are objective and cognitive in kind. For the former, the dynamism involved is not a subjective projection of the self but "an objective ontic dynamism of the experienced reality."[95] It is not a subjective affirmation rooted in the subject's finality, but a "discovery" or an implicit awareness of the objective relatedness of the contents of any thematic knowledge to an unthematic, pre-conceptual grasp of the whole multi-dimensional universe of real being. It is in this sense of a seizure of the real in its totality by virtue of its immediate presentiality to the knower that Schillebeeckx's cognitional theory is markedly intuitional. The conceptual perspective upon reality, by contrast, while authentic and true, is necessarily partial and never able to exhaust or even adequate the mystery of the real.

The transposition to supernatural knowledge, to the order of faith, does not involve any departure from this basic structure of knowing. Public Revelation is always historical; first God acts in human history, then, concurrent with this deed, are the explanatory and interpretative words of the prophets. All of this supplies the concepts with which faith has to do. Behind the concepts, but "pointed to" by them, lies the reality of God acting to which the believer attains non-conceptually. This latter encounter is made possible not by the very nature of intellection itself but only by a transforming opening of that natural light by God to himself — in the "anointing of the Holy Spirit." This is the non-historical aspect of the Revelation as present (and dialogic) address. So viewed, God's Revelation is but the explication of man's self-understanding of existence.[96] Faith comes *ex auditu* as St. Paul explains (*Romans* 10:17), but this refers to its material objects, i.e., to the objective meaning of events in history and those propositions and formulae derived from them that orientate the believing mind to an implicit intuition of God himself who alone is the *formal* object of faith.[97] Through these "categorical" realities (historical or conceptual) man "rejoins" the Absolute, now explicitly recognized as God — but in an experimental way that remains not susceptible of objective expression. Every human formulation of faith is thus intrinsically inadequate, including those of Scripture itself.[98] At the same time, the non-conceptual attainment of God is possible only in the direction indicated by the objective contents of such formulae, so that the latter are true, and when their status is that of a dogmatic pronouncement they become themselves secondary objects of faith and irrevocable.[99]

The simple meaning of this is that our knowledge of God, while impossible apart from concepts, cannot be limited to conceptual contents. Such knowledge is not the mere transfer of the latter (even as "purified" or "corrected") to God.[100] Rather, the intellect uses the idea (the *ratio concepta*) to *signify* God in another distinct and altogether surpassing operation (*actus significandi*).[101] This is indeed to "know" God but, as St. Thomas noted, *non definitive vel circumscriptive.*[102] Thus there is a distinction in every dogmatic formulation between what is affirmed and what is only the vehicle of expression, between "the real essence of the dogmatic affirmation" and "the form in which the definition is couched;" it is the former which is unchangeable while the latter admits of modification.[103]

The validity of this cannot be done away with by insisting that the concepts involved are employed solely in an analogical sense. Schillebeeckx's interpretation of St. Thomas' understanding of analogy strengthens considerably his whole theory; for he finds there no basis for the analogy of proper proportionality as developed by Cajetan. As long as it is the God-world analogy, the only possibility that he finds St. Thomas allowing is that of an intrinsic attribution.[104] In attribution the extension of the name is founded not on an abstract idea common to many but on a reality that is one numerically.[105] Some causal relationship justifies the extension; only thereafter is the meaning of the name broadened out to where it signifies all the analogues but *per prius et posterius*, that is, in terms of the various proportions they bear towards the prime analogue. In the assignation to God, the *ratio analogica* that is used retains its creaturely limitations, but it can be "prolonged" to God by reason of the rapport existing between the creature and himself. The attribution is an intrinsic one because it is founded upon a causal nexus, and because the perfection in question is of the transcendental order.[106] However, unlike an intrinsic attribution restricted to the creaturely realm, the analogous extension to God of a perfection leaves its formality as divine unknown; the divine *modus essendi* of that perfection remains shrouded in mystery.

Here analogical knowledge is only capable of conveying that God, remaining unknown in himself, is properly named *in the perspective opened up by the conceptualized perfection.*[107] This is more than to name God merely relatively (e.g., the Cause of goodness) or negatively (e.g., not evil). It is to signify his very substance but without constricting that substance within the range of even an analogical concept. God is intellectually located, as it were, at the open end of a transcendental concept.[108] So understood, analogical knowledge of God designates quite simply the proportion of creature to God; what it does not designate is any internal relationships in God (purely of reason) that are themselves proportionate to real relationships in the creature, i.e., a proportion of proportions, or proportionality.

The prospects for dogmatic development opened up by this theory are abundantly clear. The non-conceptual aspect of our knowledge of God is outside all such advancement, save in terms of a personal inexpressible penetration. The explication of such experience in conceptual terms is, on the contrary, necessarily developmental. Even in this latter phase, there is an unchangeable "core" but this lies exclusively in the orientation and direction that such concepts supply, the perspective they give onto an unknowable God; as partial expressions of a continuing experience of the Unknown they are themselves the elements of an evolutionary process. The ensuing development while not limited to drawing out *logically* the virtual intelligibilities of existing formulae, is at the same time, dependent upon the objective cognitive contents of existing dogmatic statements.

Reflection upon Schillebeeckx's solution to the epistemological problem of God raises two important questions: one concerning the basic postulate to his entire theory of knowledge; the other concerning his minimizing of God's objective intelligibility for man.

(1) In the former, the basic premise is that all knowledge is a gradual unfolding of a primary consciousness of self; an explicit awareness that is simultaneously an implicit intuition of being itself, including, in however vague a fashion, Absolute Being. Undoubtedly, the inspiration here is phenomenological but Schillebeeckx's position needs to be carefully differentiated from radical Phenomenology which, interpreting the world as a world-for-me or a world-for-thought, gives to it no truth or meaning apart from the knowing human person. Schillebeeckx on the contrary understands external reality has meaning of itself, indeed man must go out to that reality before arriving at self-awareness, and such consciousness is itself orientated towards an external world. At the very outset then he avoids all subjectivism; human thought is not of phenomena or pure objects but of the real and existent outside the mind. Thus there is no need to bridge the hiatus to the real order of being with a subjective dynamism of spirit, as Maréchal was forced to do. But what is problematic in Schillebeeckx's theory, especially in light of its claim to Thomistic parenthood, is not so much the insistence upon an intuition of being as the virtual *disengagement* of such intuition from the conceptual process as its subsequent explication.[109] All knowledge must then be given

a dual aspect: intuitive and conceptual. The concept "represents" and by means of this the mind "signifies," but only by recourse to the intuitive aspect does it attain the real. The concept thus lacks all noumenal value apart from the non-conceptual dimension of intellection, and is always a deficient rendering of what the knower grasps in a certain totality. All this marks a departure from the more common understanding in Thomistic tradition, but there are more intrinsic reasons for calling it into question. What needs to be asked is whether man's intellectual life is indeed so totally radicated in a primal consciousness of the self that is an implicit awareness of all that is, and whether the original grasp of being is indeed an intuition that is neither conceptual nor judgmental. Granting this premise, it is considerably less difficult to see the conceptualizing process as a continual effort to express what must always elude the intellect's representational powers.

(2) Secondly, is this an overly agnostic position where man's categorical (conceptual) knowledge of God is concerned? Granting that the Divine Reality is not enclosed conceptually within our concept of the transcendentals (a point that Schillebeeckx has, I think, forcibly demonstrated), are those concepts merely tendential, giving no more than an orientation or perspective within which God remains unknown and merely signified? These perspectives are at any rate multiple and varied — e.g., being, truth, goodness, knowing, loving, etc. — and retain (in the created order) a formal distinctness, i.e., the objective concept of knowledge is not that of love. Are we justified in attributing all these perfections to God *in their formal distinctness,*[110] or are we able only to affirm a Reality who is not these distinct perfections even in an infinite mode, but Something beyond as an unknown but unified prolongation of them?[111] The limitations upon intelligibility in this latter view render it impossible to conceive any relatedness within God of essence to existence, of both of these to Person or Persons, of being to operation, between knowledge, love, and power, etc. The question is whether or not an available intelligibility

is being closed off to exploration. The deepest analysis of intellection, for instance, discloses it as formally an assimilative action
necessitating a formal (not necessarily a real) distinction
between knower and known. The intentional "becoming" or
"being" the other is the foundation for a theory of immanent
forms or ideas, enabling us to speak of Divine Ideas, and to
enter more penetratingly into the mystery of *Intelligere Subsistens* and God's creative causality; and all of this without
any implicit denial of the real identity of *esse naturale* and
*esse intentionale* in God. Without distinguishing knowledge
and love (or intelligence and freedom) in God, is it possible
in this explanation to even raise the question as to the formal
medium of God's foreknowledge of future events arising from
man's freedom? The impossibility of even venturing such a
question also closes off a revealed source of further understanding the mystery of human freedom. But it is perhaps our
understanding in faith of the mystery of the Trinity that is
most of all lessened. Does this theory allow the immanent
procession of the "verbum" in intellection as such to throw
any light upon the mystery of the Eternal Logos, and of
Christ's identification of himself as consubstantial Son of God?
At least the analogy of the mind's presence to itself in human
knowledge loses much of its illuminative power regarding the
Trinity. In raising the question as to the possibility of something
more than Schillebeeckx appears to allow, there is no suggestion
of a rational demonstration of something Divine from the
created order; the theological uses of analogy are rather inverse,
the very process originating in God's self-revelation. The question is of the intrinsic intelligibility of the concepts delivered
to us in faith.

In fine, Father Schillebeeckx's theologizing leaves ample room
for a revision of our conceptual presentation of God; indeed,
demands such a constant revision. What he calls into question
(and here lies whatever weakness the position has) is the
genuine intelligibility and lasting value of any phase of objective
representation.

97

## 5. Leslie Dewart: Extreme Empiricism

*Gnoseological Background.* If Rahner and Schillebeeckx have attempted to translate many of the insights of modern thought to within the perspective of the older learning, finding there a congenial soil; and if Lonergan is seeking to re-think the old by deploying a new phenomenological methodology; Leslie Dewart,[112] on the contrary, in a fresh and thoroughly contemporary approach to the problem, inclines towards a displacement of the old by the new, stressing rather a radical break with the intellectual past[113]. The distinctive element here is an almost total emphasis upon the empirical. Acknowledging an indebtedness to Wittgenstein, Dewart begins with minimizing the distinction between thought and language.[114] Far from being an arbitrary set of symbols "representing" ideas and devised for the mere sake of communication, language has a certain priority over thought in initiating the thinking process. Even more, it would appear to be itself the very formal element of which thinking is dynamically structured. To think of something is simply to acquire and use its name.

Underlying all thought, as the ontological root of its very possibility, is human consciousness, not however as the operation of a faculty of man who pre-exists his conscious state as "substance," but as the very mode of existence proper to the human reality — a mode best described in terms of "presence": "man is the being who is present to himself."[115] Consciousness so conceived demands its intentional horizon. This is not, however, any implicit intuition of all reality (Schillebeeckx), but is supplied empirically in the varied ensemble of experiences which emerge into consciousness in such fashion as to "objectify" it.[116] The emergent process is achieved in the grasp, experientially, of language and in the resulting or perhaps accompanying occurrence of conceptualization. It appears that Dewart sees consciousness as originally pure subjectivity, one that is "formless" to begin with, and that discovers its object in and through the experience of language. The latter initiates and governs the conceptualizing process which constitutes the phenomenon that we call thinking.

The linguistic-conceptual process is necessarily socio-historical.[117] This leads rather readily to acknowledging a certain arbitrariness to the conceptual equipment to which any of us is heir and which is available in any given intellectual epoch. Any conceptual system is basically an historically determined cultural form. Transposed to the realm of Christian faith, such a theory of human knowing offers possibilities for doctrinal development that are vast. If Dewart makes some concessions to the need for continuity, this is not a continuity in the line of conceptual formulation. The latter is not necessary to preserve the unity of the faith, and indeed frequently is undesirable as actually impeding progression in the understanding of the mysteries. Human subjectivity (i.e., consciousness) is thus indigenously progressive; knowledge is process and a self creative one; it is the coming-to-be-of-the-self. Any newness of conceptual view and vocabulary entails a heightening of consciousness, with the consequence of an eventual jettisoning of past articulations of thought, whether of reason alone or of faith.

The question can be asked, however, as to whether Dewart's fusion of thought and language does not unavoidably lead to a complete neglect of the former, a denial to it of its own distinctive nature as an objectifying power not totally subject to the vagaries of ever-changing language. He seemingly eliminates the sources of stability and continuity in the history of human thought, and this poses the question as to what if anything remains unvarying in man's cognitive life. Even religious consciousness, as faith-response to Revelation, is here apparently deprived of all objectivity, at least of a cognitive kind. It isn't merely that religious formulae are inadequate, partial expressions of an inexpressible yet definitive encounter with the Divine, but rather that they are mere temporary symbols approximating in a totally functional way something that lies on the perimeter of human consciousness, an expe-

99

rience that is not only beyond man's powers of representation but is even non-objective in character. Yet even granting a primacy in faith to experience — still such experience cannot reasonably be reduced to acts that are exclusively projections of a subject; there must needs be some material content that is trans-subjective, whether God's deeds or the prophetic interpretation of them. And why do not these as experienced convey an intelligibility which must be (though not exclusively) cognitive and so objective?

*Epistemological Foreground.* The epistemological theory operative in Dewart's thought opens up broad horizons for doctrinal development. Its empirical emphasis lends itself to seeing Revelation not as a message (to be handed on, as in the Patristic *"paradosis"*) but as the Church's present experience.[118] Experience is necessarily changing; it demands that the old continually give way to the new. To admit this where Christianity is concerned is to realize that one conceptual form of faith supplants another, with an accompanying heightening of religious consciousness. To impede this growth-process would be to fossilize the *depositum fidei;* the Church would then be no more safeguarding the Word entrusted to her than would parents be nurturing the children they prevented from growing. The development this allows for is perhaps better designated a genuine evolution, i.e., while it remains phylogenetic, it is not restricted to being homogeneous in kind.

In the present state of Christian affairs, it is the Hellenic acculturation which Dewart sees as, in actual historical fact, rendering belief static, and today impeding the emergence of Christian consciousness in new conceptual and linguistic forms.[119] What he would seek then is a de-Hellenization of dogmas akin to the attempts to demythologize the Bible.[120] Unlike Harnack, he does not maintain that such Hellenization was in its own time a corruption of belief. It can be seriously questioned if this assumption of "Hellenism" is not overly narrow, i.e., not leaving any room for other possible explanations. Is it not just as true, for instance, to understand that Christian reflection

100

transformed at their very interior the concepts taken over from pre-Christian Greek philosophy? The meaning that the Council of Nicaea gives to the concept "person" is far removed from anything expressed in the Greek use of *prosopon;* and is really of Christian inspiration. Another instance of this has been pointed out in Gregory of Nyssa's use of the category "participation."[121] There is an alternative in all of this to seeing a "translation" of primitive belief into an alien thought system; it is quite as defensible to see Christian insights liberating virtualities of truth already glimpsed imperfectly, but in a universal and enduring way in the Greek experience. At the very least, this is a necessary qualification of Dewart's gratuitous assumption.

It is Dewart's concept of *truth,* however, that affords him a proximate principle for viewing doctrinal development as radically as he does. Because knowledge is not a subject's assimilation of objects but the subject's emergence into consciousness, it is more accurate to understand truth not as conformity (i.e., of a mind with reality), but as *fidelity.*[122] There is an obvious shift here away from the cognitive order; one that will allow for infallibility without any insistence upon immutability of doctrine. "Fidelity" lays emphasis upon the conative and moral dimension to Christian response; Dewart by locating truth there does not wish to eliminate intellectual elements altogether (in this he is faithful to Gabriel Marcel), but he does appear to reduce the value of concepts to a totally pragmatic or useful one. The dynamic reference of the one who knows truthfully back to that which he regards with fidelity is not a dynamism by way of the objective contents of such mental words. In its conceptual expression, at least, no truth is timeless, absolute, or trans-historical. Christian truth is thus unavoidable contingent and open to complete historicity. Dewart insists upon a continuity, but the question is how that is possible within the framework of the theory that he has constructed. Can there be continuity without at least some minimal content that is objective in a cognitive sense and so to its own degree unalterable? Even if fidelity to a non-intellective event, encountered in lived experience rather than in abstract representation, be stressed, does not such experience necessarily demand its own truth content? To take one of Dewart's own instances — the use of a phenomenological understanding of personality to conceptualize anew the mystery of the Hypostatic Union — in what sense does this maintain continuity with, let us say, the definitions of Nicaea or Chalcedon? There seemingly is no cognitive continuity at all, unless knowledge be understood as formless and voiceless, as utterly lacking in content.

*Re-conceptualization of God.* Unsurprisingly, Dewart's theory calls for radical re-thinking of traditional belief and, most fundamental of all, a re-conceptualization of God. Needless to say, his own attempt is tentative and exploratory, and remains well within the bounds of Orthodoxy.[123] The search for a new understanding of God will not be conducted, first of all, within the ambit of being; this has been true in the past due to an inheritance from Greek metaphysics. God is neither a being (supreme among all others) nor being itself. He has no essence and cannot properly be said to exist.[124] To exist is "to come forth," to "emerge," and attributable only to essence; moreover, whatever exists in this sense is actually self-creating. It follows that, lacking essence, God cannot be an object of thought, that is, he is not intelligible in and of himself (nor for himself), although he can give meaning to us — as indeed he does in Revelation. The only two concepts that will serve contemporary man's awareness of God are *presence* and *reality*.[125] God is known in our empirical experience — and this is by no means to say that he is himself the object of an empirical intuition — as a Reality beyond being who is Present to us. Understandably, in the light of such a conceptual framework there are no "proofs" or demonstrations of God. The *Quinque Viae* of St. Thomas are without final validity since they establish a "God" who is within the spectrum of being.[126] What lies at the bottom of the outmoded Hellenistic concept; what made its use possible for Medieval Christian thinkers, is analogy. Dewart is inclined to view this as mere semantic gymnastics; an attempt to say at one and the same time "God is being" and "He is *not* being." The universal use of analogy only betrays an underlying suspicion that God cannot be conceptualized in terms of being.[127]

The unsettling thing about Dewart's God — who is not being — is that he remains faceless and nameless.[128] It would seem improper, or at the very least meaningless, to conceive of Him as Creator, i.e., the pure source of what man is in his own finite being. Dewart in fact prefers to bypass this question in favor of an approach starting with man as, in his own being, he stands open to God as to a Reality beyond being. But what clues are available to His identity? Is experience of God here anything more than a heightened consciousness of the negatively unlimited possibilities of mankind, remaining as it does non-objectified and contentless? All this is a consequence of the dismissal of the analogy of being, which Dewart surprisingly misrepresents when he characterizes it as ". . . supposing that concepts derived from empirical intuition can *adequately* reach an object beyond empirical intuition . . ."[129] (italics supplied). The whole medieval postulate in the use of analogy, and most clearly in the case of the God-world analogy, was precisely that it attained (i.e., named) its secondary analogates only proportionately, that is, in an imperfect and merely relational way.[130] What analogy guaranteed in predications about God was the truthfulness of a knowledge that could not be other than inadequate.

The assertion that God is not being and yet is reality, has to presuppose that the former term is taken in a very narrow sense; it has to mean in actual fact only one of the limited modes of being. Without such restriction, as designating ultimate actuality whereby anything is posited outside of nothingness, "being" is the absolutely primal predicate. This is "be-ing" in its verbal or participial form, but Dewart is apparently limiting the word to its form as a noun where it signifies something having existence. In this latter sense it is true that God is not a being among beings, not even the supreme Being among such. It is unlikely Dewart could object to even raising the question "Does God exist?" if he understood existence as only the denial of nothingness, rather than as a perfection proper to an essence, i.e., what "ex-sists" in the sense of coming-to-be.[131] Arthur Gibson may be right in discerning a tendency on Dewart's part to reify being, to see it as a perfection superadded to something more basic than being.[132] This would appear to open the door to "nothingness" as a reality prior to being.

This prime assumption carries many other conclusions in its wake, e.g., God is not a person, the reason being that personality is limited to a narrow anthropological sense, intrinsic to a human mode of existence, and inconceivable apart from "the act by which it creates itself."[133] The eschewing of analogy precludes any possible understanding of Divine personality; Dewart makes no advertence to the notion, developed during the high Middle Ages, of the Divine Persons as Subsisting Relations — a concept that goes far beyond the limitations of created personality.

To refuse to conceive of God as the fullness of being is, of course, to deny Him the properties of pure being. Omnipotence ". . . insofar as it means . . . the possibility of violence to the spontaneity of existence . . ." might be conceived more meaningfully, not as a power of acting upon (the Christian God is not Zeus), but as a "reciprocal being-with."[134] The significance of this is that then the world and history would remain "totally open to future creation by man."[135] What is missing from this view of things is any indication of how man's exercise of freedom remains God's gift (creative, in nature; saving, in grace), and how the sovereignty of God in his own initiatives is any longer preserved.

God's eternity, as conceived in traditional belief, should similarly be rejected in favor of Temporality as "the mutual presence of God and man in the *conscious* creation of the world."[136] In fine, "The Christian God's substance is not above history; (but) is the substance of history itself."[137] Dewart makes abundantly clear that he intends this in no Hegelian sense, adding by way of a clarification that "history is made by man, but in the presence of God."[138] But what kind of contribution by God does this make allowance for? Dewart is at least logical in admitting that at best this would be a contingent influence. Certainly, it leaves no room for a predetermining or predestining God, and logically allows for a God who is himself determined. The saving events of Christ's earthly life are undeniably contingent, yet if these are truly the concrete implementation of God's saving intentions then at the same time they must possess a hypothetical or conditional necessity within the Divine mind. Dewart's failure to acknowledge this amounts, at the very least, to a shallow understanding of God's uncreated freedom, or perhaps a confusing of the latter with mere contingency.[139]

Another classical distinction that Dewart would jettison is that between the natural and supernatural orders, which he sees as "a mere play on words, irrelevant to reality."[140] His intentions here are to avoid any extrinsicism, to see nature not as "in every way opposed to grace" but "as naturally apt to receive grace, because that is how it was in fact created." Grace is thus "a historical fact, God's presence to man, which existentially qualifies the historical intelligibility of nature in a definitive way"; the difference ". . . is not in the abstract spatio-temporal *content* but in the existential historical form of the event or reality. . . ."[141] Dewart's position here bears marked similarities to that developed by Max Seckler,[142] an explanation which, while it has the advantage of bringing to light the universal order of grace in which alone man finds himself, does call into question the genuine gratuity of that order. The universality of such an order is no argument against its own unique unexactedness, an unexactedness that cannot be reduced to that which attends the unqualified freedom of God as Creator, as bringing forth persons out of nothingness or endowing some individuals with unique resources of nature not bestowed upon others. Christian tradition has always viewed grace as some sort of ontological elevation of man, the offer of a destiny which is a real and new trans-finalization of his being. The real distinctness of the supernatural order rests in the fact that what grace offers is personal communion with God that comes precisely as God's free gift and not as due to man's nature.[143] Otherwise such communion must be seen as an end intrinsically possible to nature itself (at least in theory), and is in effect to view God as homogeneous with natural creation. Unlike the "supernatural existential" of Rahner and Balthasar (involving, however, theological difficulties of its own) — which attempts to distinguish the *order* of grace common to mankind universally from the actual acceptance of grace by way of a personal, conscious decision — Dewart's explanation apparently equates grace with nature in its *de facto* historical situation.

Noting that the notion of God as "being" tends to resist expansion into the central Christian mysteries of the Trinity and the Incarnation, some similar re-conceptualization is also attempted here. *Logos* conveys not a Word-Son proceeding from His Speaker-Father in consubstantiality, but God in His presence and meaningfulness. It means God incarnate in this world, present in our history as *logos,* i.e., meaning. Dewart arrives at this view by seeing the origin of *logos* in pre-Christian Greek thought as the intelligibility of things, the divine element in reality; Christ, as the personal *Logos,* thus walks in his own footsteps as it were.[144]

In a similar vein, the Holy Spirit is expressive of God's gift of self, his self-communion to men. There is, it is true, a further dimension to this revealed truth: the realization that ". . . this religious experience 'in' us reflects what is true of God 'in' Himself. . . ."[145] Dewart's avowed intention here is merely to point out the drawbacks of conceptualizing the Trinity in the opposed concepts of nature and person; and, making his own a suggestion of Rahner's, he succeeds in drawing attention to the inadequacies resultant from too uncritical a pre-occupation with these categories. His charge of the popular conception being in fact a "crypto-tritheism"[146] is not entirely without foundation; certainly, fuller explorations are called for, and along the very lines that Dewart proposes. But caution is needed lest the reaction bring one to the opposite pole of a "crypto-modalism." The fact that the believer has no choice but to start with the inner or "economic" Trinity of itself affords such a danger. This suggests the necessity of carefully distinguishing such phrases of Dewart's as ". . . the different persons *are* different modes (albeit not successive ones) of his self-communication."[147] In short, it is of paramount importance to distinguish the Uncreated Trinity (present within the soul by grace) from its created facsimile in the soul achieved by way of created graces which are effects of the Persons.[148] Also, the ultimate explanation of the immanent processions *within* Divinity is that these are an inner necessity of the Divine Reality itself and not simply for communication and manifestation to the creaturely order.

If it indeed be impossible today to understand personality other than as a center of consciousness, then there is a good deal to Dewart's contention that the traditional explanation of the Incarnation as a Hypostatic Union, i.e., two natures united in one person, suffers somewhat in its conceptual viability.[149] The granting to Christ of a human consciousness is then the admission in Him of a human personality. At the same time, there has to be avoided any tendency toward a "crypto-docetism" in the mere repetition of the orthodox formula. This is a warning that needs to be heeded; but the suspicion remains that Dewart has not taken seriously enough the genuine and lasting truth value in the Fourth and Fifth Century definitions. Acknowledging that Christ was possessed of a human consciousness may intensify our awareness of the genuineness of his humanity. What it leaves unsaid is the believer's primary conviction that this was (and is) the human consciousness of God.

In summary, it is Dewart's understanding of truth that is the linchpin upon which his whole enterprise depends; it is here that his effort is most questionable and in the end unconvincing. Underlying all else is a rejection of knowledge as intentionality. Unlike thinkers such as Tillich and Schillebeeckx who accept the subject-object polarity as something irreducibly given, or Rahner and Lonergan who unify the opposition transcendentally in the *a priori* conditions for knowledge, Dewart insists that the opposition is *posterior* to knowledge: "the introduction of . . . an

intentional dichotomy into that which was originally undifferentiated."[150] Thus truth cannot be the conforming of mind to
what pre-exists it, rather it is an anterior quality of knowledge
which has as its consequence this relationship of conformity.
Essentially, truth is that objectification of being that is involved
in knowing, whereby the self is differentiated and acquires new
being as a knowing subject. There is a conformity achieved but
this is merely *de facto* and it is not a goal to be sought but only
a point in the on-going process of creative self-realization; it is
precisely something to be revised, to be overcome. Thus, "there
is no empirical reason whatever to suppose that, prior to the
truth of knowledge, there is a truth of things, constituted by
God's knowledge of things, which is the measure of the truth
of human knowledge."[151] Error or falsity, then, is simply the
normal failure of consciousness to be fully faithful to itself, and
so in a relative way characterizes all knowledge quite as does
truth.

Since Dewart sees faith as the religious dimension to experience, the truth of faith is not human correspondence to God's
Revelation of himself or to man's own identity and destiny discovered therein, but fidelity. But fidelity to what? It is difficult
to see on what basis this could be anything more than fidelity
to the religious self-achievement of consciousness, to man's own
religious potentialities. God would appear to be only the indeterminate horizon or focal point of a striving that lacks all determining finality; that is less freedom than radical contingency.
The transcendence of God has disappeared or at the very least
has been deferred by Dewart. The only God with whom man
enters into relationship is one of pure immanentism, and one
surely devoid of all identifying marks as a Christian God. Even
Dewart's presentation of the Trinity is not easily differentiated
from a God of Religious Naturalism, and his basic idea of God
does not yield to concretization as Jesus, the God of history.

In fine, the reconceptualization he envisages is not one of
homogeneous development; its extreme empirical basis does not
allow to human knowledge any invariant hold, even one of mere

directedness, upon a revealing God. What cannot be dismissed in Dewart's work, on the other hand, is the attention he has focused on the partial and relative character to all knowledge and truth. It cannot be denied that the correspondence theory of truth has for too long been presented as a noetic reduplication of reality rather than a tendential conformity thereto, a conformity unique in its own order of intentional immanence.

*　　*　　*

The epistemology represented by Rahner and Lonergan savors somewhat of an intellectual immanentism, which finds its way back to reality only in a highly involuted and extra-cognitive way. The extreme empiricism of Dewart, in effect equating knowledge with constant conceptual revision as a process of self-achieving consciousness, is at the opposite end of the spectrum. Schillebeeckx's position, while balancing to some degree the intellectualism of the former with the realism of the latter, does nonetheless demand an initial option of intuitionalism that is perhaps less than adequately substantiated. All three positions take Catholic thought irreversibly beyond the impasse of an earlier "conceptualism"; they render the reconceptualization of God not only possible but necessary.

# CHAPTER FOUR

## ST. THOMAS REVISITED:[1] ANALOGICAL
## KNOWLEDGE OF GOD

There is little doubt that man's knowing is focused directly upon the sensible things that make up his environment. This is true whether the explanatory theories one adopts will allow an immediate awareness of things in their extramental realness or will prefer to focus upon the objects that come to be within consciousness; and whether one admits a passivity on the part of the knowing subject before the intelligibilities that stream from without, or insists rather that the knowing subject is a contributor to and constitutor of that very intelligibility. Irrespective of all this, St. Thomas' Christian vision of the surrounding world that presents itself to man's consciousness sees it as leading him by some sort of inference to an obscure recognition of the face of God. This occurs when the intelligence penetrates through the phenomenal and the quidditative into the mystery of being itself. The inner structure of being is revealed as having a *logos* character that initiates a dynamism of responding intellect that brings man cognitively before God as the Source of all that is. Even the qualitatively higher encounter in Revelation and Faith is, in its cognitive elements, situated within this basic relatedness to God by way of the analogy of being. The primal creation undergirds in this way the "new creation" unto salvation. The clue, then, as to how authentic our knowledge of God be, whether by way of nature or by way of grace, lies: (1) first, in the mysterious occurrence or "e-vent" of being within man, and (2) secondly, in its analogical power, i.e. that indigenous capacity enabling it to open up a perspective onto God.

## 1. The Psychogenesis of Being

An oft-repeated accusation against the theology that has continued the Scholastic tradition is that its procedures are abstract and detached; the being with which it is concerned is fixed and static — whereas what "is" in the primary sense is the concrete existent or actuality, being as historic, dynamic, self-creative process. That there is truth in the charge perhaps goes without saying. But welcome as it indeed is, as a corrective to one misplaced emphasis, it all too readily lends itself to a simplistic and one-sided exaggeration. It is seldom acknowledged that very abstract thinking and objectifying by way of ideas is the sole way to an understanding of what existential encounter is, and an explanation of its distinction from and primacy over abstract concepts. Anyone who has labored with the thought of Heidegger knows this to be so. It still needs to be asked then if the "being" that comes to be in man's consciousness, (and that will determine his view of the world and so his understanding of God) initiates him into a world of abstract universals to be contemplated or does it constitute his "world" as a context of meaning, in existential encounter with all that is real in a primary sense? Or is it possible that the choice offered above cannot in fact be made, since it assumes an either-or situation, whereas it would be truer to think in terms of complementary dimensions to the mystery of human knowing? To inquire thus is to ask how the "e-vent" of being comes to pass within human spirit.

One contemporary effort at explanation is that found in the more recent writings of Lonergan, Coreth, Rahner and others, making use of the transcendental method creatively suggested by Maréchal.[2] Being is not abstracted from the surrounding world, nor intuited therefrom, but is somehow already within the ambit of the intellect, entirely if confusedly so. Being is "given" to intellect in the latter's character as spirit or as transcendental subjectivity; this "a priori" dominance over being in its entire analogical range establishes the very possibility of intellectual knowledge. This is not a naïve idealism that would have being welling up from within the depths of the knower and bestowing itself upon the objects of consciousness, but it does involve a projecting act by the subject that is "anticipatory," "intending" reality. In this context, being is not so much characteristic of existents, somehow deriving to intellect therefrom, as it is consciousness itself, an awareness of self as an unrestricted horizon for or openness to being.[3] This is a distinct epistemology, radicated in a distinct metaphysics, and if true qualifies considerably the manner in which man comes to know God. Thus serious consideration must be given to the foundation upon which it rests. Three general but basic difficulties assert themselves. First is the total gratuity of an "a priori" grasp of being. It is true enough that other theories of knowledge are just that too — theories, with their own assumptions. But the assumption here appears to operate out of a sort of "angelism," a conception of spirit as transcendental subjectivity which seemingly does not attend enough to the empirical fact that man's spirit is totally immersed in matter, even as it retains the power to surmount the limitations of that matter. Is it not part of the human condition that our cognitive life originates with the material singular and always remains bound there as to the existential touchstone that authenticates the essences it knows universally?[4] Secondly, in so far as man's subjectivity eventually emerges into his consciousness and renders him aware of his unlimited openness to being, is this anything more than *potential being?* Is the horizon that opens up anything more than a vague recognition of possibilities for the mind? What is then demanded is not a mere affirmation out of transcendental subjectivity but the painstaking process of apprehensive objectification and discursive reasoning. Lastly, is not the tendency of the Transcendentalists to structure man within a world of persons, to isolate him from the world of cosmological objects, in fact to forget that even man's proper universe is not purely personal but individual as well, i.e. radicated in existents that are sigularized by matter? This is only to acknowledge that material things also participate in being and that entering into communion with them man realises a cosmic dimension to his humanness.[5] What those who work within the Transcendental Method continue to contribute cannot, of course, be neglected, scil. the ultimate primary of the personal and subjective or intersubjective; and some qualification of the subject-object scheme to knowing, i.e. an awareness, against naïve realism, of the subjective contributions the knower brings to his knowing.

At quite the opposite extreme is an option for almost total objectivity, one seeing the ultimately real as so exclusively extra-subjective that only after coming to recognize its range of unity in the order of actual existents is it possible to engender the construct-concept imperfectly reflecting that unity.[6] At the very outset this attitude poses the dilemma of making a choice between two opposed Thomistic metaphysics—one taking as its point of departure the structure of reality itself, the other choosing rather the inner structure of the *concept* of being.[7] The complexity of real relationships can, of course, be known and given mental expression, not however by way of an abstraction or an intuition, but rather by a process beginning with induction. What is meant is not mere numerical addition, but an act of intellection that requires a greater or lesser number of singular instances to bring "being" (which resists conceptual grasp) into focus in its complexity and remoteness from matter. This is but the first step; it is completed with the negative *judgment* which *separates* being from its realized modes, a separation that is not to be confused with an intuition.[8] The mind's contact with being thus lies outside of its apprehensive powers and is only achieved in the subsequent act whereby the intellect composes and divides, i.e. affirms and denies; this led St. Thomas to explicitly teach that the attainment of being is a genuine separation.[9] The idea

114

eventually formed in an attempt to represent being is then a construct, a pale mental reflection of the complexus of real relationships, ultimately causal in kind, between actual existents. The latter is realized only in a restricted way on the predicamental level; its full realization and thus an adequate awareness of the unity of being is achieved only in the transcendental order, when the relationships of finite beings to their Uncaused Principle is surmised.

In all of this there are two questionable assumptions. First, are there, indeed, two Thomistic metaphysics between which one is obligated to choose — one building from being itself, the other from the *idea* of being? Is it not more accurate to acknowledge at the very beginning the necessary distinction between the real and the noetic orders, emphasizing their mutual complementarity so that the idea of being expresses in its own cognitive order what the diversified beings *really* have in common? It is the real unity of being that is seized in the concept, a unity that outside of the noetic order lies concealed beneath a more obvious multiplicity. Secondly, the reading here of St. Thomas' famous text from the *De Trinitate* appears overly narrow and restrictive. It is one thing to point out the invaluable nuance that Thomas brings to light in expressly opting for the term "separation," and to contrast this favorably with the choice of Cajetan and John of St. Thomas to work within the schema of three degrees of formal abstraction.[10] But a careful reading of similar texts in St. Thomas' other works suggests that the development in the *De Trinitate* is not meant as the rejection of an earlier teaching but merely as a more precise expression of the uniqueness of abstraction in the third degree.[11]

The main difficulty with this position, however, is its implication that the awareness of the real rapports between beings, and thus the unity of created being and its underlying analogical structure, come only after a recognition of their causal dependence upon Absolute Being, even if surmised only as the Source of their being.[12] This appears to demand an acknowledgement of Subsistent Being prior to any discernment of the

115

unity of finite being. Apart from having in common such real and qualitatively distinct relationships to First Being, the complexus of finite beings would, on their own predicamental level, seemingly offer nothing more than a chaotic multiplicity. At bottom, this theory would appear to understand the separation of which St. Thomas speaks as positive in kind, i.e. yielding a notion of being that not only is open to the possibility of an immaterial order of being but that postulates such an order, immediately rather than inferentially; and envisions finite reality on this prior assumption of a First Subsistent Principle.[13]

A more integral reading of St. Thomas, however, points the way to seeing the "separation" of the *De Trinitate* as merely *precisive* in kind, attaining the being common to finite things, which is not itself subsistent but rather inseparable, positively, from its modes. The negative judgment that being is not dependent upon matter is, in fact, an *abstraction* and an abstraction of what is most formal, even if, unlike other formal abstractions, it can be called a "separation." The uniqueness of this abstraction is somewhat revealed in that it takes place not in apprehension, but in a second intellectual activity, that of judgment. This is to say in effect that the total actuality of real being will not admit of compression within a concept. What is conceived is the finite quiddity or essence, which as determined in a limited, specific way so offers itself to the intellect's conceptual powers. The existence or "esse" thereof is not a limited perfection, but *of itself* bespeaks pure perfection, i.e. it is the pure but not subsistent actuality of the perfection in question, limited in fact only by the essence it actualizes. As such it can only be *affirmed*: "the first operation of the mind regards the nature of a thing, the second operation regards its existence."[14]

As no mere mechanical joining together or dividing of two concepts in the mind, but a spontaneous, perfective, and completive act by the mind of the apprehension, the judgment "bears on the surintelligibility of the act of existing."[15] Since the latter resists conceptualization, the judgment which affirms existence amounts to a genuine intuition at the very heart of the abstrac-

116

tive process. Such abstractive intuition is a true dynamism of the intellect, but not one that affirms the reality of its objects out of a projecting subjectivity (as for the Maréchalians); rather it intuits the real being of existents. This trans-conceptual dimension to all intellection assures its termination at the real and the actual. But this is only to say that it achieves the quiddity or essence *as it is actual or really existing.* The metaphysical counterpart to this is the implication that the essence has no actuality whatsoever, and thus no intelligibility or value of the real, apart from its act of existing, its "esse". Whatever it has of formal perfection in the hierarchy of being comes entirely from its existence, so that essence is only a mode of existence, i.e. it is the existence as the latter undergoes the modal limitation imposed from the side of essence. This is no denial of the real distinction in finite entity but only a recognition that the co-principles are inseparable, so that essence does not, as in a Platonic scheme, bespeak perfection apart from "esse." It is a case of "causae ad invicem"; the essence specifies and determines in a positive perfective way only in virtue of the actuality it itself receives as potency.[16] Such a manner of seeing things precludes the possibility of considering essence as a pure form awaiting, as it were, actualization. It avoids at the very beginning a view of essence enabling it to *have* intelligible value of itself and only needing existence for the *exercise* of that intelligibility.

The import of this abstractive intuitionalism is that it offers safeguards against the charge of "conceptualism" or "essentialism." With Cajetan, the stress upon the concept is such that it is seen as rather too exactly reflecting the totally real; it achieves within the mind an exact parallel to the real order without. Its limitations as abstract and universal, while acknowledged, are not taken seriously enough and the unique, concrete realization of the formal perfection within the existential order is not given its due. The disastrous consequence of this is a refusal of the mystery of concrete existence as something that always eludes the representational powers of intellect. Abstract conceptual contents are then projected outward and mistakenly taken by the knower as a noetic replica of reality.[17] In developing his understanding of analogy this leads to four notable results: (1) the doctrine of the analogy of being is investigated from the side of the *concept* of being; (2) it expresses primarily the relationships between distinct formal perfections, i.e. the proportion of the *ratio* of one perfection to the *ratio* of another; (3) when translated to the real order this is expressed as a proportion between proportions or as a proportionality, and is considered the sole genuine analogy; (4) the contents of concepts representing the transcendentals can then be transferred to God, but analogically. The theological implication of this last is major; it is to say that the concept of being and the perfections interchangeable with it such as truth, goodness etc. are capable of functioning as concepts of God. This is so only in virtue of analogy of proportionality: these concepts in their proportion to the Divine Existence represent God, as the same concepts in their proportion to various levels of finite existence represent creaturely perfections.

The "essentialism" implicit here is not nearly as marked as it is in the thought of Scotus, who readily acknowledges that the concept of being is univocal.[18] It applies to God exactly as it does to creatures — precisely because of its abstractness. What it sets aside entirely are the existential realizations of the perfections expressed within concepts. What this is tantamount to saying (and the Scotistic school makes it explicit) is that the difference between God and creature is only quantitative — identical perfections are possessed by one infinitely and by the other in a finite way. It is at this juncture in theological thought, when Cajetan re-thinks St. Thomas' own dominant insights in express confrontation with the extreme essentialism of Scotus, that what here is called the "Thomist tradition" begins to develop. Cajetan's fidelity to St. Thomas obligates him to deny the univocity of being and to insist upon its analogical character. But the very problematic which he allows Scotus to set for him exacts its price; following the Franciscan's lead he attempts to develop the doctrine of analogy less in terms of being itself than in those of its concept. Thus, the cognitive way to God is from within that concept, implying that somehow the concept can be extended to God — in a non-univocal fashion. Whereas Scotus would allow a transcendental concept to be predicted of God exactly as of creatures, Cajetan resolves the difficulty by supposing that one and the same concept is predicated *differently* of the two — not so differently as to end in equivocation, however.[19] The *ratio* of the creature thus becomes, but only in a higher order of being, the *ratio* of God. The perfection is grasped within the concept as capable of multiple proportions to existence, i.e. it includes actually if confusedly the different degrees of actuality which characterize the perfection existentially. With this, Cajetan discovers what analogy really is for him, scil. proportionality. To avoid caricaturing Cajetan's understanding it is necessary to realize that God is still known only *ex creaturis*. Because the transcendental conception is not limited to any of its modes, it can be separated from all of them, and this is how it represents God, i.e. as leaving unexpressed, because unknown, the mode-less fashion in which he is the perfection in question. It is the *ratio significata* that does service for us in making God known, the *modus significandi* is dropped.[20] Nonetheless, the *ratio* of a creaturely perfection is transferred to God, even if in a mode-less or all perfect way, and to this extent Cajetan does introduce a qualified essentialism into Thomistic tradition.

It is Schillebeeckx's refusal to extenuate this tendency in Cajetan's thought that has led him to adopt a quite distinct theory of intellectual knowing which explains the attainment of the real, existent order by way of an act of intellect that, while making use of a concept, is not itself conceptualization. Neither is this simply explained by the judgment as the termination of the conceptual act, a judgment spontaneously called into being by the apprehension. It is something more radical and primordial, an original intuition of the entirety of being, but in an undifferentiated way that is gradually differentiated

119

and thematized by the secondary process of conceptualization. Here, concepts have no value of the real whatsoever — unlike the theory of abstractive intuition outlined above, which will allow such value in a radical way, one that becomes explicitly recognized in the judgment — they merely give a *formal* directedness to a dynamic of intellect enabling the latter to explicate the vague, prior intuition it has of real being.[21] It is within this non-conceptual dimension to knowledge that analogy of being comes into play, leading to the affirmation of God. There is no question of transferring the contents of transcendental *concepts,* which merely "represent" essential perfections of finite being, to God — even if one adds the qualifying phrase *"modo analogice."* Such ideas merely give a direction or formal orientation to the mind in its trans-conceptual experience of being, and finally of the unknown Source of Being. Schillebeeckx is saying explicitly that the transcendental perfections lose their transcendentality when they become the *ratio* of a concept.[22] The transcendentality is regained only by falling back upon the other indispensable aspect to knowing in which the idea merely gives focus to an intuition. This is the plane on which God is encountered, in the realm of existents lying outside and beyond what man's concepts represent. Such representations, objectifying the creaturely order, and solely what is quidditative in that order, can never be transferred to God. He is acknowledged non-conceptually, dimly recognized from a vantage-point that those concepts provide.

Though laying claim to inspiration from St. Thomas, this theory of knowledge marks a radical departure from what has been the more common understanding by Thomists. It certainly precludes any latent conceptualism that may be a weakness of the more traditional position; and it focuses upon analogy as a dynamic structure of the ultimately real and existential order, rather than as a characteristic of the *idea* of being. It does not, however, avoid certain basic weaknesses or at least obscurities of its own. One of these is the absence of any satisfactory explanation as to how the primal intuition of all being occurs, if this is not accounted for by either apprehension or judgment. Seemingly, this would have to be non-abstractive in kind, and it can be questioned whether such a gratuitous assumption takes seriously enough the limitations inseparable from the human condition, the strictures imposed by man's materiality and individuality.[23]

Secondly, conceptualization is presented as a process of detaching quiddities from reality, with the result that the intelligibility they give expression to remains unreal or merely ideal. The necessity of recourse to an ever accompanying intuitional process appears to introduce a dualism into the very cognitive act itself, i.e. something more than the duality between the intentional and the ontological orders. It then becomes necessary to seek a foundational distinction within the ontological order, and this could be nothing other than the real distinction (in the finite order) of essence and existence. The implication then is that the mind can disengage the essence abstractly, which possesses an intelligibility that is purely formal or ideal. True enough, Schillebeeckx has, in another context, explicitly rejected this way of thinking of being,[24] but it does seem to re-appear here as underlying his epistemological position. There is moreover a possible explanation of this ambivalence. The intuitionalism that lies at the heart of Schillebeeckx's theory owes its inspiration to Phenomenology; the latter as a philosophical methodology has led (above all with Heidegger) to a discovery of the "ontological difference," i.e. a clear distinguishing between the ontic (*existenziell*) and the ontological (*existenzial*) levels of reality. The former is the domain of metaphysics, of the beings (*das Seiende*), even taken collectively; the latter is the realm of Being (*Sein*), of the process that enables the beings to be. The former is open to man's conceptual grasp, the latter merely "casts itself" into *Dasein* as consciousness. This helps to explain, then, why for Schillebeeckx there is really no concept of being at all or of its transcendental properties; why all our ideas *as such* are limited to the categories merely clarifying the being already intuited. It is here on the intuitional level that one encounters the analogical structure of being, which as belonging to the ontological rather than the ontic level of reality culminates in the intuition of God.

Two reactions to this theory come immediately to the fore: one positive, the other negative. First, positively, this draws attention to the dynamic character of analogy as a vehicle of knowing the ultimately real. It locates analogy within the ontological and existential order and saves it from relegation to the logical and the realm of essences. This is to say that it corrects the prejudice of Cajetan that analogy is ultimately proportionality, founded on formal causality with the possibility of an abstract concept representing the multiple proportions of various essences to their acts of existing. It enables analogy to be seen as founded upon a causal dependence of the efficient order, so that (viewed transcendentally rather than predicamentally) it becomes a matter of the real rapports between finite and infinite being. In a word, analogy becomes expressive of the relational or participationist character of created being; it is not proportionality, but some sort of intrinsic denomination or attribution.

Negatively, however, is the fact that this theory does not provide a *concept* of finite being that can do service as the *point de départ* for a dynamism of analogy. This means that our concepts, while they can give direction to our mysterious knowing of God. cannot function as prime analogues in the analogical denomination of God. God is not then, for example, a father *formally* but only in some virtual sense. This appears to be at some remove from St. Thomas' own literal affirmations.[25] If the grasp of being be seen as an abstractive intuition, on the other hand, then what is realized is not a Phenomenologist's Being (*Sein*), but *ens in commune* restricted to the finite world of which man forms part, and "separated" negatively not positively, from its realizations within matter. The termination of this judgmental intuition is nonetheless the visualization *in a concept* of the being objectified in the judgment of separation.[26] This is not a concept of existence, which remains non-conceptualizable

122

as such and can be conceptualized only in its limited modes as essence; it is not a concept of *esse* but of *ens*. What the intelligence grasps is that existence is not limited to any given mode of actualization; the resulting conception expresses being as it can be achieved in subjects which differ among themselves essentially. In a word, what results is the analogical concept of being, embracing somehow an *actual* multiplicity. This occurs at the very dawn of the intellect's activity, for being is the *primum cognitum,* and the condition for the knowledge of everything else.[27] But obviously its character and structure are at first perceived only dimly; a true epigenesis then begins, a gradual clarification of what is originally undifferentiated all the way down to the ultimate refinements of the idea by the metaphysician. Somehow then, the concept of being envelops the multiplicity of its finite modes — unlike the univocal concept that abstracts from its differences, excluding them actually and only potentially relating to them; and in this lies the possibility of its leading inferentially (rather than intuitionally) to an awareness of the transcendent principle of being. Such a concept does not enclose within itself the Divine perfections, as though a single idea can be predicated of the creature in one way and of God in another; it is not, in other words, expressive of a proportionality, even an un-measurable one. It does however express, at least implicitly, a relationality to God, on the basis of which it can function as the prime analogue in the intrinsic denomination of God. This is to say that while the *ratio* conceived by the mind cannot be transferred to God, it does more than give an objective perspective to the mind so that it can affirm God without representing him. The "representing" of course is only that of an analogical extrapolation but it does convey and express something of what God is formally. The concepts in question here are no wise concepts of God, but they are concepts of perfections deriving from, imitating, and thus revealing God; the *ratio* within the concept does have a real rapport to the Divine *ratio,* a rapport that (in the case of the transcendentals) is formal and not only virtual.[28] What must *not* be forgotten

123

is that our concepts retain a modality of finiteness that must be explicitly denied to God when the *ratio significata* is projected onto Him.[29] The concept of being thus conveys an intelligibility in virtue of which God is at once known and unknown. But this is to take the problem of man's original openness onto being to its more proximate basis in the mystery of analogy.

## 2. Analogy as Denomination

Analogy is itself an analogous term; its radical meaning is "proportion," yet proportions are found on all levels of being and knowledge: in mathematics (where Aristotle first employed the term), in empirical science, in poetry, in philosophy, theology, etc. Its employment within the philosophical realm alone involves multiple approaches: the psychological (seeking the origin of man's awareness of proportion); the epistemological (seeking the authenticity of knowledge by proportion); the logical (investigating analogy as a second intention); and the ontological (investigating the proportionate structure of the real, especially the transcendentally real).

Any investigation of the understanding and use of analogy by St. Thomas faces two immediate problems: (1) he nowhere has developed a formal treatment of analogy as such, (2) his own use of the term, while owing a great deal to Aristotle, marks a decided departure from the original and basic understanding of the latter. Aristotle originally uses the word to designate mathematical proportions, i.e. similar relationships between quantities; what is really then proportionality — with an eventual transference of the term from the realm of quantity to that of quality. Cajetan assumes at the very inception of his *De Nominum Analogia* that St. Thomas understands the word in exactly this Aristotelian context.[30] However St. Thomas' access to Aristotle's *Metaphysics* was by way of Arabic-Latin translations in which the disputed term is rendered *attributio*, rather than *proportio*. Uppermost in St. Thomas' mind is a

124

notion of analogy as expressive of *order,* a relatedness of a plurality to what is first, a designation *"secundum prius et posterius."* How this radical shift in emphasis came about has been convincingly suggested by H. A. Wolfson.[31] In his *logical* works, Aristotle speaks of a mode of predication that while not meeting the demands of univocation, cannot be dismissed as pure equivocation either; since it bears closer resemblance to the latter, however, he characterizes it as an intended and purposeful equivocation (*equivocatio a consilio*) rather than an accidental and random one (*equivocatio a casu*).[32] Alexander of Aphrodisias labels such terms as these "amphibolous"; later Arabian thinkers such as Averroes, Avicenna, Algazel, and Al-Farabi, (later to be followed by Moses Maimonides), give an Arabic semantic turn to this Greek word so that it appears as *analogikos* — a word that Aristotle does use but never in this context of predication, of extending a *ratio* and a name from one subject to others. It is true that St. Thomas' most common rendering of this word is "proportion," but this is because he is referring to the underlying ontic structure in the real order that will allow for the attributive predication; he takes proportion to mean not a similarity of proportions within distinct substances, i.e. a proportionality, but the hierarchy of causal dependence of the many to what is, in some order, first — founding a predication that expresses this ordered unity, a predication *"per prius et posterius,"* or *"secundum magis et minus."*[33]

That this is indeed a proper interpretation of St. Thomas is borne out by adverting to what is the strongest textual evidence against it: the clear references by St. Thomas to proportionality that occur in the Third and Fourth Books of the *Commentary on the Sentences* and especially in the early questions of the *De Veritate.*[34] What is of telling importance here is the limited period within St. Thomas' writing career during which such designation occurs; the word does not appear before the year 1256 and is not to be found in any work of St. Thomas after the year 1257. This suggests a chronological development in St. Thomas' own understanding of analogy, one that appears to build

125

constructively towards proportionality only to culminate very quickly in its definitive rejection. Interpretative clues are not lacking both as to the motive for this development and the actual course that it assumed. The earlier theological writings of St. Thomas, especially the *Commentary* on Peter Lombard, were worked out within the prevailing Augustinianism and Neo-Platonism of the times; thus great stress is laid upon exemplarism. From the very beginning, St. Thomas understands the necessity of seeing this as a *real* exemplarity, one existing within the framework of efficient causality. But he is somewhat ill at ease working within a Neo-Platonic scheme and feels the need for a more explicit emphasis upon the order of *esse.* Even more than this is a growing awareness of the major difference between transcendental analogy and predicamental analogy. In viewing analogy as a unity of order there is the danger, at least, of reducing the principle of being to the quasi-genus that it principles.[35] To forestall this, St. Thomas throws emphasis upon the infinite distance separating created and uncreated being, stressing not the direct proportion of one to the other but the indirect and more remote *proportionality.* The similarity now is not that of divine to creaturely perfection, but of the relationship between divine perfection to divine being and creaturely perfection to created being. In short, the focus is now the qualitatively infinite difference distinguishing God and creature; a difference which cannot be measured because one of the terms remains unknown, and so cannot adequately be expressed within a system defining one in terms of the other (scil. analogy as an order to something first).

Why then the sudden and resolute abandonment of proportionality? The express treatments of analogy subsequent to this period, notably in the two *Summae* and in the *De Potentia,* invariably refer to two kinds of analogy — scil., the proportion of many to some one third reality or *ratio,* and the direct proportion of one thing or *ratio* to another.[36] The implication is that St. Thomas came to fear that proportionality lent itself to the first kind of analogy; that it tended to compare God and creature in virtue of their diverse proportions to some third thing which thus assumed a primacy over God. If it were unthinkable that such primacy be real, the way was still open to thinking of it as ideal. In effect, this would be to posit an idea whose very abstractness would allow it to somehow incorporate the divine and the creaturely. The most constant and clear reiteration of St. Thomas on transcendental analogy after 1257 is that the sole possibility is that called *"unius ad alterum,"* to the exclusion of what is designated *"plura ad unum."*[37] Cajetan in developing his ideas within a logical scheme insists that attribution as such can be only extrinsic denomination and that the sole instance of intrinsic denomination is proportionality. He is thereby constrained to fall back upon a *concept* expressive of this proportionate unity; e.g. "goodness as such" can be said in one way of the creature, in a distinct way of God. This is precisely what St. Thomas is at pains to avoid. Is he then reverting to his earlier position? If the "proportionality" of the *De Veritate* runs the risk of subordinating the Divine Being to an abstract idea, the "proportion" of the early *Commentary on the Sentences* veers too closely to a hierarchical structure of formal perfections in which Divine Being is merely the maximum within an implied homogeneity.

The key to St. Thomas' resolution lies in his perception of the ambivalence that characterizes analogy, i.e. the fact that it is indigenous to both the real and the ideal orders. Any failure to distinguish these two realms is self-defeating for any system of thought. What the distinction demands here is acknowledging that analogy as a metaphysical structure is one thing and as a logical instrument in the noetic order is quite something else.[38] The importance of keeping the difference clear led St. Thomas to deal with analogy on two distinct levels: on the first of these he develops his doctrine of the *analogy of names*; on the other he concerns himself with the *analogy of being*. It is the first of these that becomes paramount *as analogy*, and that gains a certain primacy where the use of the latter term is concerned; the metaphysical structure undergirding analogous naming is henceforth more frequently presented in another metaphysical term — that of participation.[39]

The unity of real being is such as to sustain within itself (and with no detriment to that unity) a real plurality. The consequence of this is that one thing can be known by way of another thing essentially different from it because of a direct proportion between them, or different proportions to a third thing; this is analogical *knowledge*. Analogy itself is the *naming* of things as they are known in this way; it is the designation of the relationships or proportions between things not as they are in real existence but as they are in knowledge. It is the transferral of a word, and the *ratio* it signifies, from one reality to another because the latter is known in virtue of its rapport or similitude to the former. Analogy, in fine, is a being of logic; it is a *second intention*.[40] Cajetan, it is true, also sees analogy as a mode of predication, and his division of it is a logical one; the subtle but radical difference is the latter's assumption that things in the mind exactly parallel things in reality so that attribution expresses only extrinsic causal relationships, and the sole expression of intrinsic convenience is proportionality. St. Thomas is much more cautious on allowing such transitions between the logical and ontic orders, the noetic and the entitative; he tends to emphasize rather the inverse directedness of the two, i.e. the *a posteriori*, effect to cause, direction of knowing as contrasted with the *a priori*, cause to effect, relationship that has priority in the extra-mental order.

If this assumption be correct, then the determination of what analogy is lies not with the metaphysical structure of the real (except in a fundamental sense) but rather with the limitations of human knowing in its seeking to grasp that structure. "We name things as we know them" which is not exactly to say that we name them as they are in themselves. So seen, analogy is a transferal of a name originally signifying one reality to another, not because the *ratio nominis* embraces both from the very beginning but because the second is known in virtue of some relatedness or proportion to the first. Obviously there has to be

128

a basis for this transposition and this is always some quality intrinsic to the thing to which the name is transferred: the accident has its own being which enables us to designate it by a name that originally means the being of substance; the medicine has intrinsic qualities causative of health so that we can call it healthy; and in metaphor, there is some real basis in virtue of which one thing resembles another. On the other hand, what the name originally signifies in a proper, non-analogical sense may be found in the secondary analogates either intrinsically, extrinsically, or merely by supposition; it is incidental to analogy as formally a naming which of these is the case. When the quality the word bespeaks is intrinsic to both analogates (differently so, of course) then the use of analogy of names takes one out of the logical world into that of metaphysics; analogy of names being now a noetic instrument for disclosing the structure of the real, i.e. the analogous character of being itself. The rapport between things in our knowledge is the clue to discovering their unity and interrelatedness in real existence.[41] Of itself, being precedes knowledge, but within the universe of man's knowing it is the knowledge of one thing that leads to another, so that we come to a grasp of the ultimately real only in inferential ways. The *raison d'être* of analogy lies with the limitations of incarnate intellect, of spirit that exists within bodiliness.

Analogy of names, then, involves but one concept, which properly signifies only one analogate of which it is said *per prius*. When it is extended to the other analogates, however, it undergoes an expanding process to the point where it becomes a common *ratio* of them all. But what this expanded concept gives expression to is an intelligibility of relatedness; and it is this that is the analogical concept properly so-called. One of the problems with the position that became entrenched from Cajetan's time onward lies with the question as to how one concept can embrace multiple intelligibilities actually and yet only confusedly. It is far easier to understand a concept expressive of one intelligibility yet with distinct proportions to varied

129

subjects. In this latter view, analogy is always *ab uno* or *ad unum*, the naming is always *per prius et posterius*.[42] Always demanded, then, is a prime analogue; the meaning of the name and *ratio* when extended to secondary analogates derives from the first so that the definition of the latter necessarily enters into the definition of all the others, *as analogically considered*. In the one instance where St. Thomas clearly denies a prime analogue the context is that of transcendental analogy, and what he is rejecting is a prime analogue such as is had in predicamental analogy where all the terms are finite.[43] When one term is infinite then it remains ultimately unknowable; the proportion between it and the finite terms is not such as to lead to a proper knowledge of the former. In this sense, the Principle of being is not a measure of other beings, i.e. it is not a homogeneous measure reducible to the order of the perfections it measures.

There are only two modes of analogous naming; for St. Thomas this is a taxative division. It is indicated more clearly perhaps than elsewhere in Question 13 of the *Prima Pars*: two or more realities receive a common name due to the diverse proportions they bear to some other one reality (*"multa ad unum"*, or the proportion is direct of one to the other (*"unum ad alterum"*).[44] The example given is one where the denomination is extrinsic: healthy said of medicine and urine in their relationship to organic health of an animal; and the same term used to designate the well being of the animal and medicine in virtue of a direct relationship. It could just as easily be illustrated by proportions that are intrinsic, e.g. quantity and quality are called being in virtue of their distinct proportions to substance, or in another knowing frame of reference, quality can be named being in virtue of its direct proportion to substance. This clarifies the point that, whether the ontological substructure be the intrinsic possession of a formality by all subjects or merely an extrinsic causal relationship, the analogical function is itself formally one of pure attribution or denomination. What occurs is less a common designation than a transfer of the name of one to the other.[45] It would seem that St. Thomas should be taken literally here when he writes of names common to God and creature as said *"secundum analogiam, idest proportionem"*; he (1) is talking about commonness not in being but in designation by name, and (2) indicates that this occurs in virtue of analogy as proportion, no mention being made of proportionality.

### 3. Analogy as Participation

Analogy is itself an analogical notion. St. Thomas came in time to give a certain primacy to its localization in the domain of logic, to look upon it in its purest form as a mode of speech. Analogy is thus first and foremost analogy of names; a mode of signifying that occupies a middle position between univocation and equivocation, which like analogy are beings of logic or second intentions of the mind. Perhaps the most serious reservation to this theory is that it abstracts entirely from considering whether the perfection conveyed by the transferred name be intrinsic or extrinsic to the secondary analogates. How valid after all is a linguistic theory in which language does not reflect the real situation of those things about which it speaks? But the point is that analogical language *does* express whether the perfection be intrinsic or not to those subjects to which it is attributed; it does this, however, not insofar as it is analogical naming but in virtue of the content of the predication. The question of intrinsicality is set aside only in the purely formal consideration of analogical attribution, one that looks only to the form of the "saying" and not to "what" is said. Still, all language must have some material content, and on this level the existential order is reflected (or, in the case of falsity, not reflected). But this is to take one back into the real order, to the relations between things as they exist rather than as they are in knowledge. Logical concerns are now altered into metaphysical ones, and on the noetic plane the conceptions of the mind are no longer second intentions but first intentions.

This descent or return to the order of real being is absolutely necessary; the logical world exists only on the assumption of a prior contact with the real world that is the metaphysical experience. Analogy of names, in short, if it be the purest instance of analogy, is not anything autonomous or self-sustaining. It is completely grounded in an underlying ontological structure. And on this level — both that of the beings themselves and the mind's knowing of them — one necessarily deals with such truths as whether the common perfection be intrinsic to all the analogates or not, whether the convenience be formal or virtual etc. This too is analogy, but analogy of being, not the analogy of names. This is the context within which St. Thomas first develops his understanding of analogy, notably in the *Commentary* on Peter Lombard. Here he sees the modes of analogy not as *plura ad unum* and *unum ad alterum* but in a tripartite division as *"secundum esse tantum," "secundum intentionem tantum,"* and *"secundum esse et intentionem."*[46] But the perspective adopted here is that of the metaphysician or more often the theologian; it is the *content* of the analogical predication that concerns him. The later division of analogy into its two logical modes (as in *Prima Pars*, Question Thirteen) is such as to allow for a subdivision of each of these modes into either *"secundum intentionem tantum"* or *"secundum esse et intentionem"* (leaving aside *"secundum esse tantum"* which as Cajetan notes is analogy only *"abusive dicta"*).[47]

Metaphysical analogy, however, is like analogy of names in that it is a structure of proportions and not of proportionality. Even in the case where there can be no question but that the analogous perfection is intrinsic to all the analogates, there is still a prime analogate, and the unity of being is one of order or proportion "to" or "from" it. Even if expressed in the formula of a proportionality, this is still verified; what is being said in effect is not simply that e.g. substance is to its existence as proportionately accident is to its existence, but something more, scil., that substance is to its existence *per se* as accident is to its existence *in alio*, i.e. in substance. Otherwise there is no unity of order or proportion, that is to say no analogical oneness. Cajetan's objection that the predication here (which he sees not as a second intention but as an exact reflection of the real order) is absolute with no necessary relation to a prime analogue because the perfection is intrinsic to all, would seem to demand logically a concept that is not analogical at all but abstract in a totally undetermined way, for example "goodness as such". It would abstract from the order of being of those things about which the predication is made. In Cajetan's proportionality an accident is said to have being *quocumque modo,* with no indication of what that being is in its proportion to the being of substance. The properly analogical notion assigns being to accident precisely as being *per aliud,* as relational to being *per se;* it locates the accidental *esse* within its proper perspective on the spectrum of being.

This hierarchical structure to the universe of being establishes its unity and is constituted ultimately by the vast complexus of proportions of each being to a Primal Being. Man, for instance, is a being of a definite proportion to Subsistent Being, which proportion is greater and more proximate to First Being than that of a vegetable, and at the same time lesser and more remote than that proper to an angelic being. Thus the direct proportions of man to vegetable and to angel are in virtue of their distinct proportions to Infinite Being. This can be understood and labeled as the analogy of being, either transcendental analogy as in the example above or predicamental analogy when the proportions are limited to those between substance and its various accidental modes. If it be a question of the proportion of one finite substance to another or to others, this too is analogy, but not the analogy of being; it reduces itself rather to a comparison between essences.

This, of course, is the age-old problem of the one and the many. The irreducible key to its resolution is causality — the very origin of things from others, whether of the entire finite order from Infinite Being, or of an individual within a species from another individual of the same species. Such causality is first of all efficient, and immediately explains the distinctness and multiplicity of things. Of itself however it opens up another deeper dimension to causality, an intelligibility that lies concealed within efficiency, namely that of exemplarity. It is here that the unity of being begins to assert itself, or perhaps better, to explain itself. *"Omme agens agit sibi simile"*: an effect must be something of its cause. Exemplarity explains similarity; and when universal, the oneness that is immanent at the heart of beings. If there be one supreme Exemplar, then each being communes with every other being in a resemblance that lies at the deepest core of its being. To encounter, however dimly, the being of any entity is thus to enter into the mystery of being itself and of ultimate intelligibility. This communion of all reality nonetheless does not do away with the more obvious plurality and diversity, and this serves to show that the exemplarity in question is not univocal in kind. The power and richness of this causality are such as to allow for an inexhaustible range of effects. Thus the assimilation which results is not at all homogeneous in kind; the unity of being is, in a word, only proportionate. Everything imitates the one Source of being in a diminished way; the degrees of being are the various proportions, of greater or lesser remoteness, to that pure Source. The explanation of this lies in a principle of limitation that enters into the makeup of finite being which, metaphysically speaking, is grasped as potentiality.[48] The very notion of a limiting principle demands a corresponding principle that undergoes the limitation, scil. actuality. The latter by itself, even as created actuality, bespeaks unlimited perfection but such as is non-subsistent, non-existent outside of the composite being it actualizes. This potency-act *leit-motif* becomes in the order of being the essence-existence relationship. Thus seen, actuality or existence is the unifying force in being, potency or essence is the divisive and pluralizing factor. Obviously these cannot be thought of as distinct realities or things; they are only co-principles of a reality, which "are" by and for each other, distinguishable yet inseparable. Essence is only the mode of a creature's being, the perfection it bespeaks is one that comes to it from existence.[49] Essence is then prior to existence only logically; in the real order there is only simultaneity, with existence enjoying priority of perfection. Similarly, the proportionate unity achieved here is something real and not to be confused with a Platonic hierarchy of formal perfections. The Supreme Exemplar does not simply measure *ideally* the diminished being derived from it. Put another way, the unity here is not achieved originally within the *concept* of being. Rather the concept expresses the prior oneness of reality itself; the knower is assimilated to, "becomes" in the intentional order what the entitative order already is.[50]

What all this strongly suggests is that the multidimensional character to the universe of being is perhaps best thematized as *participation*.[51] This would appear as the irreducible structure of reality and thus the most adequate conceptual category with which to express its unity within plurality.[52] To designate this as analogy is to run the risk of confusing the logical and ontological orders. There is an advantage then in restricting the term analogy to its most precise and primary sense as something operative within the noetic order — as the process of *naming* which derives from our *knowing* of things in their inter-relatedness. The former is *analogy of names,* the later is *analogical knowledge;* undergirding both is the ultimate ontological structure as *participation.* Another advantage to this terminological and conceptual scheme is a clearer indication of the limitations indigenous to human knowing as abstractive and inferential. Analogy as designation conveys that dynamism of intellection in which an original concept is enabled to undergo a process of expansion and projection onto other subjects. This is especially true in the case of seeking to know God, where the direction of the knowing as *a posteriori* reverses the causal order within being.

To participate (from the Latin *partem capere*) is to possess in a partial or deficient way something subsisting in total perfection as a pure, unlimited source whence alone the partial realization can proceed. As characterizing the real, participation

135

always bespeaks an intrinsic communion. This is by no means to imply that the intrinsicality is always formal; indeed it can frequently be only virtual.[53] All it demands is that the mystery of causal origin be recognized as necessarily assimilative; every effect precisely as such must be somehow like its cause (and vice versa), and in virtue of what it is really and intrinsically. Within the order of finite being, there are, of course, the instances of similarity or formal convenience which seem to stand outside of the causal proportion of exemplified to exemplar. Ordinarily, here, the situation is one of identity or of mere metaphorical likeness. The former usually can be reduced to a common causal reference to some third reality, and thus reductively to participation; the latter, on the contrary, does not involve any real resemblance but only an imaginative one (though it is the real characteristics of one thing that suggest the real qualities of another) and so the mysteriousness of metaphor is perhaps properly located within analogy and not within participation.

It is in the transcendental order, however, that the participationist schema offers the fullest intelligibility, expressing the real proportions of various *entia per participationem* to the *Ens per essentiam*. Creatures are here seen as ranged hierarchically according to greater or lesser approximation to Subsistent Being. Their real relations of dependence upon the Maximum constitutes their proportion one to another as well as that of the entire finite order to the infinite, and is the proportionate unity of created being.

## 4. Analogical Knowledge of God

In the foregoing view, analogy is a matter of attribution, a process within that human sphere where knowing and speaking converge. It is rooted in man's linguisticality as that is inseparable from discursive knowing and learning, and is the rendering into speech of an awareness of one thing from another. Proximately this rests upon the discerning of a proportion between things, direct or indirect, which amounts reductively to some kind of similitude, though not ordinarily a formal similitude. Ultimately it is based upon the rapports — real or imagined, intrinsic or extrinsic — between realities within the community of being, and can be traced back to the mystery of the causal origin of things. The deepest explanation for this lies in the phenomenon of activity itself as self-actualization, given clear expression in the adage *"omne agens agit sibi simile."*[54] This is the ontological substructure to analogy, and it is here suggested that it can perhaps be best conceived in metaphysical categories as participation.

For the Scholastics, the naming process is revelatory of meaning; language is the bearer and the mirror of thought. Wittgenstein most clearly represents the Copernican revolution which sees meaning as emerging from the use of the word. In either case, what is incontestable is the unity of thought and speech. Two very disparate examples serve to make this unity graphic: one is St. Thomas' understanding of Divine Life as an eternal and necessary speaking of the consubstantial Word — a "diction" that is the ontological prerequisite to an equally necessary spiration of Personal Love; the other is Heidegger's development of "primal speaking," i.e. of a primordial speech anteceding all of man's cultural languages, which is the mode in which Being (*Sein*) "comes to pass" within human consciousness.

Readily discernible then is a parallelism between knowledge and language, but in any philosophy of Realism both are subsequent and subordinate to the order of the ultimately real, that of being itself. The Scholastic vision of things saw thought and speech as measured by reality, and thus as reflecting the latter. Reality itself, however, was recognized as a multiplicity that could not immediately be grasped in its unity. The multiplicity was, nonetheless, an ordered one and thus a unity. The ontic order of things among themselves deriving from a Pure Source, however, had to assume an inverse directedness as a logical order indigenous to discursive knowing. Having come forth from the Source of being, man was by his very finiteness constrained to grope his way back, cognitively first of all, from the multiple and the imperfect to the All-Inclusive. In effect this was to discern in time the analogical (or better, the participationist) structure of being, and to enter thereby on a projecting dynamic of intellection towards the One which served as the measure of all else. Analogy is attribution "from" or "to" something first. As a naming process, however, and so parallel to knowing but inverse to being, analogy is the designation of God from creatures. "The invisible things of God are made known by way of the things he has made."[55] It is the name proper to the creature that is projected somehow onto God; it is the creaturely perfection that functions as the prime analogue and which is the "source" (cognitively) that measures the mind's reach into the Divine, which latter remains truly transcendent and so unknowable. What value then can possibly derive to the conceptual contents so employed? Can the power inherent in the analogical reach of intelligence expand the concept to where it somehow "represents" a perfection of God himself? Demurring from that, are we left with what cannot escape the limitations of symbolic speech, i.e. with a God that we somehow "attain" to, but not conceptually?

By way of an initial clarification, it should be noted that the problematic is basically the same whether the cognitive process be that of reason with only its natural resources or that of the Christian intellect suffused with light of faith and in actual response to the Revealed Word.[56] In either case, it is the representational value of concepts originating within human, this-worldly experience that is being questioned. A deeper intelligibility is conveyed within the faith-experience,[57] but this is not to suggest that such faith-response is no longer man's own cognitive consciousness even though delivered to him at God's initiative, and that it thereby evades the limitations of the finite concept. If God speaks to man this can only be in human words. The projective power of analogy within faith, its "reach" towards God, is of a higher order, but the concept so expanded remains creaturely, limited in its representational endowments. Do even the conceptual categories and images of Revelation "represent" God's perfections as properly his own?

Secondly, this is not to raise doubts as to whether or not there are any ideas that can truly *designate* God himself. There are only three possible categories of such names: relative ones; those that are negative; and substantive names that are at once absolute and positive. In the first two cases, the names used do "signify" *only how* God is related to the world or what He is not; both stand for the Divine Reality but only as it is so related, and insofar as it is not, or positively lacks a given imperfection. In neither instance is there intention of applying the meaning of the name to God as if it were capable of "representing" him; we are merely saying that God who remains unknown does exercise a causal influence upon our world, and that whatever he is, he is not in bodily fashion.[58] But with the third category of names the problem comes into sharp focus; these do signify *substantialiter*, i.e. naming directly what God is in himself.[59] Obviously some analogical expansion of the concept is demanded but does this enable the latter to somehow include, even imperfectly, the *ratio* of a Divine perfection? Schillebeeckx vehemently denies this, refusing to the concept any value of the real; God himself is "affirmed" and "signified" in a non-conceptual cognitive act (inseparable nonetheless from an objective perspective opened up by the concept); he is nowise "represented."[60] This, as was shown above, is a corrective to those theories which interpret Cajetan's analogy of proper proportionality as allowing for a *ratio* that includes actually yet confusedly the divine as well as all creaturely modes of being.[61]

Much of religious language is metaphorical and here, of course, the images and symbols, even when they are neither relative nor negative in kind, are not intended to be taken literally; they are in obvious ways non-representational. God is indeed a "consuming fire" but no one confuses him with corporeal flames. The representation at work here is inseparable from conditions of materiality and imperfection, though possessed of a power to evoke another intelligible world of which it is a shadowy symbol. In itself, the image remains in the realm of the univocal, but can function as a linguistic artifice in the suggestive and imaginative summoning of another realm, really equivocal to its own. There is an underlying proportionality in metaphor, which enables Cajetan to categorize it as a mode of this analogy of proportionality.[62] It is an instance of analogy but improperly so; one thing is known in its rapport or similitude to another, but the proportion while intrinsic is not proper in kind and is not of the ontic order.[63] There is something in the arrangement of stars that suggests an animal or a dipper, but the similitude is in the order of shape or figure not that of natures, and even in the former there is lacking any real causal nexus. The similitude occurs in imagination, and ordinarily in virtue of appearances; if I look with the poet's eye, the clouds do appear "as spectral hounds scudding before the storm." But there is no common *ratio* here; in simile the semblance is expressed in terms of an analogy of proportionality (God in revealing his Word is like the sower who sows his seed) whereas in metaphor it is a case of supposition (God *is* a tower of strength). Metaphorical speech is born in the sudden perception of those mysterious affinities for which the world offers untold possibilities, usually discovered in a spontaneous, creative play of imagination. Its immediate effect is astonishment in which one is led to see an unsuspected similitude, that is illuminative and truth-bearing. This symbolic mode of knowing and expressing, indigenous to poetry, is then no denial of its truth value. When we say with Luther, "a mighty fortress is my God," we acknowledge that God is an unfailing refuge, but this is the truth, not the metaphor. The theological use of metaphor ordinarily suggests a semblance between some effect of God's and an action characteristic of the creature, thus what is actually being illumined is a certain similitude between causalities. The point here is that metaphorical speech about God does not

140

imply any proper conceptions of the Divine Being but only makes possible a knowledge of his operations indirectly known through a concept of the appearances and operations of his creatures.

Beyond all this, however, is speech about God that cannot be dismissed as metaphorical. The ideas involved now are limited to representing perfections of the transcendental order, scil. being, and whatever is interchangeable therewith as goodness, truth and such quasi-transcendentals as life, intelligence and love.[64] Still, such notions originate within the creaturely sphere and initially at least there is a transferal to God of a name properly designating not God but his creature. Obviously, if the term is to designate God some transformation of its meaning has to take place. The first stage in this expanding process occurs when one of two constitutive elements in the total signification of the word is simply dropped.[65] The original signification of the term, achieved in a unique abstractive process proper to the analogical act, includes both a *perfection* and its various finite *modes of existing*. This is unavoidable since the mind can only encounter the perfection as concretely existing and thus with its various modes of limitation. The latter's inapplicability to God is obvious and so in a mental process is simply eliminated. The process is itself the dynamic of analogical knowing and occurs not only explicitly in philosophical reflection but spontaneously and implicitly in a pre-philosophical phase.

The *ratio* that is retained is *not* so purified, however, that it can designate equally creature and God, one in a finite and the other in an infinite mode. To so think is to endow an abstract idea which excludes all imperfection with priority over God: logically such a notion could then be sub-divided into a created and an uncreated mode of realization; metaphysically, God would be understood as participating in a source prior to himself. The *ratio* that remains is not then a proper concept of the divine prerogative it designates because it leaves unexpressed the incomprehensible divine *modus essendi*. What is signified is a divine attribute that remains beyond conceptualization, yet knowable in a partial though authentic way in terms of a proportion to the objective contents of a creaturely concept. That concept already has an expandability in virtue of its not being limited to any modal realization of the perfection it signifies. Because of this it can be used as the *point de départ* for a projection by the act of judgment onto God. God is thus known through this concept; the judgment attains the existing order, in this case that proper to God — thus one is not left in the ideal order of an abstract concept. But the concept in no way represents the manner in which God is this perfection, so the judgment is not one of identifying God with the *ratio* in its modelessness but rather of understanding him as lying in the direction of the pure perfection it bespeaks.

In the constructing of the concept, should the modes of its actualization be entirely abstracted from, then the resulting idea would be univocal, not analogical. On the other hand, there seems no possible way of understanding them as actually included within the one idea, as Cajetan seems to suggest, without destroying the unity of the concept. This latter is certainly out of the question where predication about God is concerned. St. Thomas, however, offers an alternative by insisting that the analogical idea is not common in either of these ways but in virtue of a predication according to an order to something first, *secundum prius et posterius*. He clarifies this in the *De Potentia,* distinguishing between a common or generic element and a proper or specific one in the original construction of the concept.[66] The generic is set aside and the remaining proper notion which *of itself* is univocal, is extended intentionally to signify the proportions and rapports of certain other realities to the one that is prior in knowledge. It is this latter that constitutes precisely the analogical idea. The prime analogue will be the reality which answers to the proper meaning of the term, and this meaning will enter into the definition of all the other analogues as they take upon themselves the common name.[67] In "God-talk", the proper meaning of our

142

words is creaturely and finite; the analogical projection of them onto God is a designation of God relationally. When this latter play of analogy occurs within the light of faith, it achieves a deeper level of expandability and becomes Revelational analogy or what Maritain calls "sur-analogy."[68]

As long as the concern is merely with the *ratio nominis*, that is, with the notion to which the name gives linguistic utterance, the proportion is *to*, or better *from*, the concept representing the finite perfection. Even though divested of its finite modes of signifying, its meaning is available to us only by reference to such modes. When attention is shifted to the *reality* so named, i.e. to the *res nominis*, then the noetic direction is inversed. The perfection as divine, as beyond all modality and thus as constituting an attribute of God, measures the real existence of that perfection in its various participated modalities. In the ontological realm, God is the One to which and from which all things are proportioned. But this is the proportion prevailing between God and world as they exist and not as they come to be in knowledge; it is a rapport between realities *in se* and not *in mente*. As they fall within cognition the proportion between them enables man to know God in virtue of the creature, and to attribute to the former a name properly representative of the latter. The meaning of the term is not common to God and creature as if somehow embracing the specific ratio of both; the essence of God after all cannot be constrained and represented within any concept or name. It is rather proper to the creature and extended to God in the intellectual project which is analogical knowing. Simple as it appears in our psychological experience, it is on analysis complex.[69] Basically it is a dynamic of relational knowing, issuing in a predication *per prius et posterius*, or *secundum proportionem*, or *secundum ordinem*, which is to say it is an analogy of attribution. The knowing itself is accomplished in a judgment which affirms God as an infinitely removed and unconceptualizable term, but within a perspective opened up by the intelligible contents of a concept. Indigenous to such analogous speech is that the meaning of the word as said of the secondary analogates is discernible only by reference to what it means as said of the primary analogate. This is to say that the definition of the prime analogue enters into that of the secondary analogues in so far as they are known and designated analogously. Since God is the secondary analogue where the *meaning of the word* is concerned (it will be exactly the inverse if it is rather a question of the *reality* conceived in the mental word or *ratio* and expressed in the word of speech) every divine name bears a meaning for us that is derived from the sphere of God's effects. Thus God is being known and named *relationally*, i.e. by way of a proportion to the contents of a created idea. When it is said therefore that there is no concept of God,[70] this means that even in the case of the transcendentals the so-called analogous concept does not "include" a *ratio* of the divine; it does not "represent" anything proper to God. At the same time, such ideas — both as naturally held, and as further expanded within the illuminative experience of faith — do render possible an authentic knowledge of God. All human awareness of the divine then is without any proper conception of God and at the same time totally by way of a concept. Such ideas are not representational but they do allow for a consciousness of God that, while partial, is nonetheless cognitive, objective, non-metaphorical, and non-symbolic.

# CHAPTER FIVE

## ORIGIN OF GOD - LANGUAGE AND THE DYNAMISM
## OF RECONCEPTUALIZATION

### 1. Origin and Authentication of Symbols and
### Concepts about God

The all pervasive starting point of contemporary Western thought is human consciousness and subjectivity. This is recognized as the irreducible differential of human being and life. Similarly, it is commonly acknowledged that consciousness is bipolar: there must needs be a self *who is* conscious and something *of which* he is conscious. This is only to state that consciousness is never without contents and doesn't engage the question as to whether such objects are noumenal (classical realism) or totally phenomenal in kind (post-Cartesian thought). Human existence then is precisely inter-relatedness to a world. Further, the tendency is against seeing consciousness as purely creative or constituting consciousness; at least, the idealist hypothesis is as suspect in the modern restatement of it by Hüsserl (during one phase of his work) as it has been historically. If so, then, though man is "in a world," that world is not, or at least not entirely, of his own making. The givenness of reality to experience cannot be easily gainsaid, which means that reality is not finally at man's disposal; it is something that we do not determine but that determines us. Part of experience then is a sense of the limits to one's being, an awareness of radical contingency. At least in this sense, something transcendent, i.e., something over and against the self or human consciousness in general *(Dasein)*, is part of experience. And in such fashion, man comes to recognize his own transcendence, his power of transcending, a liberating movement beyond the self and the limits of time and place.

Thus human experience is made aware of a certain gratuity at the base of human existence that spontaneously is symbolized either as a Void *(Dasein* is grounded in nothing beyond itself; yet the implacability of *être en soi* means a final absurdity for human existence) or as a Presence. Langdon Gilkey contends that experience on the ontic level, prior to all ontological analyses, reveals a dimension of ultimacy in human existence.[1] At this point a fundamental option concerning ultimacy has to be made at least implicitly, for ultimate questions force themselves upon man even if below the threshold of conscious reflection; indeed this heuristic dimension to existence is itself a symptom of transcendence. The implication of this is that man's freedom is a co-constitutor of the integral experience; what the experience will actually be is partially determined by the free decisions which constitute a basic disposition or attitude, an *élan* towards the raw materials of the human world that are merely "given." Heidegger's analysis in *Sein und Zeit* discovers the meaning of *Dasein* to be temporality, but a temporality unto death, the anticipation of which leads to living one's life in the face of ultimacy and thus authentically. Remotely parallel to this, Lonergan has recently spoken of four "conversions" (respectively, the intellectual, the moral, the religious, and the Christian) that lead to an authentic possession of the truth. What is significant in both is the emphasis upon the moment of freedom in man's positing of his authentic self.

One lives one's life in the presence of reality that is freely experienced as either meaningless (thus as negating the question which human existence poses) or as holding out promise of some sort of meaning; on this basis the experience is symbolized in terms of either a Void or of a Presence. Should the latter be the case, it amounts to an act of transcendence, and is covertly and negatively an acknowledgment of some sort of transcendent. The symbolizing process itself is spontaneous and indigenous to human consciousness so that experience and symbol are co-principles of consciousness and mutually inter-active; hylomorphically, the experience assumes a natural form as symbol, and the latter informs and illumines the experience. This occurs first on the level of the lived-world where reason is subordinate to feeling and mood arising in turn out of a pre-conscious oneness with all of being. Thus the symbols which directly come to birth are emotive and conative in kind, assuming the outward forms of image and myth. Mircea Eliade has made the point that the ultimacy of this presence has meant that the symbols in which it is primitively articulated are in fact "religious," so that symbolizations on the profane level are subsequent to and derived from these primal ones.[2] The term "religious" here, of course, does not imply a recognition of the transcendent as God in any personal or theistic sense, much less as conceived in terms of an explicit Revelation.

The inter-action of experience and symbol is a dynamism that is prolix, growing more complex and refined and quickly becoming communal and cultural. At this point, a conscious, critical reflection upon the symbols comes normally into play, largely by way of correlating them to what is more directly known and apprehended non-symbolically. The numinous element attending the symbol, itself impels towards seeking greater certitude and clarity on the more purely cognitive level, on another stratum of consciousness, namely that of conceptual apprehension, judgment and reasoning. The symbol "points" to the symbolized only in dark fashion, though it does articulate a primal unity of man the symbol-maker with reality that cannot otherwise come to expression, and is not rendered superfluous by the concept. And even the concept can be used symbolically to give expression to what is dimly surmised as lying beyond its immediate range, but such usage in its turn

147

seeks its own ground and certainty in knowledge expression that is non-symbolic. The transferal from the language of symbol to that of logical conceptions means a transposition from the ontic order to the ontological, and the interpretative act is now in fact a doing of philosophy whether that of rational metaphysics or of eidetic analysis.

To summarize: the experience of ultimacy finds expression first of all in image, symbol and myth, but the very nature of this kind of knowing inaugurates the attempt to overcome its own deficiencies through transforming the concepts already possessed — once sense intuition naturally engages the intellect's power to penetrate reality in its intelligibility (concepts) and in its existence (judgments) — so as to bring to more purely cognitive thematization (to the extent that such is possible) what is encountered in experience as ultimate and unconditioned.

Nonetheless, the articulation of experience through symbol into concept has not always issued historically in conceiving of ultimacy as personal and absolute. Merleau-Ponty renders it as Contingency itself; Heidegger — as Absolute but non-divine; Whitehead — as Divine while still finite and relative. It can quite as readily be conceived as Process, as History, as the Material Dialectic, etc. This probability suggests that the project attempted by Gilkey in *Naming the Whirlwind* is not quite enough by itself, is valid only as a prolegomenon. It is at this point that the need for Revelation makes itself felt; some explicit content not available in ordinary experience has to be supplied by God himself; only he can disclose his own identity.[3] The occurrence of Revelation within consciousness demands its objective pole,[4] supplied by the mighty deeds of God in history and the interpretative words of the prophets — proclaimed by the Church as the authentic community of believers. God's self disclosure, in his revelatory act, must come to linguistic expression in an appropriation of existing human language (figurative and proper), which appropriation invests them with elements of originality but without dislocating the language as such. Thus, as the influence of Wittgenstein is serving to confirm, there is no such thing as a special religious language, but only the religious *use* of ordinary language. If God is to speak to man he must do so humanly, and so within the confines of our conceptual and linguistic world. The place in language where we do speak about God is, granted, at the very limits of language; the use here is a considerable transformation of ordinary words achieved by the total religious life-context that shapes them. Further, it is a question, not of a mere transfer of even such altered contents, but of a function as objective reference points in designating what lies beyond the perimeter of experience. Still, the designation must be from *within* our language, unless all ideas of God are to be dismissed as Fideism or Nominalism.

God's unveiling of himself, however, is at the same time a veiling. For the expressive power of our notions is always relative, relational, and indirect; man's historicity means that none of them escape a cultural and historical conditionedness. The root of such inadequacy lies in the inaccessibility of the Divine to intuition or empirical experience in which all our ideas originate. Thus though finite ideas are indispensable and offer an authentic *point de départ,* an objective perspective out of which to designate God, it is this very use which imperates a continuous noetic dynamic of reconceptualization.

## 2. **Reconceptualization: Its Necessity; Some Theories and Their Limits**

Clearly undeniable to the Christian (though admitting of divergent interpretations) is the inaccessibility of God from any initiative of man's. Apart from this, the whole notion of Revelation becomes watered down to near meaninglessness. At the same time, the very possibility of the latter demands making room for some receptive capacity within the limits of human consciousness. Unless one is prepared to run the risk of a total dualism, some coordination of these two truths has to be allowed. Revelation must needs have some point of insertion within the pre-Revelational life of man. In effect this is to acknowledge the pure possibility of a natural theology. It is not necessarily to admit the actual existence of any such thing. Indeed, what our contemporary vantage-point within history seems to compel us towards is seeing so-called natural theology as something that occurs and is nurtured within a religious faith response, within theology properly understood.[5] This is only to say that human faith must articulate itself in human concepts, and that such concepts no matter how transformed must derive from a phase of existence that precedes the faith experience. Some such concepts then possess an expandability, an intrinsic openness that enables them to function as the raw material in a cognitive awareness of God.

But the general truth remains that of God's unknowability, and consequent ineffability. He is transcen*dent* in the absolute and radical sense of the term: man's transcen*dence* as a capacity for "passing beyond" the limits of himself, is relative, and stops short of any direct cognitive grasp of the mystery of the Divine. It is a serious misunderstanding to suppose that man has some sort of radical power to know God that merely has been impaired by sin, or that we know as little as we do merely because God has chosen not to unveil himself fully, preferring to keep man in a faith situation that is arbitrarily obscure. On the contrary, it is proper to God that he cannot be known as he is in himself.[6] One of the truths owed to Revelation is that God is to be found as God only outside of the perspective of nature or the world,[7] and thus the Christian affirmation of him calls for radical obedience.

The first sign of this ontological unknowability of God in his total otherness is the proliferation of images and metaphors that Christianity must fall back upon under penalty of impoverishing itself, but which are no more than symbolic and relative. The history of Christianity offers ample evidence of this, beginning with the Biblical accounts themselves; indeed the latter appear to have an enduring quality suggesting that the modern attempt to dismiss them as archaic is rooted in a failure to perceive their genuine truth value. So basic and unavoidable is this sort of language that there always has been the tendency to interpret even statements whose linguistic form is literal rather than metaphorical in a symbolic way, leaving them with no other truth value. Paul Tillich has built his entire theology on this premise, but he would seem to be not far removed from St. Anselm when the latter writes of God being at once compassionate and not compassionate, i.e., compassionate in terms of our experience but not compassionate in terms of his own being.[8] Ideas are here used in a paradoxical and self-negating way, much like the way Bonhoeffer interprets the dogmatic propositions of the Council of Chalcedon.[9] It is to this tradition that Protestantism has by and large allied itself.

But there is a second truth: underlying and authenticating these non-literal expressions are others whose meaning is proper and literal rather than metaphorical and symbolic. It is these that enable theology to assume, in a genuine if unique sense, the status of science, rather than confining its task to the interpretation of religious poetry. If mystical theology surpasses in its own way *notional* theology, there remains a fundamental dependence and subordination of the former to the latter. But the point is that even these concepts and the language in which they come to expression for all their non-symbolic character, can never be other than relative. The knowledge they bear, while true and authentic, is always inadequate and is only a perspective onto God. Their analogical character means that while *signifying* God they necessarily fail to *represent* him; with them we know God relationally, i.e., in virtue of that relationship whereby God super-exceeds in an unknown way the participated creaturely perfection that we do know directly. What this prohibits is any absolutizing of our ideas of God, consistent with what Protestantism has interpreted as the Bible's continual protest against any finality to human knowing of God. Not that such ideas are false and must be continually denounced, not that they can ever be abandoned even — as long as it is a question of truths whose meaning is clear within Revelation itself or that are authentically propounded by the teaching authority of the Church. Dogmas are irrevocable. But because such knowledge, as human, is conceptual and analogical — the knowing process is a projecting dynamic from the finite to the infinite with the consequence that it ever remains *developmental in kind.* The projection is open-ended in its *terminus ad quem,* so that the noesis that occurs has principles of limitation as well as of extension. There is an indigenous element of reserve in the affirmations of consciousness; it is recognized that God lies beyond whatever is thought and said. This is betrayed in the use of complementary statements as correctives, e.g., a concrete term to counter-balance an abstract one, as well as in the fact that a vast number of distinct concepts are employed in speaking of God who is simple. In short what seems called for is a process of continual reconceptualization where God is concerned. But the keynote of that endeavor is *continuity* — the concepts of the past cannot be rejected anymore than they can be fossilized. It is they that serve as the authentic springboard into the future of Christian thought; their inadequacy initiates our effort to expand them; their present authenticity gives an objective directedness to that deepening and expanding process and is the guarantee of new truth rather than mere corruption of the old.

At this point a caution is required. What has just been said is not to deny that some expressions and ideas are, or were in the past, erroneous; nor that there are others whose presentation of the truth is so partial as to be a liability. Obviously such should be abandoned in the interest of a deepening faith. Also, even in the case of dogmatic statements within authentic tradition, a careful distinction must needs be made between what is being revealed or defined and what is rather an accompanying and underlying conceptual vehicle of that truth. This does not mean that the Revelation itself is non-conceptual in kind and the concepts are mere objectifications of a truth seized somehow non-conceptually. It rather indicates that a varied com-

152

plexus of concepts are involved in a total truth and not all the conceptual elements are necessarily being presented as Revealed. Especially where the Christian mysteries are involved some of the notions may be only attempts to grasp in idea what might otherwise be left vague and ambiguous. The clearest illustration of this at present is in all probability the difficult exegesis of the pronouncements of the Council of Trent on Transubstantiation. It is hardly allowable that the Council intended to bind in faith to the Aristotelian teaching on substance. The exegetical task, then, of determining what is an authentic and irreversible concept of Christian faith and what is only a cultural and conceptual elaboration of the latter must be carefully undergone. And perhaps the greater danger here is that of absolutizing.

It is the indigenous conceptual element to Christian faith that demands: (1) that our faith-knowledge of God be developmental — for there is no proper concept of him and (2) that such development occur precisely on the level of conceptualization. Granted that the terminal object of faith is the reality of God and not our idea of him, still he is able to terminate our belief only from the vantage-point of one formality of intelligibility, namely that expressed in the concept. To be an object is not to exist as such (i.e., to be a thing) but to exist for a subject, in a determined proportion of attainability for some faculty. Likewise, the continual transformation of concepts cannot be understood as it was in Modernism in the initial years of the Twentieth Century. What underlay the latter was an epistemological assumption that religious experience was preconceptual, and merely found its way thereafter into concepts as a means of self expression and conscious explication. The concepts to be used were those already available within existing cultures; the advent of a new cultural milieu then would not merely allow but necessitate jettisoning the old formulae and substituting new ones. Since Revelation itself was not notional or linguistic in kind, dogmas were only symbols fashioned from ideas appropriated from the cultural environment.

The position recently elaborated by Leslie Dewart,[10] at once challenging and controversial, evidences an intellectual kinship, though not a genetic one, with the Modernist theory. It cannot however be dismissed as only a sophisticated restatement of the latter, and differs from it radically on at least two basic points. First, is the acknowledgment of a personal and historical Revelation that is more than an evolving expression of an immanent religious instinct within man. Secondly, and more to the point here, is a distinct epistemological pre-supposition. Unlike the Modernists, Dewart understands all human knowledge to be conceptual, thus there is no question of a *pure* religious experience that afterwards comes to expression in various conceptual systems.[11] Conceptualization, however, is a process of objectifying and thereby differentiating what is known from the self, implying some sort of original identity.[12] Apparently Dewart is willing to acknowledge substantial distinction and individuality among existents but this is radicated in matter and is proper only to the cosmological universe. Spirit or consciousness is precisely a transcending of the separateness — not as a power to attain to and absorb the other as object (what he calls "intussusception"[13]), but as somehow already embracing the total range of meaning and intelligibility, yet in an indistinct, pre-conscious, unthematized way. Initially then, there is no subject-object dichotomy at the basis of knowledge.

The real affinity with Modernism appears more clearly in Dewart's empiricism; in the contention that the raw material, so to speak, for the conceptualizing process is already provided and available in the concrete experiences shaped by one's cultural, socio-historical environment. As that cultural inheritance alters and progresses, so do the ideas with which faith is rendered conscious and thematic. There is continuity in man's faith-response itself (as well as in God's continuing self-communication) but not in any cultural, i.e. conceptual, form wherein it is explicated.[14]

In effect, Dewart is saying that faith bears directly on God as he is in himself; the propositions and formulae of Scripture and Tradition are only the *"conceptualization, culturally and historically conditioned* of the Christian religious experience of belief in God"[15], and as such are not part of the object of faith. Dogmatic truth is a matter of fidelity, not of objective cognitive correspondence. This is, on Dewart's own admission, a rejection of St. Thomas' theology of faith which he sees as "pre-critical."[16] In St. Thomas' view faith does terminate at the very reality of God — only thus is it a theological virtue. But being man's act and having a necessary cognitive element it must operate by way of a concept — one which *represents* not God but something created, yet which can by the projecting dynamism of analogy *designate* God and sometimes properly so (i.e., non-metaphorically). Thus it is God who is known directly, and not e.g. our idea of him; still he is known only from the angle of intelligibility afforded by the concept. This is what St. Thomas means by calling God the *formal* object of faith; the formal object is not the entity as such but precisely *as known*, under the limited aspect of its attainment — the formal object of faith is the God of Revelation, i.e., God *as known by Revelation.*[17] In this way the propositions and formulae of Scripture and Tradition are themselves indirectly the objects of faith — which is only to say that as a cognitive act, belief must have some content. The concepts involved have an enduring character at least in the sense of being irreversible; they cannot be rejected though they may be expanded, enriched, and surpassed. Thus an objective cognitive continuity is assured. For Dewart, on the other hand, though concepts are indispensable for belief, none of them are enduring and thus *they* do not develop. In time they are rejected and new ones achieved in their stead.

There are two truths that appear as normative in this area:
1) the knowledge we have of God by way of our faith-response to his self-communication is, like all human knowledge, conceptual; and 2) the ideas employed are, even more than other ideas, partial and inadequate but yet authentic and true; that is to say, in one way mutable, in another way immutable. This is to understand that the intentional character to faith-

knowing demands that the latter be seen as developmental; dogmatic evolution is then necessary and indigenous to faith itself. Further, it indicates that such a developing dynamic occurs on the level of the ideas themselves; they stand in need of a continual re-working. Where God is concerned this amounts to a process of reconceptualization.

The implications of this are such that it must be maintained that Revelation itself develops — not as God's own act but as man's seizure in faith of the content of that Revelation. And indeed this appears incontestable in both Testaments. Israel's temptation is to regard as final what is only a partial fulfillment, and to counteract this God delivers them into exile, sends suffering upon them, leads them to an awareness that the world is still marked with sin and yet to be judged by him, that he has not yet spoken his decisive word. One outstanding illustration in the New Testament is the late appearance in St. John of a highly developed teaching on the Holy Spirit.[18] This perhaps affords no problem in light of the fact that God continues to reveal throughout this period. Once he has acted definitively in the Christ-event, however, so that *in this sen e* Revelation is closed,[19] the problem does become more acute. Henceforward, development will be basically an explication of the Revelation already made, and this will initiate the age of Tradition. But this very "transmission" is, on its own level, developmental in kind. This can also be considered a development of Revelation, not now in its *constitutive phase* (marked by inspiration), but in its *explicative phase*. The relationship between the two is such that the latter always occurs by way of reference back to the former or constitutive phase. The transmission, then — as a living tradition — is itself a constant reinterpretation, occurring in one fashion *on the level of faith*, in a less restricted fashion *on the level of theological science*. The process of change is both by way of *additions* to the existing deposit and of refinement; in the latter case, certain conceptual elements may be altered qualitatively or even eliminated. What remains constant is a certain objectively determined and irreversible directedness. This precludes the reconceptualizing process being understood in so broad a sense as to amount to *transformism*, understanding by this latter an evolution that is heterogeneous in kind, in which no continuity of meaning is discernible in the transition from one conceptual scheme to another. Much of contemporary Protestant thought, at least that which is heir to Liberal Theology, is attempting just this. Within Catholicism, the Modernist Movement was an abortive attempt in this direction. The project of Leslie Dewart, while differing on the important point of allowing a uniqueness to the historical Revelation in Christ, is in its own way an advocacy of transformism. It is not entirely clear how some of the Catholic theologians who re-posed the Modernist dilemma in the Forties have avoided it.[20] Their solutions in general called for some sort of separation of the act of faith as an *affirmation* from its conceptual or notional representation, allowing for an almost total relativity and mutability of the latter.

Preferable to transformism, then, is a genetic evolutionism, one allowing for change within continuity. This has emerged on the present scene in the form of three distinct theories. First is the *historico-religious* theory which would give to the Apostolic Revelation a totality in its historical origin. Some of this original plenitude of truth is temporarily lost from sight or de-emphasized during one period of the Church's life only to be re-discovered or recalled in another. What this theory demands, however, is the discovery someplace in the archives of the Church of evidence for the original Revelation long neglected and now newly emerging into Christian consciousness. It is apparent that this position has been discredited by its failure to be able to do this, even with all the resources of modern historiography, in cases such as those of the Marian dogmas.

More successful is a second theory, which has prevailed over the past four centuries, and might most aptly be called the theory of *logical explication*. Here the development is a process of drawing out and making explicit what is implicit in the central concepts of the faith. This explanation is one indigenous to

Scholasticism and finds at least its roots in St. Thomas; its fullest elaboration is perhaps to be found in the early Twentieth Century work of Francisco Marin-Sola.[21] There is little denying that the process it explains *does* have a role in dogmatic evolution and one that notional theology cannot afford to neglect; the question is rather as to its adequacy as an explanation. A general objection is that it isolates development on the cognitive level alone; but the more significant question is whether it be adequate even there. It would appear to stricture the movement of human consciousness too narrowly within the logical and rational sphere. Without allowing that cognitive progress is other than conceptual, judgmental, and especially by way of reasoning — it seems restrictive and unreal to confine that process to the level of reflective thought, to the activity of analysis and demonstration, of induction and deduction. The very existence of a reflective realm of thought manifests a prior world of spontaneous and implicit growth in consciousness. What seemingly lies at the bottom of this theory and explains its shortcomings, is a failure to distinguish the psychological and the logical aspects of human reasoning.

The rationalism that is latent here appears in what became in time a *scholia* to the position, namely the acceptance of so-called "virtual Revelation." When the implications and virtualities of a revealed truth were brought into light, they too were characterized as revealed "virtually." But if the explication or deduction is the work of reason (even under the light of faith) it is difficult to see how the motive of assent can be other than the power of reason, no matter how metaphysically close the conclusion be to its premise. If it be a question of a deduction *from* truths of faith (through the medium of a middle premise of reason) then what develops is not faith-knowledge itself but the explanatory science of theology. If it be rather a reasoning process *within* faith, there are two possibilities: the acquisition of a new truth (in a truly illative syllogism), or the mere explication of a presently held truth (in the merely explicative syllogism). In the latter case there is growth, it is true, but

158

only in terms of greater precision and clarity. In the former instance, the new truth if it is to be of faith must admit of being revealed, which is to say that its emergence into consciousness must be ascribed not to reason but to the light of faith.

The issue in all this can be seen in the question: what exactly is it that evolves? If we take as a concrete case our belief in God, surely it is not the reality at which our faith terminates, scil. God himself. Nor, at the other extreme, is it merely the language and formulations with which we speak about God. It is then faith itself which develops — not as a subjective intensification of the virtue but as an objective increase in the content of faith, a progression in what is believed. That is to say, it is our understanding itself of God in the light of his self-communication that advances. How? If all human understanding is conceptual, then what occurs is a reinterpretation or a reconceptualization. But the process cannot be narrowed down to a critical analysis of certain focal concepts and the logical derivation therefrom of new ones. One reason is that the original conceptions give only a limited perspective onto God and there is always the danger of falling back upon intelligibilities and virtualities in the concept that do not refer to God, of failing to observe the limitations inherent in all analogical knowing. More generally, however, this only allows for a clarification of an original all-sufficing though implicit knowledge. Development then would be limited to greater articulation, to rendering faith-knowledge more submissive to the rigidities of logical science, or to putting into new words an original and unaltering understanding.[22]

It is possible, however, to conceive of the very deposit of faith itself as evolving, in virtue of a continuing Revelation — a process that is at bottom cognitive, necessarily conceptual, and with a homogeneous continuity between present and past conceptual schemes. For lack of a better name, though with some propriety, this might be designated a *theological theory* of development. It allows for a reconceptualizing process that occurs initially on the pre-critical, pre-reflexive level by reasoning

that is spontaneous and implicit in kind. Though some anticipation of this theory can be found in the Nineteenth Century
work of Newman and Moehler along with others of the Catholic
School of Tübingen, it represents in fact an outlook that only
began to find expression in the mid-Twentieth Century, with the
re-emergence of the unresolved problem of the Modernist crisis,
and owes much to the heightened awareness of the historical
dimension to religious existence. The *status quaestionis* from the
Sixteenth through the Nineteenth Century was quite different
in focus. This new approach makes room for sources of doctrinal
growth that are not directly in themselves cognitive, e.g., the
affective, and that of lived experience, especially liturgical and
sacramental. Newman's influence can be detected here, though
it should be said critically that he perhaps overstressed the
moral elements in development to the detriment of the objective
and cognitive. Likewise there comes to mind the perhaps exaggerated role given to "action" in the thought of Blondel. At
any rate, allowance is here made for the origin of conceptual
schemes from outside of religious thinking and the realm of
classical philosophy already utilized in the Middle Ages, e.g.,
those of Personalism, Phenomenology, Existentialism, the newer
philosophies of language, etc. But underlying all else are the
epistemologies — or better, the ontologies of knowledge — at
work within this theory; the envisagement of how man knows.
One is the heuristic theory of knowledge to which Rahner and
Lonergan have contributed, seeing man as a questioner who
already possesses in some preconscious way the answers to the
questions he poses for himself; this is a condition for the very
possibility of inquiring in the first place. Each answer, no matter
how tentative, is the horizon for an entirely new question.
"Insight" becomes the means of the progression of knowledge
rather than discursive reasoning. In any case there is a homogeneous continuity on the conceptual level that is accounted
for here. The same is true with Schillebeeckx's "implicit intuition." Concepts of themselves have no value of the real but
they are the indispensable means to the intuition of the real,

160

and the service they perform is the supplying of an objective, cognitive directedness to that intuition. But the very primacy of the intuitional or non-conceptual element means that the partial and inadequate character to the concepts one is using at any given period keeps the latter in a state of flux, a state of constant alteration. Where faith-knowledge is concerned, it is the illuminative power of the light of faith itself that continuously refines and purifies the intelligibilities inherent within our concepts.

In an earlier chapter it was suggested that the basic assumptions underlying both these metaphysical stances, i.e., the Transcendentalism of Rahner and Lonergan on one hand, and the Implicit Intuitionalism of Schillebeeckx on the other, are open at the very least to qualification. Nevertheless, each of them has shed some positive light on the mystery of human knowing, especially in helping to explain its dynamic and developmental character. And these same preconceptions are intelligible within a distinct metaphysics and epistemology, i.e., that developed in Chapter Four as an Abstractive Intuitionalism by way of the consummation of the concept in the judgment of existence.

At any rate the possibilities afforded for a theory of doctrinal development, one beyond the narrow scope possible within what has been designated the logical explication theory, are quite clear. Concretely, one of the more promising attempts to elaborate and explain the epistemology operative in what has here been called the *theological theory* is offered by Schillebeeckx in his expansion of the *sensus plenior*.[23]

# CHAPTER SIX

## THE GOD WHO IS KNOWN ANALOGICALLY

Some shift in conceptual perspective onto God is a *fait accompli* in modern theology. What is offered however ranges broadly from an outright denial of God's reality in the "God is Dead" Movement to a near anthropomorphic emphasis upon his immanence and presence. The one common note is perhaps the dissatisfaction with a neutral and disinterested transcendence — e.g., Bishop Robinson's recourse to "depth" images in preference to a God "out there," borrowing from Tillich's "Ground of Being;" and Bonhoeffer's thesis of "This-Worldly Transcendence." The question, once again, is that of the value and meaning attending the ideas with which we strive to know an unknowable God. The theory sketched above of abstractive intuition (Chapter One) and of analogy (Chapter Four) might be tested by an attempt to implement it in the actual reconceptualization of God. This can be done best by focusing upon five central areas of mystery attending the search for God: (1) the problem of his very being or existence; (2) his transcendence and/or immanence; (3) his attributes in their multiplicity and simplicity; (4) the particular attribute of immutability; (5) the attribute of eternity; and (6) the central Christian mystery of the Divine Triune Personalities.

# 1. **The Being of God**

The concepts of "being," "existence," "is-ness," etc. are meta-physical notions and any introduction of them apropos of God must face an initial prejudice. As the achievements of natural speculative thought they are thought to be of no avail in the affirmation of the Christian God who discloses himself only in faith; as predicated of God they are idolatrous and to that extent "a-theistic." The normal process of reconceptualization which historically developed from a mythological understanding of God to a metaphysical one must continue into a further stage that overcomes such limited categories proper to the finite and the created. This reaction against setting up human ideas of God in place of the Divine Reality owes more today to Barth than to any other man; he attempted to do in his own age what Kierkegaard had done in his a century earlier. The question, however, is whether it be possible to know God even by way of faith apart from some human idea. Barth avoided the dilemma by assuming that it is, and setting himself against any possibility of an *analogia entis*. The clue lay in an understanding of Revelation as the initiative of God in so exclusive a sense that it implied in fact no human correlative or response. The use of religious language, the act of preaching, etc. were no more than occasions wherein the act of Revelation might occur. Its even-tuation as a grace implied a requisition of language, e.g. that of Scripture, by God for a meaning not available in the words themselves. In such a fideistic view the believer has no "idea" of God at all, nor can he evolve such from any philosophical system to objectify his faith experience. God encounters him in the act of belief which is self-authenticating and beyond noetic representation. God is not a being and does not exist because he is "Wholly Other" than what these categories convey.

Bultmann, who represents the alternate position into which Dialectical Theology polarized between the Wars, qualifies this extreme transcendence and allows for some language contact with God on man's own level. Biblical language is an instance of this, but that language is mythological in kind and as such suffers two shortcomings: (a) it is a dead language in a culture whose world-view is no longer mythological, and (b) it object-ifies God, who cannot be so objectified, as an object of thought. What is called for then is "demythologization" or "reinterpre-tation." The neutralizing of myth leaves us with what revealed religion is all about, scil. existential self-understanding. What is delivered to us is not so much knowledge about God as knowledge about ourselves as authentically related to a God who remains concealed though encountered in faith-experience.[1] Here, for Barth as for Bultmann, God in himself cannot be rendered into an object of human thought; there is neither concept nor language to justify saying that God "is," "exists," or has "being." The use of such expressions, whether by believer or non-believer, is a philosophic act and has nothing whatsoever to do with the Christian God.

Tillich, seeing the inconvenience of this unbridgeable hiatus between God's revealing and man's language-response, realized that the question could not be so readily disposed of and offered an alternative explanation. Words, images, and ideas about God have a symbolic value; this is possible because they are grounded in the one non-symbolic statement: God is, or is Being Itself. Whereas God is not *a* being nor does he "exist," still the notion of being is the one point of contact wherein man can radicate his attempt to know God. To this extent alone Tillich is allowing some basis for a natural cognitive approach to God, granted that it is one to be sub-sumed and deepened in faith. The difficulty with his position lies in its ambiguity. No sooner does he assert it than he backs away from its unavoidable implications.[2] In final analysis MacQuarrie's interpretation would seem to be correct, namely that the affirmation of God as Being is merely intended *as a definition*, i.e. as the radical sense in which Tillich intends to use the word.[3] Thus, there is no dialectical process, natural and spontaneous in kind at first and then subsumed within the act of faith, establishing that God "is" and leading logically to the

*Esse Subsistens* or *Ens a Se* of Classical Scholasticism.

Dewart accepts the challenge implicit in Tillich's ambiguity with a definitive rejection of classical metaphysics. God quite simply is not Being at all; he was so conceived only in a period characterized by a quite normal under-development of theism. The normalcy of this is explained by the fact that until recent times the only thought categories available with which to elaborate the experience of faith were those of the Hellenistic metaphysical outlook. The new cultural age has delivered to us a radically new conceptual scheme in which it is possible to reach the Christian God beyond theism.[4] Whereas Tillich is insistent that God is not *a* being, not even the Supreme Being, Dewart's contention is that he is not being at all. God is rather the "open background of consciousness and being;" the only category offered as expressive of this is "presence."[5] Operative here is a totally non-traditional understanding of being. Man's transcendence is precisely his consciousness, which latter is a capacity for constituting objects of consciousness, thereby endowing them with being, or "creating" them. Things in themselves are given being by man as he assumes them into his history, and he "creates" thereby even himself. God is experienced as lying beyond this, as uncreated, as not being.[6] God is not then an object of thought. "Our concepts are in principle unable to make known to us the existence of God."[7] "Religious experience, then, does not reveal a transcendent being: what it reveals is that being exists in the presence of a reality which transcends it."[8]

At the core of this theological agnosticism is a rejection of analogy. And for all the illuminative insights from contemporary philosophy (somewhat eclectic, actually) that Dewart brings to this task it must be seriously asked if they do in fact justify such a rejection. A major suspicion that this is not the case arises from his surprising but clear misunderstanding of analogy. He rightly sees it as a matter of *predication* but denies what such predication is grounded in, namely, analogical *understanding* (in turn made possible by the participationist structure to reality). Such arbitrary predication is for him simply a way of admitting the insufficiency of concepts without consciously acknowledging it.[9] To say that God exists and then to add that the statement is analogical is simply to say that he doesn't exist. Analogy does not in fact provide a metaphysical knowledge of God at all, it merely serves "to introduce a qualification to every positive statement about God."[10]

As was earlier observed, Dewart is inclined to reify being; to use the term as a noun; when he allows it the connotation of a verb it is always the "be-ing" of an essence as something prior and distinct, i.e., "ex-sistence," and never being as pure actuality. Thus he is understandably sympathetic towards Gilson's project of denying that God has any essence at all; but the conclusion he sees this logically culminating in is the consequent denial (against Gilson) that God has being. He is right in seeing Maritain as a better guide to St. Thomas when the former maintains that we must attribute to God both essence and *esse*, though only as *conceptually* distinct.[11] From this it follows rigorously that "There is, therefore, an unbridgeable difference between the way God is *in himself* and the way in which he is *in our knowledge*."[12] But Dewart views this in the same light as Kant, namely as rendering every affirmation of God's being by intellect an implicit instance of the ontological argument. In actual fact it only manifests the impossibility of any proper knowledge of God. Only by way of conceptual distinctions is it possible to know that God lies beyond such distinction; not only beyond essence but beyond existence, beyond anything we can conceive of. The truth arrived at here is not assumed in some masked form of the ontological argument but reached to; it is the terminus of the thrusting act of intelligence.[13] Thanks to the judgment of analogy we can say "God is" but in a radically other fashion than finite things "are." One way of expressing the radical difference is to deny of God in a *via negationis* any *real* distinction of essence and existence, for this is the source of finiteness. Yet we must rest content with no conceptual envisionment of that real indistinctness.

All this is at a far remove from affirming, in an existential judgment,[14] that God "is," making use of a concept that represents the perfection of creaturely existence, without limitation to any one of its modes, to signify, but authentically so, that God has this very perfectness though in an unknown divine way surpassing all conceptual representation. At least something like this is necessary because the affirmation (or negation) of being simply cannot be avoided — or transcended — in any human speech. The very effort to do so is itself an implicit positing of being. To speak of God as present (and as not being) is surely to say that he *is* present. The primacy and irreducibility of this category are such that outside of it lies only nothing — meaning by the latter not Heidegger's "no-thing" *(Das Nichts)*, nor the transluminous darkness of the mystics, but the utter void in which and of which no word can be spoken.[15] In actual fact, the dismissal of being is possible only on the condition of defining it in such a restrictive fashion that it can be gone beyond. This is what Dewart does in restricting it to mean the product of man's creativity: man "creates" his objects and thus himself as subject, and only these are said to "be." But surely the givenness of the preworld out of which he creates his objects and so himself, and especially the givenness of human consciousness itself has to be explained ultimately as *"being*-there" *(Da-Sein).*[16]

At the same time, the mind's vicarious living in its own way, through the existential judgment, of that very existence that is exercised extra-mentally is not any conceiving of the very *actus existendi;* it is merely the affirmation of a subject enjoying whatever actuality it has (known or unknown) as over against utter negation. It is a true knowing, but only in a sense analogous to the conceptual grasp of essence. Even finite existence cannot be enclosed within a concept, and its affirmation demands a range of concepts representing the limiting modes (essences) within the spectrum of being; thus univocal or generic speech in its regard is impossible.[17] Moreover, God's being is not affirmed within this spectrum but *from* it. A second level of analogical speech comes into play here, one that projects from the level of the transcendentals where one is dealing with concepts that already are analogical in their own order. The very way we say "God is" affirms that such beingness is unknown and unnamed. The negating quality of analogy is operative in the sense that there is a quite clear if implicit denial that God is being in any of the modes which alone offer themselves to our experience. Neither is this the attribution to him of an abstract modeless idea, scil. being as such, (as Scotus thought to do) but it is to reach the divine reality in one of its intelligibilities, in a purely relational way *ex creaturis,* in a projective act of analogical knowing that is open-ended. Thus while it is true to say that God is, it is not true to say that he is not, except syncategorematically, i.e., he is not in this or that limited way of being. Thus, insisting upon the meaning of the word "exist" in its etymological sense ("ex-sist," to come to be out of something), it is improper to speak of God's existence. This is why St. Thomas' question is *"an sit Deus?"* (whether or not God is); the Latin equivalent for "exist" or "existence" does not occur in the entire question.[18] To exist is to be in a way that man can grasp; it is the actuality of an essence that finitizes the act of being and enables it to be conceived. What is acknowledged in the affirmation of God's being is the fact *that* he is, not *how* he is. St. Thomas' succinct advertence to this absolutely primal distinction was by way of pointing out that the verb "to be" is used in two senses — to signify the act of existing, and the mental conjunction of subject and predicate in the judgment. In the first manner we do not know the being of God anymore than we know his essence; all that analogical knowledge permits is the second.[19] But we know that this judgment is true; not merely correct according to the rules of formal logic, but attaining to the real situation *that* God is, leaving unattained *how* he is. This follows with all subsequent predications, as e.g. that God is good; the goodness of God is affirmed without any grasp of what divine goodness consists of. On the reflective level, this is mediated by the work of reason, whether a *posteriori* discursus or transcendental reflection, but in any case it is made possible by the

169

relationality of finite participated being to the unknown Being that is its source or ground. To attempt to speak of God apart from affirming his beingness is not to speak of God at all.

## 2. The Transcendence of God

All of the foregoing leads to at least two conclusions: that the mind of man is naturally capable of affirming that "God is" and, that whatever direction the reconceptualization of God takes it must be in terms of "being." The negative element in our knowledge of God (which can never be forgotten) prohibits saying that God is *a* being, for the connotation here is of an essence that has received a really distinct act of limited existence. To call him the Supreme Being does not avoid a similar misapprehension because of the implication of substance, even though unique in kind which reductively locates God within a genus proper to creatures.[20] Christian theology never intended any such unjustified application of the term "substance"; the point is that it tended to fall back upon this abusive extension of the word for lack of more accurate categories. Certainly God is not the sum total of all the beings, nor the expression in an abstract idea of what all beings share in common — *ens in commune*. But if God is not any being why then is he not nothing? This draws attention to a certain unsatisfactoriness with the expression Being Itself; if this idea be voided of all determinateness it comes uncomfortably close to Hegel's nothingness.

Some advance can be made by having recourse to Being in the sense of Heidegger's *Sein*: here Being is nothingness (*das Nichts*) only in the sense of being "no-thing." It is in this sense an Absolute, transcendent to the world of existents (*das Seiende*). But is this in final analysis anything more than the being-process? After all, Heidegger only sees Being as "coming to pass" *within* the beings enabling them to appear for *Dasein*. Seemingly, this makes God, as *Sein*, immanent to the world; his transcendence is

170

one within the world, and rests upon Heidegger's Ontological Difference between Being and the beings. John MacQuarrie attempting to show the applicability of the concept to God writes of the essence of being as "precisely the dynamic 'letting be'... of the beings,"[21] and "as a kind of energy that permits beings to be," though he goes on to suggest that "perhaps the word 'act' would be better for it suggests a more highly organized energy." This "letting be" is understood in a positive and active sense "as enabling to be, empowering to be, or bringing into being."[22] The *logical* implications of this are, *prima facie,* pantheistic, and MacQuarrie does not succeed in dispelling them merely by insisting that "Being 'is' the *transcendens,* and this term indicates not only God's distinction from the world but his 'wholly other' character as over against whatever is in the world."[23] Here he is obviously having recourse to something not objectively in the concept of Being as "letting be." How is it possible to see Being as set over against whatever is in the world and still to acknowledge that "there 'is' no being apart from beings"?[24] It is perhaps a clue to this ambivalence that in one place MacQuarrie writes of "the *incomparable* that lets-be"[25]; the definite article and the adjective suggesting grammatically something more than mere process. The motives at work here are clear enough: to avoid supposing, on one hand, that God is some being among beings and, on the other, that he is pure being in the Hegelian sense of total indetermination. But what such a view fails to acknowledge is that determinateness is itself a perfection, since it enables anything to be what it is rather than nothing.[26] The power of analogy then can enable us to know that God is total determination — not the sum total of all limiting determinations of existents, but a transcendent plenitude. God is then not so much "letting be" as an unknown one who "lets be" and thereby grants to men some faint glimpse into the mystery of himself. It is not a valid objection to this to say that it simply puts us into the position of asking the further question about the "being" of this Being. For that presupposes that whatever "has" being is an essence in the sense of a mode or a limitation of being, and that is exactly what we know the essence of God not to be. His essence, or *what* he is, cannot restrict his being and so does not enter into real union with it. The remaining alternative is that it *is* his being, that essence and existence are identical in God. Thus, one can preclude MacQuarrie's objection that such a being even if the most "being-ful" of all beings would still be transcended by Being itself.

Underlying this new conceptual approach is a recognition of process and change as a perfection and the tendency to see being as static and thus imperfect. The need then is to give to being an existential connotation it lacks in traditional theism. This is done in passing over from the ontic (*existenziell*) realm to the ontological (*existenzial*) one where Being (*Sein* rather than *das Seiende*) now includes becoming. The metaphysical insight here is a valid one and cannot be neglected; and it is true that traditional theological usage of the idea of being did tend to convey the notion of a God whose transcendence was a sort of neutrality towards a universe of change. But the insight needs to be carried one step further. Becoming, like being on the ontic level, is limited perfection. What characterizes God is the formality of perfectness in becoming without the restrictions that necessarily attend all the manners of becoming that we can conceive of. Immutability, as a verbal designation of a divine attribute, is not an entirely felicitous expression; it is entirely negative in kind. It needs counter-balancing from such expressions as "Pure Act," and this may be the traditional category that comes closest to the existential meaning of Being. The God conceived as Actuality is not any super-substance, but *Esse Subsistens* (unreceived "is-hood"). However, such Being is not restricted to process within the world but is a pure Source of inexhaustible process lying itself beyond process in any finite sense. God is changeless because he is the full realization of all that is perfect in change in a purer sense, in a way that is "wholly other." Cajetan, in a different context, insists that it is not quite precise to speak of God as, on one hand, absolute and, on the other, relative; he is rather some one perfection whose intelligibility lies beyond what we can grasp in these two combined concepts.[27]

The Absoluteness of God, in short, is also something we can affirm only analogically; the limitations or "agnostic" elements in such a knowing have to be acknowledged. In the light of this the Christian understands readily that Merleau-Ponty's denial of all absolutes is not necessarily atheism.[28] What makes his thought important are the careful nuances he gives to it. Seeing reality as a horizon for man, as a preworld (*pré-monde*) that is unfinished and must be co-constituted by man, it cannot itself be misapprehended as an absolute. But (especially with the development of his thought) it is quite as much an error to make man as co-constitutor of the world into an absolute. The sole possibility for transcendence here is that originally allowed by Hüsserl himself, scil., that of phenomena — not as the appearances which conceal reality (phenomenalism), but as reality itself as it appears (Phenomenology). This movement towards ontology, albeit an existential ontology, has obvious kinship with the thinking of Heidegger; and the latter's eventual designation of *Dasein* as the "Shepherd of Being" is paralleled by Merleau-Ponty's notion of man as "inhabiting Being": "it is being which speaks in us and not we who speak in being."[29] Even what is "pre-given" here, however, is not an absolute in Merleau-Ponty's precise sense, namely something already defined and self contained or "finished." His rejection of theism is in terms of a God who is presented as an absolute in this objectivized way. It is God as a rationalistic projection of man's experience of his own finiteness, a God who escapes this finiteness into infinity, that Merleau-Ponty cannot find room for. He wishes to say in Frans Vandenbussche's lucid phrase that "Divine Existence is not human existence freed from all its limitations."[30]

But what is it then, what possible clue do we have to the identity of what might be a God beyond theism? Merleau-Ponty offers little more than a tentative hope that there is a hidden, ultimate meaning to human existence and history. He gradually

173

came to find meaning in excess of what consciousness can achieve by itself, a meaning radicated in the primacy of Being "which speaks in us."[31] But reality is still phenomenal, i.e. meaningful structure. And the most that he can say of Being is that it is "the frame of the phenomena, it is *dimensionality* itself"[32] (italics supplied); elsewhere it is referred to as *Openness*,[33] that is, the open background to all of human existence and history. What Merleau-Ponty's thought refuses is any supposition that God is *absolutely* known, i.e., an absolute in his technical sense of what can be objectivized by us. Here his negative contribution to the Christian search needs to be welcomed. But it would be going too far — beyond what his thought will justify — to deny that God is an Absolute or is known to be such. There is no reason why the infinity attributed to God should be "spurious,"[34] as long as it is recognized that God's infinity lies beyond any of our concepts and is understood as qualitatively something more than human existence without limits. It seems, too, that Merleau-Ponty does allow for one absolute (if not in certainty, at least in hope), the absolute of "directionality." But that directionality appears immanent within the world of the word and of history. And surely the Christian must hesitate to give to this the name God. That it provides a focus for encounter with God may be readily admitted. But is it itself anything more than Tillich's "Ground of Being," which he himself came to see as having a certain ambivalence on the transcendence-immanence axis. Vandenbussche's critical comment on Heidegger, scil. "that one may wonder whether (he) does not allow the autonomy of the world to vanish into the mundanity (the *In-der-Welt-Sein*) of *Dasein* itself,"[35] seems to fit Merleau-Ponty nearly as well.

In fine, the very way in which one affirms that God "is" means saying that he is as other than and so metaphysically "outside of" the entire order of finite being; in a word, as transcendent to it, no matter how this be conceptually nuanced. This may well give rise to further problems of explanation, but these cannot be allowed to negate the truth that the concept of God does express his absolute transcendence.

## 3. The Immanence of God

The conception of God as Pure Actuality is not an idea of him as a being among the beings, nor as the supreme substance, nor as the sum total of all beings, nor as an abstract idea. But on the other hand, neither must this reduce itself to the being-process, to "letting be," or "dimensionality." The human motives for falling back upon these latter are easy to see: an acute awareness of the misconceiving which the former categories involve, and a desire to re-establish God's immanence. Historically it owes something to a reaction against the extreme transcendentality that serves to isolate a Barthian god. The strength of this new approach is that God is discovered, or discoverable, not within nature or the context of the cosmological world but within a context of meaning, a world of the word and of history that man himself creates. But it is precisely here that it must be seriously questioned if this leaves God with any genuine autonomy over against the world. Can indeed his sovereignty be truly safeguarded without explicitly giving to God the prerogatives of subsistence and personality? It may be easier to reverse the problem and ask if a subsistent and personal God is necessarily one without immanence to the world, an immanence other than that of an arbitrary intrusion into it — for this appears to be an assumption of those who seek the reality of God in the being-process.

The Biblical God, in a surmounting of paganism, was freed from nature, but at the same time the major emphasis was upon his *presence* by an initiative of his own to the community that was Israel. This was an implicit recognition that God was both transcendent and immanent, but without any explicit conceptual working out of their compatibility. The Middle Ages, absorbing and at the same time transforming the Hellenistic metaphysical outlook, was able thereby to do just that. Their conceptual terms so stressed the transcendence that the very existence of anything else at all could only be explained by the immediate causal presence of the Source of being to whatever was of that Source.

175

St. Thomas' technical phrase referring to God as the *proper* cause of being means that God is more intimate to each and every existent than the latter is to itself.[36] The precision of thought here, however, was such that this involved no diminution of God's own being; it all occurred on an utterly free initiative of God's knowing and loving, and precluded even any real relation of God to his world. Briefly, this was to affirm what has been constant in the Catholic tradition, namely the simultaneity of God's transcendence and immanence. The reaction of the Reformation against Scholasticism resulted in an abandonment of this position. In its place was an understanding of immanence immediately in terms of the Incarnation: God remains transcendent as God but comes among men in the flesh of Christ. To some degree this occasioned the collapse of theology into Christology, and not the Nicene Christology of *homoousios,* but the Lutheran Christology of *kenosis.* Today, the Post-Bultmannian School has sought to recover a sense of God's immanence by recourse to an existential encounter with a God who is in himself utterly transcendent and inaccessible from man's side; an encounter by way of the Word which calls for demythologization and makes the theological task that of Hermeneutics. The newness of this project lies with its introduction of existential categories with which to reconceptualize.

But a conception of God as Subsistent Being, as sheer Existence whose very essence is "to be," or as Being *per essentiam* which means that everything else *is* only in virtue of a participation in what God is of himself — when properly understood — demands a God who, remaining transcendent, is at the same time totally immanent to his creation. It is unthinkable that there could be anything at all without the presence of Being to and within it, accounting not only for its having come into being but for its very perdurance in being. No being of our experience then, and notably human "being," is of itself or by itself; its hallmark, as Merleau-Ponty so lucidly saw, is contingency, relatedness, ambiguity, historicness, etc. Not that God in this conception is formally the actuality of the creature but he is its source in so exclusive a sense that the communication of finite actuality demands his immediate presence; a non-mediated presence, it might be noted, not merely of his power but of his very Self. This divine actuation, further, is not realized only in the instance of things or substances, but of every least operation, tendency, recoil, relationship, etc., for these too are in their own way being. So universal is this in-existence of God to the world that what is called his providence should not be misconstrued as an intervention from without but as a meaningful (or beingful) directionality inherent in the dynamism of being itself. The very causality of creatures is itself exercised only in virtue of the supercausality of Pure Actuality that penetrates and suffuses it.

However, God also *is* outside of creation; his being is not, as it were, exhausted by all that he does. He *is* not merely to explain the universe or to supply for it an *a priori* ground for its being. Few tenets of classical Theism have been perhaps as commonly misunderstood as that which maintains that God is unchanged by his acting in and upon the world; that he bears no real relation to that world. This is frequently misread to mean that God is at an ontological remove from and without concern for the world he sustains in existence. In actual fact the classical position, properly understood, means exactly the inverse of this. What it wished to deny is that God's knowing and loving of the world are mere accidental relationships, acquired as it were extrinsically and contingently; on the contrary, there is a sense in which it is necessary on God's part and constitutes his very Being and Self as the Plenitude of Being.[37] This does not mean that God necessarily creates the world; all that is necessary is that Pure Actuality should freely choose either to create or not create. Nor does it mean that the *de facto* relationships which here and now prevail are the only possible ones. It only means that once a world is posited, some relationship is absolutely neces-sary. That is, it pertains to the very essence of God that he be in rapport at every moment and on every level with the world that "is" only by participation in him. St. Thomas' constant denial that there can be any real relationship of God to creature means that the penetration of our being by God cannot be reduced to Aristotle's category of "relation" as something accidentally accruing to and inhering within God — except in our thinking, except as a relation of reason. Relations, properly taken, are contingent, matters of facticity, whereas God's rapports with the world are essential to his Being as Knower and Lover of what he has freely summoned into existence. We conceive of this after the fashion of a relation since it is the only category available to us, but the impropriety of it is brought to light when we reflect that we merely construe God's involvement with us in terms of our own real and dependent relationship upon him. Because God is the Plenitude of Being he does not merely enter upon a relationship rendering himself adjacent to or alongside his creatures, by contacting them from a situation of prior isolation, as it were, in and through an operation distinct from his Being. Rather, the creature issues from "within" the divine fecundity as a finite concretation of what God is, and is totally sustained "within" that fecundity. Of course, this must not be misconstrued to imply that the very essence of God is itself a relation, i.e., that God is, as the Scholastics would say, related *transcendentally* (rather than predicamentally) to a world of creatures. Apart from implying the necessary existence of creatures, this would leave God's being incomplete in itself and actually perfected by the creaturely termination of that relationship. In effect, God would then be part of a larger universe of being superior to himself alone. This view of the matter fails to see that if God is Subsistent Reality then his every communication is altruistic; his super-abundance of being is such that he can only give, not acquire. It is the creature who is the beneficiary of God's creative activity; his own being is neither enriched nor diminished. Thus, the world, ordered ultimately to God's glory, is created for us and not for him. In short, the transcendence and the immanence of God cannot be separated; it is well to avoid a certain conceptual ambivalence by insisting on the real simultaneity of these two attributes, and perhaps even clearer to try to understand them as indistinguishable in God.

Still, this traditional picture may well be thought to be less than an adequate explanation of God's love for the world. It cannot be repudiated but does need to be carried further. The clue to doing this may well lie in recalling that God's immanence to the world is, in the end, a presence. The latter is a *personal* category (as Hermeneutical Theology has insisted in seeing God's relation to the world in terms of his Word), and must be understood as distinct from, but not opposed to, categories of *nature*. To do full justice to the immanence of God, then, demands approaching this not only ontologically in terms of the presence of Being to being but also existentially in terms of personal disclosure within the human world where man as a co-positor of meaning constitutes himself. The two approaches are complementary to one another for the reason that man is both nature and person, and that God's nature is, and identically so, personal; in fact, he is Tri-Personal. The category of relation then can be transposed to another level of meaning without rejecting a prior one. Ontological relations, whether transcendental or predicamental, if real in God, would bespeak imperfection and thus be destructive of his nature. Existential relations, on the contrary, as "real" are precisely constitutive of personhood — thus is the Trinity precisely constituted by Three Relations. Such relations must not imply real dependence *of nature,* it is true, (as once again, they do not in the Trinity), and so must be seen against the background of denying real ontological relations of God.[38] On this basis, the complementarity of the two conceptions at work here precludes understanding relation in a Whiteheadian sense with the logical consequence of finitizing God's (subsequent) nature. But what it allows is a conception wherein God freely wills to constitute himself personally — not simply as God, but as a creating and saving God — by his concrete and actual knowing and loving of the world. Properly understood, this could include his choice to concur with man in the latter's self-constituting creativity, to thus wait upon man's free moral decisions.[39] What is suggested here is not an eclecticism of two disparate conceptual schemes, but a movement of understanding from an ontology that underplays the personal into one that recognizes the personal as identical with the ontological at its apex in God. But this divine identity can be reflected humanly only as a unity, thus the ambivalence.

## 4. Distinction of Attributes

The human cognitive search for God *de facto* issues in the attribution to him of multiple perfections which since they are not intended as synonyms are in some sense distinct. The question here is that of God's knowability, i.e., the concrete objectification in varied human categories. Transcendental Thomists fear that the tradition which ignores Kant has fallen into a quasi-rationalist excess in delineating in such detail those divine perfections, in over-stressing the applicability of the intelligible contents of our ideas to God, giving them in effect a representational value. A focal point of this fear of a hidden anthropomorphism is the discussion on what kind of distinction prevails between the divine attributes. Such distinction, of course, has never been presented as anything more than rational, i.e., the work of reason in its attempt to analyze the being of God which is in reality one and simple.[40] But it is being asked, still, whether the basis which validates such a work of reason be the distinction of created perfections which form the *point de départ* for our knowing God, or rather the very eminence of God as the plenitude of Pure Being. Unquestionably, the ideas are distinct among themselves, and *de facto*, they are predicated of God in a distinct fashion, but is such distinctness in God in any manner whatsoever or does it derive *entirely* from our limited mode of knowing? The question is of some import because if the Divine Reality offers some intrinsic basis for the distinctions which are formally the work of reason, then the ensuing relationships in terms of

an order among the attributes, a logical anteriority and poste-
riority, are likewise verified. Is the relationship of love to knowledge *in God* somehow, or is it only a relationship between our
ideas of knowledge and love? The genesis of an inner word at
the very heart of intellection and the eruption of such intellective
generation into love that is spirative of an immanent term is a
profound cognitive reach into the mystery of a God of Trinitarian
Processions.[41] But does God himself offer a fundament for such
an analysis or is this is an unjustified projection onto God of our
human mode of knowing?

Rahner, as we have seen, tends to circumvent the problem
as posed in these terms. While not denying an ontology of God's
perfections (one which survives within a faith context) and even
allowing for the conditions of its possibility, he is aware of its
inherent limitations and noticeably shy of pursuing such an
approach.[42] Though valid, its intelligible yield is slight and
readily lends itself to mis-apprehensions. If knowledge is the
conception of something against the pre-conceptual and unthematic prehension (*Vorgriff*) of being as an unrestricted horizon,
which in its turn demands an implicit affirmation of Absolute
Being, then the dynamism of human knowing in its analogical
reach to God assumes a different starting point and an inverse
directedness. While allowing full scope to analogy both in the
order of being and knowing, Rahner's Transcendentalism alters
considerably what analogy means; this is especially apparent
of analogy as operative within the order of knowing, as offering
an epistemological structure. Analogical knowing is here the
thematic clarification of prehended being which "posits" God
as the Unconditional who is merely the condition for limited
beings, as the unknowable Ground of the finite. The process
of rational demonstration is here being radically curtailed; thus,
Rahner's "proofs" for God, while *a posteriori* are quite other than
the *a posteriori viae* of classical Thomism. In accord with this,
Rahner's efforts are directed towards the New Testament's presentation of God's presence through Revelation as an existential
event unveiling to us not *what* God is but *who* he is. It is the

personal attitude (*Haltung*) that God freely adopts towards man within salvation history that comes to the fore, which as personal does not easily surrender itself into the categories of ontology, but finds expression in the paradoxical utterances of Christ and in the final paradox of the Cross.

In fine, Rahner's position represents an option or preference of theological procedure; he simply eschews the question as to how the various attributes of God are ontologically related. Schillebeeckx, by contrast, does urge the question in this perspective and clearly insists that the attribution to God of multiple perfections must not be misconstrued as a virtual distinguishing of these attributes within God. To do so is to push theology beyond a reserve it must honor, a silence it must maintain. Though our ideas are distinct in themselves, they are not predicated distinctly of God. Their distinctness is traceable to their creaturely character, and to carry this over onto God is to suppose that they can somehow "represent" divine perfections, whereas in fact they can only be used to "designate" them. The error is that of presuming to enclose the reality of God within a human idea.

Schillebeeckx discerns two underlying errors at work here — the first is a misunderstanding of the analogy between God and the world as that of proper proportionality; the other is endowing concepts with the power to attain the real whereas this is possible only in virtue of a nonconceptual implicit intuition of being. Both of these represent profound insights that do carry theological speculation forward; at the same time, the conviction perdures that both are an over-stressing (by way of reaction) of one facet of the total truth. Some reservations on the two theses are thus called for; reservations, nonetheless, which hopefully will preserve the advance that Schillebeeckx's thinking represents over past theological statements on the issue. The two truths not to be lost are: we do not have proper concepts of God, and our concepts *as such* lack actual existential reference.

The import of the famous text from the *Contra Gentiles*: "We are not able to know of God what he is but only what he is not and how other beings relate to him"[43], is that God cannot be known (apart from the Beatific Vision) *"sub ratione propria."* By this he means to say that the only knowledge we have of the divine quiddity, of God as he is in himself, is negative and relative. What this does not mean is that there is no positive knowledge of God at all, although this latter knowledge derives from the reproduction in creatures of God's prerogatives. His perfections are known and named in a *human mode,* that is, *"secundum quod inveniuntur in creaturis."*[44] The very substance of the Deity is cognitively attained but only in virtue of concepts whose intelligible contents are directly representative of the creaturely. This is as true of analogical concepts of pure or absolute perfections (the transcendentals) as it is of others. God is the Transcendent, he is not a transcendental. Even when the *"modus significandi"* of the concept, which gives existential reference to the perfection expressed, is dropped, the *"ratio significata"* which remains is not a proper ratio of God because it leaves unexpressed the divine mode of existence. Secondary reasons are the abstractness and plurality of such *rationes;* God is the concrete plenitude of being and is one. Still, the above process reveals that the *ratio* is not necessarily bound to its finite conditions of existential realization. Thus, the mind can affirm that this perfection is in God, though in an unknown way, *modo divino.* Thereby it can be known, e.g., *that* God is good but not *what* his goodness is.[45] Nonetheless, the predication is intrinsic, saying more than that God is the efficient cause of the created perfection. In effect, by recourse to exemplar causality, a formal convenience is being acknowledged between a finite and an infinite perfection, but a convenience that while formal is only *by analogy understood as a proportion,* and radicated in the causal derivation of one from the other. As a consequence, the "likeness" is non-reciprocal in kind, and one of the extremes remains unknown in itself. God who is *toto caelo* other than the creature can be known only in virtue of the creature's limited resemblance to himself. Because the analogical notion ranges over all the instances of its finite realization, including all of them actually and not limited to any one, it can serve to open up a conceptual perspective

183

enabling man to say God is good, etc. In this, the idea retains its positive value, functioning as the objective focal point of a judgmental affirmation of God. Through such a created idea we "intend" an incomprehensible God in a conscious unknowing.

This proportion is ontologically the analogy of being, wherein created being is a finite participation in Uncaused Being, arising out of the mystery of creation. But, more properly, analogy is a matter of knowing and naming something in virtue of this proportion, in this case the knowing of God from the proportion that known finite being bears towards him. It is a relational knowing in which God is known to be the perfection in question without there being any proper conceptualization of that perfection as divine. The proportion here is immediate or direct, what St. Thomas refers to as analogy *"unius ad alterum";* that is, it is not a knowledge of God and creature in a common relation to some third thing, the *"plura ad unum"* analogy.[46] The significance of this is that the *"analogatum"* (God) remains a *Deus Absconditus* who is only named, but truly so, from the *"analogans"* (the created perfection). One term of the proportion evades conceptual expression because the "distance" of the proportion is unknown, because the unlikeness of the two extremes is infinite and unmeasurable, so that the two terms cannot be compared except as exceeding and exceeded, as unknown infinite to known finite.

In short, this is, as Schillebeeckx has strongly argued, an analogy of proportion or attribution – granting that the basis for the attribution is the intrinsic possession of the perfection in question by both analogues. Univocal predication, in Scotus' solution, is out of the question since it leaves one talking about ideas and not about realities at all. Analogical predication in the sense of proportionality – which is really a proportion between proportions –[47] has the inconvenience of abstracting from the variants so that the infinite qualitative difference of God is not expressed. However, once it is understood that the relationship of God to man is one of an unreciprocal imitation, a proportion of the Uncreated to the created, *then* the un-measurable character of the proportion can be more clearly articulated and formulated *in the form of* a proportionality. But the proportionality here is one that lives within and is sustained by a prior analogy of attribution. So conceived the prime analogue or *analogans* enters into the definition of all the other analogues.[48] Thus a *name* common to creature and God is said *"per prius et posterius,"* but in this order, i.e., primarily of the creature and secondarily by attribution to God as known in terms of the created perfection. This is not always true of the actual perfection designated by the name however.

Schillebeeckx's second point is that seizure of the real can be explained only in terms of an implicit intuition that inseparably accompanies the conceptualizing process. Rahner explains this, as noted earlier, by way of the intellect's prehension of being. It follows from this that no idea is equal to the primal existential grasp of the real, and our knowledge of God is actually situated in this phase of human intellection, though not in isolation from the conceptual: "It is a striking fact that Aquinas based the analogy of names on the reality, and not on the *ratio concepta* itself."[49] A reservation on this epistemological understanding that must be felt, nonetheless, is its unavoidable tendency to minimize the role of the concept and its intelligible content, and thus its role in rational discourse whereby alone man can expand his cognition. The intuition of being which is the heart of this theory does not offer itself to reflective analysis, and is somewhat gratuitously assumed — though once assumed the remainder of the theory does fall into place.[50] Seemingly, for Schillebeeckx, the implicit intuition *is* intellective cognition, and the engendering of ideas something to which man is further necessitated only by his limited mode of being.

Knowledge does essentially "intend" the real; what is directly known (except in the science of logic) is not the object of consciousness, the concept itself, but the reality mediated by the concept, though only in the limited formality indicated by the concept. The concept as such is not however gifted with this value of the real. Recourse has to be had to the act of judgment in restoring the content of the idea to the existential order. The recognition of the identity of what the concept signifies with what actually is (though only in one formality of its total being) is by way of an affirmation, as a spontaneous completion of apprehension, that is indigenous to human intelligence. Judgment is thus the lived and intentional conformity of rational spirit to reality; it is an affirmation of the real rather than an intuition of it. Nonetheless, the being directly laid hold of in this fashion is finite being in its whole analogical range. So the knowing and designating of God have to make do with an idea whose proper representational power is limited to the created order. Affirmation of God is in virtue of a further judgment which is inferential or truly illative (though prephilosophical as well as philosophical and logical in kind), an inference of Absolute Being from the affirmation of finite being.

Man's cognitive search for God then involves the attribution to him of multiple perfections by way of human ideas formally distinct among themselves. None of these are ideas of God; they are not, as it were, expanded into *rationes Dei*. There is no common idea (analogically so) predicated of God and creature merely in a different mode. Every perfection expressed in an idea, even those of the transcendental order, is less than pure perfection from this fact at least that it is not the perfectness expressed in other ideas — the idea or formality of knowledge is not that of love, for example. But God's Simplicity is such that his oneness of perfection includes actually and identically all perfection. This is the meaning of St. Thomas' phrase: "*non communicant in aliquo commune, sed per imitatione.*"[51] The mind drives through the created idea (thus in a movement that is cognitive and objective, not affective and conative as for Rahner) to affirm that God is indeed the perfection in question but in an unknown, utterly other, way that lies shrouded in darkness beyond man's conceptual powers. The Divine Attributes then are not formally distinct *in God*; no virtuality is posited within Pure Act. The cause of such distinctness is the finite intelligence itself, its own limitations in the face of the Divine Simplicity.

At the same time, these *rationes* are predicated distinctly *of God*, which is to say that the *fundament* for the distinction is God himself. Otherwise the various names *as said of God* would be mere synonyms for the unknown Divine Essence. In fact, we seek that Essence only in affirming certain of its attributes, thereby designating the Reality of God from multiple angles of intelligibility supplied by our human concepts. Yet it is the eminence of God as the Plenitude of Being as *Ipsum Esse Subsistens*, that founds and justifies this noetic variation.[52] Father Schillebeeckx prefers not to say this much, fearing that this in effect allows for at least an imperfect conceptual grasp of God's prerogatives. But, in truth, the grounding of our distinctions in God's eminent Simplicity does not mean that we attain his attributes in their proper essence, positively.

Not to acknowledge that the very eminence of God founds and authenticates reason's distinguishing the Divine Attributes seems to preclude any objective reference in the case of those dogmatic statements whose meaning depends upon distinction. That the idea of person is other than that of nature is the basis for shedding light upon the mystery that the Word became Incarnate whereas the Father and the Spirit did not. Another central distinction — that between knowledge and love — illumines somewhat, within the obscurity of faith, the real distinction of Word and Spirit in terms of the word-proffering quality of intellection *(dicere)* and the spirative, impulse of love *(spirare)*. Still and all, this is not to say that such distinctions are in God, even virtually.

St. Thomas' own reflection on this problem of attributing varied perfections to God evidences, I believe, a nuancing of thought that preserves a subtle balance between the two facets of the one truth. In the *De Potentia* (begun in 1259) the subjective origin of the distinctions within reason is stressed; these are in God only *"sicut in radice verificante has conceptiones"* (q.7, a.6, Resp.); they are not founded in the Divine

Essence *"sicut in subjecto sed sicut in causa veritatis vel sicut in repraesentato per omnes"* (ad. 6). The text in *I Sentences,* d. 2, q. 1, a. 3 — which was written after completion of the original *Commentary* on the occasion of a disputation held at Rome in 1265 or 1266, after St. Thomas had been asked to examine the teaching of Peter of Tarantasia on this point, and inserted into the *Sentences* later, between 1266-1267[53] — stresses that the multiple conceptions *"non tantum est ex parte intellectus nostri, sed etiam ex parte ipsius Dei . . . inquantum scilicet est aliquid in Deo correspondens omnibus istis conceptionibus"* (Sol.). However, he goes on in his concluding sentence to insist that this is not to place any diversity or multiplicity "in the reality which is God." The reason for the shift in emphasis is only to safeguard the fact that theological truth is truth about God himself and not about our knowledge of God.[54] Still the plurality exists only in our minds; the attributes are not distinct in God as *rationes* (as Scotus wished). Through our distinct ideas we are obscurely oriented towards the God of Reality, known in an unknowing.

## 5. A Changing God?

One of the concepts of classical Theism — that of God's immutability — is being rather consistently challenged as a static metaphysical notion that fails to do justice to the God of the New Testament. The dissatisfaction arises largely from faith in the Incarnation itself and in the genuineness of the humanity assumed by the Logos. In a broader perspective, however, it is the underlying assumption that change and process are simply more perfect than changelessness. This is really the prior question: whether change in any sense is intrinsic to and constitutive of the Divine Reality. The question can be broached then; first, in terms of mutability as such, and, secondly, in terms of the concrete difficulty posed by the Incarnation. A slightly distinct question which the Incarnation also raises, scil., whether

188

God is to be endowed with temporality and history, will be dealt with in a later section. Those who express dissatisfaction with the traditional idea — that of immutability — are agreed that the statement "God is immutable," however inadequate and misleading by itself, is in some sense a true one. Such an admission is hardly surprising for a Catholic in the light of explicit dogmatic formulations as e.g., that of the First Vatican Council; for a Protestant its minimal truth is the exclusion from God of that kind of change that is no more than trivial commotion and obvious imperfection. Even those whose position is radical enough to call for a finite God allow for at least part of his being as immutable. Whitehead, for example, (and it is to his thought that writers such as John Cobb and Schubert Ogden are indebted, via Charles Hartshorne) distinguishes in God a *primordial* and a *consequent* nature: the former is not characterized by process: only in the latter does development occur within God's being.[55] The problem then is not the elimination of the category of immutability but its harmonizing with mutability.

Rahner, and some disciples, find a clue in the Incarnation: here God, immutable in himself, is mutable in the other.[56] Though apparent only in the Incarnation, the principle is a general one: God is subject to change. This means far more than that God is the total cause of change which as such is restricted to the world of contingency. The truth here — of God's immutability and mutability — is a dual one, or one that is dialectical in kind. It is like the truth of the Trinity giving a deepened and authentic meaning to the truth that God is One. Rahner and others see the older concept of immutability as precluding this in quite simply eliminating change from God entirely. This dissatisfaction with and desire to go beyond the traditional conception cannot but enlist sympathy; the actual employment of the older concept has *de facto* issued in an over-simplistic, one-sided objectification of God that falls short of the religious truth offered to Christian experience. Rahner's thought is a carefully nuanced attempt to correct this and is most instructive, and the feeling remains that

189

Trethowan's criticism for all its attempt at orthodoxy lacks a real appreciation of those nuances.[57]

What this serves to remind us of is God's radical unknowability; while the power of analogical knowledge enables us to know God in a way that is objective and cognitively authentic, i.e., true, still it is an encountering of God in his very unknowability. If the flux that marks the finite order is not to be said of God, neither is its diametrical opposite—static inertia. Beneath the obvious imperfectness of change is a latent perfection that must be somehow ascribed to God. It is not only *what is attained* that bespeaks perfection, but the very *attaining;* not only the known and the loved, but the very knowing and loving — yet differently in God and in creature. This is only to say that being (especially understood in its participial form) is a dynamism. In God, however, this "process" is without any limiting potentiality, and is rather Pure Actuality. The very negative grammatical form of "im-mutability" directly intends denying of God the imperfectness attending finite mutation, but unfortunately and unjustifiably it has been expanded into a positive idea of Divinity itself.[58] The perfection of process, then, is in God but in an originative way, as in a Pure Source which is *virtually* what it gives rise to. Formally speaking, God is an unnamed perfection lying beyond the alteration and permanency that offer themselves to our experience. The mind tends here to shuttle back and forth, as it were, between two ideas: that God is changeless and that he is the origin of all change — which while unopposed are by no means easily reconciled. St. Anselm seems to have grasped the dilemma this way, and very graphically so: "How, then, art thou compassionate and not compassionate, O Lord, unless because thou art compassionate in terms of our experience, and not compassionate in terms of thy being."[59] This appears to say that God is not really compassionate at all but that we are unable to think of his perfection in this area except in the images and concepts of what we understand as compassion. Setting aside the actual example Anselm uses (compassion as a passion rooted in the passivity of a material organism bespeaks a kind of change we can readily exempt God from), this highlights the truth we are searching for here. If we speak rather of clemency or mercy in God, can we do justice to. Revelation in conceiving of these as nowise involving some newness of being in God himself?

Possibly the ideological tension here can be surmounted to some degree by recalling that the concept of immutability does not at all include a *ratio* of God; it is only a jumping off place for a projecting act of analogy towards God which employs the concept to signify immutability of *Actuality;* the fuller concept here is really *Changeless Activity.* God is immutable, that is, he is not mutable at all, but the denial of this latter is not a positive designation of him as merely despoiled of change, as impassive rather than passive. Such a perfection will be so totally other in God from what we alone know as change that it is better called "changelessness," although the latter in conceptual isolation is no less misleading. This is to say, in effect, that Divinity conceived as Subsisting Actuality, as pure *energeia,* lies beyond both change and its correlate — permanence. God's dynamism, designated without being properly rendered into a concept, is then superior to what is expressed as change or process, which suggest expenditure of energy or newness of acquisition.

Something like this, at least, is what is being attempted in the redefinition of God. Schoonenberg's phrase that God is not "relative" as opposed to something absolute but that he is "relational," seems little more than a terminological sidestepping of the issue.[60] Rahner's formulation is bolder but one question has to be put to it. Does it differentiate adequately between Uncreated and created being? To say that God *becomes* even *in the other,* rather than that he is the source of the becoming *of* the other "within" himself, runs the risk of obscuring the sharp line of demarcation between God and world. What needs preserving is that God *is* all that the entire universe becomes or can become (he is the total horizon of possibilities): and much more besides that it cannot become. And he is all of this not as potency and in indetermination, but as Inexhaustible Actuality. Thus with the advent of creatures there is now being less than God's. But Rahner's way of expressing this — that God while remaining infinite has "become less than he (always) is"[61] — needs the qualifying phrase "in the creature," which is seemingly to say "as creature."

It is true that the causality of God in summoning finite being out of nothingness (which can never be conceived as homogeneous or univocal to any created causal framework) is so total that it does embrace the *formal* order — not that the creature lacks its own act of existence and exists rather by God's *esse*, but that its created being is a participation, and a formal one, in God's very Being.[62] Nevertheless, to have or receive God's being in a limited, modal way *(partem capere)* is precisely to be *not God,* to be set over against him with the consequent possibility of sin, etc. Participation is unintelligible apart from the perspective of causality; the communication of finite being is creative, unlike the communication of Divine Being from Father to Son and Spirit. It is improper to speak of the Divine Persons "participating" in the Godhead for They are that Being in identity. True, Rahner works out his categories here in the area of the Incarnation and grace (as did De la Taille with his "created actuation by Uncreated Act"). But the basic assumption is the same and remains questionable, scil. whether a "quasi-formal" causal influx of God be allowable.[63]

Martin D'Arcy has taken a slightly different tack on Rahner's attempted re-definition in this area suggesting that we "simply be done with" the concept of necessity of nature in which immutability is rooted and have recourse solely to the personalist category of freedom.[64] Whereas Rahner feels obligated to retain the category of immutability, D'Arcy would jettison it entirely, leaving God in a realm of pure creative change. But in dropping one of these do we not misconstrue what God is? The imperfection attaching to the idea of necessity is recognized, and yet those which accompany our concept of person and freedom are not strained out. The fundamental danger in this is the tendency to look upon God's freedom as inseparable from contingency, since this is the case with the only freedom we can directly experience. The human person is a body-person, a projecting subject; he creates his human world but only out of the raw material of a "given" world (the *pré-monde* of Merleau-Ponty); in Tillich's phrase, objective reason is involved over and above subjective reason. The finite person is essentially in relation to other persons, something analogously true within the Trinity. But further, are not even God's free commitments towards the world a personal disposal of himself towards others that make him to be on this level something different than he would in fact be had he not so chosen? Does he not then "change" in his free relationality towards men — in the domain of personhood transcendent to that of nature and causal influx where he already is whatever he can cause to be?

Some clarification may well develop from at least a brief reflection on what exactly the free creative act in God is. *In its very entity* that act is God's nature itself and so is necessary, immutable, and eternal; *in its termination* at any one of an infinite number of possibilities it is mutable and temporal. The Divine freedom then is the one necessary act of God as it terminates at a non-necessary object. What is unthinkable is that God not choose at all — he must will to create or not to create, to produce this kind of world or some other, to redeem or not to redeem; his willing then is not contingent; it is not a transposition from potency to actuality. Thus the motive of his willing does not impose itself from the object willed nor from "subjective" conditions on his part other than those of a loving self-determination that is altruistic. God is not obligated to his self-communication even in the moral sense that, were he to choose not to give of himself, he would be less perfect than he in fact is. Cajetan notes with perspicuity that when a relative name is assigned to God — as e.g., Creator said of him after there is a world and thus temporally — the denomination is *really extrinsic*, i.e., its real foundation is in the creature who has passively undergone change, but still it is *formally intrinsic*, for it is God about whom we are talking, and the altering of the creature is a perfection within him, scil., his very willing of it.[65] It is in this sense that God is the Creator from all eternity.

In fine, on the level of nature, God is immutable in himself; it can be said that he is mutable *in the other*, but *not as himself*. When Rahner writes that God "poses the other as his reality,"[66] this is true only if it be understood that what is meant is *his created reality, his effect,* and not an interior modification of his own proper reality. At the same time, it remains true that finite being *is* only "within" Infinite Being; the "being-in" of the former is no denial of its real and radical distinction from God.

Undeniably, however, the Incarnation does pose the problem in terms that are more urgent and less amenable to abstract categorizing. God did become man and remains such; from all eternity he did will to be something other than God, to exist humanly (without thereby ceasing to be God). The situation with God then is not exactly the same as it would be had he chosen to not enflesh himself. He now exists in a state of personal involvement (it is the *Person* of the Logos who assumes flesh) with mankind, in a state of human openness and availability, that is not compatible with a denial of this.

The change can be described as wholly on the part of the other — i.e., the individual humanity of Christ, and mediately all humanity, and remotely the entire cosmos — *only ontically*. Once again, on the Existential (*existential* as opposed to *existentiell*) level, God's communication with and self-donation to men cannot be expressed in full by falling back upon God's immutability of nature — even as we have nuanced it above. Here, being is creatively self-expressive, self-donative in a manner that transcends the causation of an effect. Such causation is not a becoming in God, whereas the free disposal of himself vis a vis other persons is that kind of "becoming" constitutive of personhood. Thus generation, a category of unchanging nature in God, explains the transcendentally free "exercise" of personhood between Father and Son — on which level alone can their real distinction be understood. God is thus within himself not only necessary but free. Thus too, it is the Logos who suffers and dies in the other, but it is not the Divinity as such that is meant. A priori, this principle would hold good, differently of course, outside of the Incarnation. At any rate, the truth which lies deep in our faith confession does demand articulation in categories beyond the essential one of Immutability.

## 6. Temporality in God?

No one single "discovery" in the contemporary epoch of the world of ideas has had as far reaching an impact as that centering on the historicity of man. Heidegger, whose phenomenological analysis of *Dasein* reveals its very structure to be temporality, is only one, though a major force, in this new direction to thought. Man, as *ex-sistence*, is the place where Being (*Sein*) occurs; he is the There of Being (*Dasein*) among beings. Thus, Being itself is variously described as a "coming to pass," a "lighting up," as *aletheia* (unveiling or unconcealment) so that it is a process, the being-process of the beings. In this is the awareness that man lives on two distinct levels: the ontic and the ontological; the realm of "fallenness" (*Verfallenheit*) among the beings and the realm of transcendence to Being. The former of these, wherein man lives but inauthentically, is the *historical* order; the latter, allowing for authentic existence, is rather the *historic* order in which past and future are assumed into presentiality. Being is historic then; it is pure creative process; it is Ad-vent or E-vent. Therefore it is true to say that all reality is itself history, or that history is the one medium in which reality appears.

The theological implications of this simply cannot be exaggerated. The most immediate is a conception of Revelation as historic; not only does it occur within history but it constitutes a presentiality that assumes within itself past and future. Some notably Pannenberg, have gone even further than this suggesting that universal history (and not just *Heilsgeschichte*) is itself Revelation. At any rate, Being as E-vent means that history is looked upon as present address. The world that supplies the context for this is a world of the word; the anthropological parallel to this view of Revelation is one that focuses sharply upon man's linguisticality. Language itself becomes event, the revelatory event in which man encounters God. Heidegger speaks of a primal language that precedes our cultural languages, and Bultmann's faith-encounter is something non-objective, out of which reflective thought and language arises. Our consciousness of God then occurs within a historic frame of reference The traditional conception of God as eternal "now" appears as a philosophic and metaphysical idea that is alien both to the God of faith and to the Being of a Phenomenologist. Another distinct way of Christianizing the Heideggerian insight (and what is most remarkable is that it is not his alone; it is proving to be a point of convergence for quite different kinds of thinking, e.g. that of Wittgenstein) is to do as John MacQuarrie has done and simply identify *Sein* as a philosopher's way of naming the Christian God.[67] But in both of these viewpoints — one seeing God as immersing himself into the historic order proper to man in the communication of his Word; the other conceiving God as pure "Letting be" — the consequence is the same: the injection of temporality into God. Hans Jonas looks upon God as having given himself up into the temporal universe in so real a sense that the destiny of the Deity is at stake in our decisions.[68] There is a curious Catholic approximation to this, though not nearly so radical, to be found in Karl Rahner when he writes of God as emptying himself, giving himself away, the κέγωσις and γένεσις of God himself.[69] Whitehead had earlier developed the concept of a God who, though not a Creator of the world, still "saved" the world somewhat in this way. This is really an attempt by Whitehead to reconcile time and eternity, and is explained on the basis of his distinguishing between a *primordial* and a *consequent* nature of God.[70] The latter is that

196

aspect of God that is first affected by other lesser beings and then as *superjective* pours back meaningful actuality upon them; in this way the past is preserved in God, given an objective immortality, and the future emerges from him. This enables Whitehead to say that while God's primordial nature is eternal, his subsequent nature is really temporal. It must be noted, however, that the temporality is of a much higher order than what we know as a mere sequence of events. James Collins has given this clarity by saying that for Whitehead God's subsequent nature is not so much temporal as a transmutation of time.[71] The parallel with Heidegger's historic as opposed to historical order, with *Geschichte* as opposed to *Historie* is unavoidable. Schubert Ogden has pursued some of Heidegger's implications, especially those to be found in a well known footnote to the latter's *Sein und Zeit*. There, in an uncharacteristic explicit reference to God, Heidegger wrote: "If the eternity of God would admit of being 'construed' philosophically, it could be understood only as a more primal and 'infinite' temporality."[72] Ogden incorporates this into his own thinking, portraying God as eminent temporality or historicity. Time in such a primal sense "is not the 'within-timeness' in which we order the objects of our ordinary external perceptions" but "the time constituted by our experiencing itself, as actual occurrence."[73] The present, so conceived, "is not an extensionless instant within our experience, but the decisive moment *(Augenblick)* in which our experience itself occurs and is constituted": here "the present extends beyond itself into both the past and the future and is, in fact, the unification of these other modes or 'ecstacies' (*Ekstasen*) of time."[74]

But how alien is this to what was meant, in a more conventional theology, by eternity? Clearly, the latter was not taken as expressive of "endless time," but neither was it taken as the "*nunc stans,*" except metaphorically. Boethius, it is true, did have recourse to this phrase in his *De Trinitate,* but St. Thomas observes that this is descriptive of eternity not as it really is but only as we conceive of it ("*secundum nostram apprehensionem*"), since it lies beyond our conceptual capacities.[75] Just as we imaginatively picture time as a flow of the "now" over a continuum, which it is not, so we picture eternity as a motionless "now."[76] St. Thomas much prefers the descriptive definition that Boethius offers in his *De Consolatione Philosophiae*, explaining that the word "perfect" there is precisely an attempt to exclude the "now," or indivisible instant, which is only proper to time, and even there represents something imperfect.[77] The operative word for eternity is *simultaneity* excluding time as succession or sequence — not only continuous sequence in a material universe of uninterrupted motion but even a succession of immaterial thoughts and affections related to one another in an ordered sequence but without any measuring of the intervals between (this was the *discrete* time of angelic activity where thoughts and affections are sequential, but without there being any transmutation of the angelic substance; the measure of the latter is not time at all but what the Medievals called *aevum or aeviternity*).[78]

When Ogden assigns a past and a future to God this, of course, is in direct verbal opposition to what St. Thomas understands by eternity, but what the latter term denies is a past and future of cosmological time, and Ogden obviously intends to exclude this. The past and future of "historic" time, the self-creating time of decision, are something else again. The Scholastic idea of eternity was never a denial of this, and, it seems to me, is open to and capable of embracing the reality of historic temporality — not, however, in a human mode but in a modeless way proper to Divinity. The concept is, though in a fashion that is not entirely clear, transcendent to both flux on one hand and stationary immobility on the other. The logical relations between the two concepts of "eternity" and "time" are then "wholly positive and mutually implicative;"[79] Ogden does see them as such, but denies that the traditional idea of eternity will allow this. This is not to suggest any exact conceptual coincidence between Thomistic "eternity" and the "primal *temporality*" deriving from Heidegger. Historicity is a concept that marks a very contemporary state of human consciousness; St. Thomas could hardly have been so in advance of his times as to have had an awareness of it. The most that can be said is that there is no denial of it in his thinking, even if this came to be the case in lesser thinkers. Thus, there is at least the possibility of a conceptual convergence of ideas, which, while representing distinct angles of intelligibility, do not mutually exclude one another, as is the case with contraries.

The motive for wanting to locate God within a framework of historicity is clear enough: the felt need to conceive of God as pertinent to our present cultural experience, and the mystery of suffering which surrenders some of its meaninglessness when God is "involved" and implicated in it compassionately. There is a perhaps not altogether strange congeniality in American Protestantism towards a God who can serve as a partner of man in his moral quest. But at the same time this serves to point up the basic and perhaps unsurmountable weakness in this posture, namely, the taking of a human structure of things as a prototype of what God himself is. There is a depth of truth to the statement that the transcendence of God is not what is farthest from us but what is closest at hand,[80] but the closeness is that of the availability and presence of what is most unlike us. Must God be subject to time in order to save those who are anguished by it? Surely, the Record of Revelation makes it abundantly clear that the involvement of God's very being in man's history is such that this is God's history too. But does this mean a history of which God is only one component, even if the primal component? Is it not a richer motion and one closer to the Bible to see it as God's history in a more radical sense — because it originates from him as the sacrament of his creative love-knowledge, and is all embraced within him who is not static but the dynamism of Pure Act. As his immutability is not impassivity but Indeficient Activity, is not his eternity not "timelessness" but a sublimation of even existential time into Divine Presentiality?

Once again, what must be allowed its full operative scope is the power of analogical knowing. Beginning with cosmological time and rising to existential time, God is dimly surmised as lying beyond all this, not negatively in a static and monolithic "timelessness," but in a perfection so pure as to elude man's exact conceptual capacities. The awareness of human historicity is an insight as illuminative as it is at first startling; its intelligibility cannot be neglected, but the problem is its reconciliation with the idea of eternity. One way is the retention of both concepts in a thinking process that is always dialectical, a constant cognitive moving from one facet to the other. But the paradoxical character of this keeps it very limited; there seems to be a call for some surmounting of the oscillation, some unification of what otherwise presents itself as an excessive polarization. The knowing act here is a dynamism of judgment which calls for a constant reworking of the concepts that objectify such judgments. The Medievals put great store by the motion of "wholeness" by which they attempted to seize in simultaneity what was in fact fragmented into past, present, and future.[81] The burden is one known in every aesthetic experience; thus Merleau-Ponty can speak of the experience of "interior time" undergone in listening to great music. Analogy demands that the perfectness of this be projected unto God, but analogy also has a power which purges temporality of an imperfection that always attends its realization as finite. The perfections of God are indistinguishable in his Oneness; the distinctness all comes from man's attempts to grasp them cognitively in concept. Somewhat in this sense, historicity is the image of eternity.

A postscript to the above reflections is supplied by those theologies which see "the future" as a paradigm of transcendence.[82] This is to emphasize a category of immanence, to conceive of God less as he is in himself than as he is for man. Yet this is entirely legitimate because God is for us exactly what he is in himself; the God who comes into our midst does so precisely as transcendent. Religiously, this can lead to an attitude that tends to dislocate the present and to render it meaningless in itself as present encounter with God. Schillebeeckx's essay

"God: The Future of Man" is not entirely free of this over-emphasis.[83] The reservations needed here, in what is actually a tendency to give primacy to the virtue of hope over that of faith, have been well noted by Langdon Gilkey.[84]

Properly understood, however, what is meant is that our future, not as terrestrial but as meta-historical, while qualitatively something new (the "wholly other" will thus be the "wholly new"), will not be a cessation or denial of man's historicity but a consummation of it. Just as God comes to us now under the conditions of present (chronological) history in Christ, so then in eternal life shall he disclose himself to us in Existential (eschatological) "time." This is only to note the legitimacy of contemporary man's inclination to experience God, indirectly of course, in terms of his own transcendental subjectivity and historicity.


## 7. God As Tri-Personal

Even the central assertion of Theism — that God is a "person" — has been re-rendered an open question in recent religious speculation. Tillich and some of the Radical Theologians have for some time thought in terms of a "God beyond the God of Theism," and on the Catholic side, Schillebeeckx eschews the word "person" for its more fluid adjectival form — "personal." What this amounts to is a tendency to view the category of "person" as proper to man and incapable of projection, even analogically, onto God — unless it be newly endowed with an intelligibility not hitherto possessed. At bottom is a dissatisfaction with the word as it denotes a metaphysical term of nature, or a mode of subsistence, rendering that nature existent and uniquely so, i.e., as incommunicable. That the word "person" has ceased to bear this meaning for contemporary man is undoubtedly true, and so the project of uncovering the intelligibility in the newer employment of the word that is applicable to God is a desirable one. But it might be asked if the meaning that the word newly takes upon itself does not *have to assume* the truth value in the older concept, especially in the light of the Christological and Trinitarian definitions. Can the newer sense to which the believer puts the word, his re-working of the concept, break continuity with the authentic uses of the past? Which is to ask if one of the burdens of the faith, in its motivating theological reflection, is not a preservation of the achievements of the past as it fosters present advance.

The overwhelming direction of our contemporary cultural experience is one that gives primacy to the human person and extols personal values. So marked is this that the immediate tendency is to conceive of God in similar categories, with a Christian reaction that is justifiably fearful of anthropomorphism. Heidegger's reflections on man have led to the insistence that internal relatedness to others is essential and not merely accidental to the latter's being as having a unique ontic priority among the beings. The essential structure of human existence, that is its very existentiality, is "being-with-others;" man is *In-der-Welt-Sein,* and his basic attitude is "care" (*Sorge*), as an internal affectivity towards others. This represents an advance over the *ego-substance* of classical Greek and Medieval thought, and as well over the *subjectivism* that arises by way of reaction in the thought of Descartes and Kant. If Hüsserl's seminal thinking, at least in the later *Cartesian Meditations,* is not entirely free of the suspicion of idealism, it does seem that Heidegger's ontology has surmounted it; and Merleau-Ponty's study of "bodiliness" as the foundation for the body-person's internal and real relatedness to other bodies and body-persons has carried the effort further.[85] This marks a retreat from any conception of man as an isolated self; only things below the level of consciousness could suffer so limited and imperfect a mode of being.

This very notion of internal relatedness however (not as an accident of substance, but as the very essence of existence, i.e., *Existenz*) rests upon the ontic and ontological foundation of *consciousness.* Thus the person is also characterized as being a center (though not in the sense of a subjective self) or focus of consciousness; consciousness looked upon not as an endowment of a nature but, as freedom, something self-creative and self-constituting. It creates its own personal world of meaning and thus constitutes its own concrete nature rather than deriving therefrom; nature is thus a terminus of personality rather than vice versa; something historical, constantly being achieved. Personality, as consciousness, does not have existence but exerts itself towards life and existence; it is the source of exercised existence, of that process out of which the being of man emerges. Its own development is by way of increased self-awareness or heightened presence to self. The person "becomes" not simply in the classical sense of becoming the other intentionally (in becoming the object known through the irruption in intellect of its intelligible form), and *affectively* (in the real, vital, and unitive *élan* towards the beloved), but in the sense of becoming something other in and as itself.

Indigenous to the above notion is an internal relatedness; man as person is "being-in-the-world," a world which in its bodiliness is "given," mediated to me by my body (indeed, the body is simply that part of the world in which the person immediately is). On a profounder level, that world is not cosmological in kind but rather a *Lebenswelt*, a total context of meaning, bespeaking a relatedness to other persons that is not accidental but essential. Significantly enough, the concepts at work here have originated in philosophy not theology, and such thinkers as Heidegger and Merleau-Ponty have explicitly refused to give them any theistic connotations. Seemingly, this calls for some clear adaptation of these concepts in their use by Christian theologians, especially in Trinitarian theology. Still, important use of the notions of consciousness and subjectivity have been made in Christology — for example, the genuineness of Christ's humanity as having its own personality in this sense (which is not the sense of the definitions of Chalcedon) has been richly developed, notably in the writings of Lonergan and Rahner.[86] If God is personal in the above way he would appear to be necessarily "in-the-world" and a focus of developing consciousness, a subject of relation and change irreconcilable with genuine transcendence. Recognition of this — that God cannot be a personal existent in the sense of *Dasein* — has led John MacQuarrie to conceptualize him rather in terms of Heidegger's *Sein*. But, richly suggestive as this is, it needs careful working out and demands a radical transformation of Heidegger's concept. If *Sein* is the "lighting-up" process within *Dasein* as the locus where *Sein* "comes to pass," then in what sense has the personal character of the Hebraic-Christian, Yahweh-God been preserved?

It should be noted, however, that emphasis upon consciousness as constitutive of the person has gone beyond mere psychological subjectivity. Lonergan makes this clear in his insistence that while consciousness is a factor in knowing it is not to be simply identified therewith; it is rather "an awareness immanent in cognitional acts."[87] The subject-object polarity is native to knowing as such, which is knowing something, or being confronted by an object. But consciousness transcends this tension and constitutes pure subjectivity. It is not knowing an object, not even the reflexive knowing of self as object, but the constitutive awareness of self precisely as subject: "this constitutive knowing and being known is consciousness."[88] Thus it is the presence of being to itself; what Augustine understood as the presence of *mens* to itself prior to any reflexive or introspective act. Presumably then, in an analogical application to God it need not imply the isolation of a psychological subject in dependent relationship to a world of objects.

At any rate, the real question for the Christian is not that of God's personality in the sense of his one absolute subsistence, but one that relates to the revealed doctrine that God is Tripersonal. This is surely God's central disclosure as to what he is in himself; the sense of his incomprehensibility and ineffability, real enough but somewhat obscure in the Old Testament, emerges as a positive "deepening of the darkness" in the New Testament revelation of the Trinity. The core of the faith-acknowledgement here is distinctness within God that cannot be expressed in terms denotive of essence, formal perfection, or even existence. With Augustine, when we are compelled to ask: "three what?" we can only reply "three Persons." The mystery, however, is available only by way of the *oikonomia*, i.e., God's concrete historical approach to his creatures in Christ. What is disclosed here is that the presence of God is not any longer mediate, as in Old Testament angelism, but immediate; it is God himself who is sent and given to us. At the same time the approach of God is *distinct* in a threefold way. Our relatedness to the Son who is Incarnate involves distinct relations to the Father whom he reveals and the Spirit whom he promises. This is the Trinity *pro nobis*, a three-fold relatedness of God to us. But part of the dynamism of faith-consciousness is the deeper awareness that God is disclosing *himself* and not merely the creative outworkings of his love, that something more than modes of appearance is at issue here. God is *in himself* Source and Word and Spirit, and quite unlike the way he is, e.g., omnipotence, knowledge, and love — for here the distinctions are *not* of man's making as are the latter. The point here is that the New Testament *oikonomia* is a self-communication of God so that the modes of that communication necessarily reflect what is true of the Divine Being itself. Thus the distinction and inter-relatedness of the two temporal missions — the visible mission of the Incarnate *Logos*, and the invisible mission of the *Pneuma* — bespeak something like this in God himself, apart from any relation to a possible world.

The conceptualization of this was, of course, fraught with difficulty and not until quite some time after Nicaea was the category of "person" (in its Greek and Latin equivalents) taken over from Hellenic thought, transformed within a faith-context, and used as a *symbolum* to articulate the mystery of the Trinity. The reason for this was simple enough — there was no other category available with which to express a distinctness that, while real, was not a difference of nature or essence. The very formula, however, drew attention away from the "economic" Trinity; the center of interest was that Trinity *in Se* approached noetically in an abstract, notional, non-historical way with the paradoxical result of "de-personalizing" God. Also, the static and non-existential formulation of the dogma did *de facto* discourage any further questing of faith into the meaning of the mystery. Little was done after the speculations of Tertullian, Augustine, and Thomas (which helped consolidate the tradition) apart from some devotional and mystical literature. Even where the Magisterium is concerned, the last significant concern with the Trinity was as long ago as the Council of Florence.

A second consequence of the practical failure to realize that in salvation-history the three Divine Persons are made available to us *in themselves* can be seen in Rahner's complaint about a theological methodology that locates the treatise on the Trinity only after and in logical subordination to a consideration of God's oneness of nature. Looked at in the least favorable light, this has too easily conveyed the impression that the Trinity was a sort of superfluous appendage to his being, that God simply happened to be Three-Personal, a fact without significance to man. Criticism on this point, nonetheless, can be overly negative and overly facile. St. Thomas, for one, did strive against such an implication; in spite of a long history of misinterpretation, it is quite clear that the *Summa Theologiae* from Question Two onward is seeking the Triune God of Revelation.[89] He also expressly maintains that, apart from an understanding of the Trinity, no genuine understanding either of creation or salvation is possible.[90] The option to treat logically of the Divine Nature before the Personalities is just that, an option — and no one schema is able to do full justice to a knowledge that must move dialectically between an existential-historical and an essential-conceptual pole. St. Thomas' own option may well owe something to his Western mentality, but is more adequately explained by his intending an *ordo doctrinae* rather than an *ordo inventionis*.[91] Still and all, that method does have to correct itself against a tendency to approach the Incarnation from the background of an abstractly elaborated Trinitarian theology. The danger, as Anthony Kelly notes, is that of failing "in some measure to appreciate the actual personal 'Self' of the divine Person in His role *pro nobis*."[92]

The opposite approach, starting with and emphasizing the Trinity of the *economia* and reaching back to an understanding of the Trinity *in Se*, is not without shortcomings of its own. The prevalent idea of "person" as a subject of consciousness cannot be literally applied without conveying the notion that the Persons in God are poles of intersubjectivity with men in the dialogue of salvation — which would be a form of crypto-Tritheism. Such an extreme error, however, has been almost universally avoided. More understandable perhaps are formulations that seem subtly suggestive of Modalism. John MacQuarrie's presentation of the Divine Three as "Primordial Being," "Expressive Being," and "Unitive Being" is a case in point.[93] Another is the Rahner-Vorgrimler *Theological Dictionary's* suggestion of "Ultimate Originality," "Principle Acting in History," and "Gift Bestowed and Received."[94] It can be asked whether these formulations adequately convey the real distinctness that the Conciliar use of the term "person" intended to articulate . . . since it is obvious none of these mean to suggest differences on the plan of essential perfections. Leslie Dewart faces up to these implications with his own suggestion: an elimination entirely of the category "person" as no longer a viable conceptual expression of faith. Seemingly, he feels no uneasiness in adopting a Modalistic posture: ". . . the different persons *are* different modes (albeit not successive ones) of his self-communication." He goes on to explain (citing the Rahner-Vorgrimler *Dictionary*) that the "Trinity of God's dealing with us is already the reality of God as he is in himself." Thus, *Logos* means the "*rationality* which pervaded all reality" and its adoption by Christian theology especially in the Fourth Gospel means not the Word who emanates from the Father but "the consubstantiality of the *Incarnate* Word and God," so that "the Christian God who revealed himself to us in the person of Jesus was in reality that which in Hellenic usage was already — indeed, had traditionally been — called the *Logos*."[95] It is difficult to see how this is not to say that *logos* (lower case) is a created effect of God's, and that *Logos* (upper case) is God revealing himself as source of that intelligibility of things or as identified (consubstantial) with it. One would be hard put to explain how the former is not Modalism and the latter not Pantheism. Parallel remarks could be made respecting his conception of the Third Person as ". . . God himself, *in his very reality*, made present to us by himself: and this is what is called the Holy Spirit."[96] Dewart is seemingly suggesting that Spirit is but a name for God as he gives himself to men. This is far indeed from understanding that the Spirit inhabits the souls of the just in his proper hypostatic character, i.e., in company with the Father and Son, but as somehow really distinct from them.

Rahner's forthright, carefully nuanced attempt to rethink the mystery begins with the Trinity within history, the Trinity of the economy of salvation. It is the Incarnate God visibly active within history who first of all takes our attention, revealing himself to *be* God because he is from the Father, his Father, who is *the* God — ὁ Θεός . This God, of whom Christ is, in his humanity, the sacrament, is not the Godhead but the First Person of the Trinity.[97] The latter phase of the self-communication is, of course, the promise of the Spirit who being sent by Father and Son is of their very substance (homooúsios); thus there is but one "nature" of the Three. The logical order here is one in which the idea of nature or essence is subsequent to that of the Persons. Admittedly, this is a more Biblical way of thinking, at least where the New Testament is concerned, and it conforms to the mentality of Greek Christianity that antecedes the opposite viewpoint originating in Latin Christianity. Also, it serves to correct what must be acknowledged as a congenital inadequacy in the Scholastic scheme of things, namely, the tendency to neutralize Trinitarianism into Monotheism, where the One God simply happens to be, for some mysterious reason, Tri-Personal. Three conclusions that Rahner draws will serve to illustrate the difference that this more Biblical approach makes.

First, is an awareness that in salvation-history the Divine Persons *in themselves* are made available to us. This enables us to appreciate that the role Christ's humanity bears towards men is something deriving precisely from his proper hypostatic characteristics as the *Second* Person of God. Consequent upon this is a positive emphasis upon the Trinitarian structure of grace. The root reason for this is that "it is of the essence and meaning of the Word of God that he and he alone is the one who begins and can begin a human history."[98] God's being is such that only the Son could have assumed flesh in the Incarnation, because of what he is personally within the bosom of the Trinity. "When God freely steps outside of himself in *self*-communication . . . it is *and must be* the Son who appears historically in the flesh as man."[99] Thus, there is a theologically misplaced emphasis in speaking of "God made man" rather than "the Word of God made man," or of "Son of God" rather than "Son of the Father." This is a genuine corrective to what has been the weakest point in past theological renderings of the Trinity, and a richer penetration of understanding into the Christian mystery.

Secondly, this calls for — indeed, itself inaugurates — a new procedure within theological science. Specifically, the theological treatise on the Trinity should assume as its starting point the Father in God as ὁ Θεός of the New Testament, conceived of as not positively absolute though not yet relative either.[100] This alternative to an older procedure is at once a corrective and an advance; as a methodological option it has to be taken seriously. But as with every limited categorical approach to a mystery that lies beyond any and every order of concepts, its strongest point is at the same time its point of structural weakness. Without dismissing the recommendation, it can be observed that what it must safeguard itself against is any emphasizing of the distinctness between the Divine Three to where it veers over from the personal into the essential order. If the distinction is not exclusively relative (relation being the least of all possible distinctions that is still real, and one that does not jeopardize the simplicity of nature because it bespeaks the pure *esse ad* of one Person to another, and not of any or all persons to the Divine Nature), there is at least the implied danger of construing it as absolute, as involving perfection, or attributes, or activity. This would

Q

amount to the very opposite of Modalism; it would be a kind of Subordinationism.

Rahner is saying in effect what must be insisted upon, namely that the Trinity *pro nobis* is the Trinity *in se;* God is in himself the Threeness unveiled to us in salvation-history. However, his theological schema may fail to make clear that the approach of the Uncreated Three in creation and in re-creation (or redemptive salvation) is necessarily creative and causal, which causality, while ultimately originating with the Persons as such, does not derive immediately from the Person but mediately through the nature and its endowments. To overlook this will demand a different understanding and explanation of how person and nature are interrelated, and thus what each of them is. Even granting that the distinction in God is nowise real, still *our concepts* of nature and person are formally distinct and such concepts, since they remain man's achievement, cannot be made use of even in speaking of God, without attending to that formality of distinction. On his own admission, Rahner's ideas in this area owe much to Existential thought where "person" means a man's disposing of himself by way of his free decision, and by "nature" is meant all that is "given" in a man prior to this disposal.[101] This gives emphasis to a dualism of nature and person, a tension between them more marked than that allowable if person be understood as the subsistence of a nature. What it tends to suggest is that the person is able to somehow operate on the nature directly; nature is required less as supplying the essence of the kind of activity able to stem from the person than as the object upon which its activity is exercised.[102] This gives to person a sort of autonomy over the nature it personifies, and approaches close to essentializing personality. What is not clear is how these philosophical considerations are purged of such finite and limiting elements as they are employed by the theologian in the effort to conceptualize objectively the mystery of the Trinity, to illumine for understanding what cannot be "conceived" in any proper sense because it belongs to the realm of "person" rather than "nature."

Thirdly, there is Rahner's contention that each of the Divine Persons has a proper causal influx upon the soul in the grace state[103] — a conclusion that intensifies somewhat the difficulties felt above. The causality meant is, of course, not efficient but of the formal order, and to avoid any suggestion that a Divine Person can relate to the soul as a form truly informing, it is designated "quasi-formal." Rahner's fear is that anything less than this runs the risk of reducing the Inhabitation of the Trinity to appropriation. But Catholic theology has always understood it as something more than this, and it is further true that the theory of appropriation always involves a Person in his unique and proper or personal character; i.e., a work common to all three Persons can be appropriated to any one of them only because of an affinity to what is a unique prerogative of that Person. At this point, Rahner shows some hesitancy: in the Inhabitation, the Divine Person does not "exercise(s) its hypostatic function in respect of that to which the communication is made" (this is true only in the Incarnation) but a "true ontological communication of the hypostasis takes place (but), to the end and only to the end that it can become in virtue of this quasi-formal causality the object of immediate knowledge and love."[104] If this means only that the Persons are the objects or terms of a knowledge and love possible to the graced soul by reason of a communication or presence of the Persons as distinct, but operating upon the soul through their common Divinity, it is not distinguishable from St. Thomas' own teaching.[105] If it means (especially the phrase: ". . . in virtue of this quasi-formal causality") that each Person exercises a communication or an influx even formal in kind, that is exclusively his own, then this will have to be explained in a way that avoids all implication of distinctness on the part of essence or perfection. And it can at least be asked if phrases such as "quasi-formal causality," "influx," "communication" etc. really succeed in doing this. The controversy is by now an old one and need not be reintroduced here: it is agreed that all Three Persons, in a proper way characteristic of each, give themselves to and enter upon familiar relations with the graced soul, and in a way that cannot be explained by mere appropriation; moreover, that this demands at least as a prerequisite an underlying efficient causality of God common to all Persons. What is in question is whether this self-bestowal, this state of presence and of inter-personal relationship, is itself another three-fold causal communication or rather a formal effect already brought about by the common causation. Rahner is quite clear that each Person is capable of a proper causality to the extent that he sees sanctification as a proper work of the Holy Spirit, somewhat analogous to the way the Incarnation is proper to the Son, and he expressly denies that this can be explained by appropriation.[106] The latter theory does assign a certain primacy to the presence of the Spirit, but in virtue of an affinity between the created effect as a work of love and the personal prerogatives of the Spirit, and not in virtue of any exclusive causal influx.[107]

The hesitancy felt before Rahner's suggestion in this area lies in whether or not he has adequately safeguarded *conceptually* the truth that the Divine Three are a Triunity. The ultimate problem is that of the relationship between nature and person, which admittedly remains elusive. Human personality, too, is an unique instance of a common nature (specifically so, at any rate) which accounts for the fact that each person is related to others (and essentially related as long as one speaks metaphysically); it is the person who is related but only within the nature and through its activities. And the grace state is precisely man's participation in God's own nature.

Rahner's most recent study[108] is genuinely inventive in seeking to transform the categories of Divine Knowledge and Love as these explain immediately the two temporal communications in salvation-history, and mediately the two inner processions. Knowledge here comes to mean a modality of God's *self*-communication in which he lets his nature come to the fore in the presence of others as faithful offer; and love is another modality wherein the acceptance of the offer is brought about by the self-communicating God himself. This is elaborated by recourse to sets

212

of polar ideas such as: origin — future; history — transcendence; and offer — acceptance. But once again, for all its challenging originality, it can be questioned whether this project actually succeeds in bypassing or going beyond what is conveyed by the metaphysical notion of "person." At best it seems to presuppose the latter and to attempt to enrich our understanding of it.

What emerges from these reflections is that few aspects of our God-idea need reformulation as radically as that regarding the Trinity and yet what has thus far been attempted offers little more than tentative directions. Starting with the abstract concepts of a theological system can run the risk of imposing these *a priori* upon the revelatory events of Sacred History itself. To begin with the Scriptural data would thus seem to be mandatory, but matters cannot be left there — to believe is spontaneously to seek to understand. Bishop Robinson is content to interpret the Trinitarian doctrine of the New Testament as telling us nothing about God himself, so that there is in fact no Divine Trinity at all.[109] Schillebeeckx has been content to develop the mystery in terms of its salvific relevance for men, eschewing any elaboration of it in a "metaphysics of faith" as a mystery constitutive of God's deepest being — apart from acknowledging that God assumes an initiative of love towards man in which He reveals that he is *in himself* personal in a mysterious Triune way.[110] This, of course, is a theologian's understanding of his task within his own age — but it observes a silence before more ultimate questions. Rahner, in venturing these, takes us farthest of all, perhaps, but the feeling persists of what appears at crucial points as an overstress of the way in which the Three are distinct, or at the very least, of certain cautions towards a conceptual system not yet fully docile to the translucent darkness of the light of faith.

In fine, the Trinity presents what is perhaps the most difficult area of all in the conceptual reinterpretation of God. The following observations, then, are at best only guide lines for a task yet to be done.

First, the distinguishing message of the New Testament, when it speaks about God is a specifically Trinitarian one, and that Trinitarian dimension needs to be recovered against a crypto-Unitarianism.

Secondly, the Scriptures do not refer directly and explicitly to the Trinity *in se* but to the Trinity manifest in salvation history, which then must be the sole starting point in the search for concepts with which to articulate faith in the "immanent" Trinity — which search, nonetheless, the believer-theologian must enter upon.

Thirdly, the Biblical point of reference may well make it misleading to conceive of God as enjoying one absolute act of subsistence (as Creator, e.g.), alongside as it were the three relatively distinct ones; at the very least, such cannot be thought of as constituting "person." Concretely, then, it should be impossible to think of God existing save as Father, and *Logos*, and *Pneuma*.

Fourthly, the category of "person" or "hypostasis" etc. is surely not *"per se"* indispensable to faith in the Trinity, as its relatively late appearance on the scene tends to confirm. But when all is said and done, is there in our present state of faith-consciousness any better term available to us; can the Trinity be satisfactorily understood without it?[111] If not, then there should be no question of abandoning the concept but rather of recovering and deepening it.

Apropos of more positive suggestions along these lines, Wittgenstein had made an arresting statement concerning human personality that strengthens somewhat the possible applicability of this notion to God: "The thinking, presenting subject — there is no such thing. . . . The philosophical I is not the man, not the human body, or the human soul of which psychology treats, but the metaphysical subject, the limit — not a part of the world."[112] This may be closer conceptually than might at first sight appear to St. Thomas' elaboration of the Divine Three as Subsistent Relations, not under the formality of relatedness but that of distinct subsistence. This was St. Thomas' attempt, at any rate, to preserve the real distinction of the Persons of the Trinity

214

without acknowledging any difference or diversity — which he did by distinguishing (without thereby eliminating) the "*aspectus in*" which is accidental to relation from the "*aspectus ad*" which alone is essential to it, thus arriving at pure relation.[113] The penetrating comment of Cajetan on this (though cited earlier) is so illuminating that it must be adverted to again:

> . . . in God, in reality or in the real order, there is one Relativity which is not purely absolute nor purely relative, nor is it mixed or composed of or resulting from both; but in a most eminent manner it formally contains that which is relative (indeed, many relative entities) and that which is absolute. . . We are wrong in approaching God through the categories of absolute and relative, imagining that the distinction between the absolute and the relative is prior to the Divine Reality itself. Consequently, we think one has to be subordinated to the other. However, the complete opposite is the case; because the Divine Reality comes before being and all its differences, it is Super-Being, and super-One etc.[114]

This understanding of Subsistent Relation as answering to the notion of person when analogically projected onto God was elaborated by Cajetan into a notion of person in general as an ultimate metaphysical *mode* or *term* of intellectual reality rendering the latter proximately capable of existing in a unique and irreducible way.[115] This bears obvious kinship to Wittgenstein's idea of "metaphysical limit." Capreolus, the first of the commentators on St. Thomas, articulated the same idea rather differently, seeing metaphysical personality to consist in a transcendental *relation* of a singular instance of nature to its own unique act of existing.[116] In both these conceptions, though especially in the latter, personality is a relatedness towards existence. It would seem no violation of this basic insight to transpose it to the order of *Existenz* (rather than *esse*) where personality would then be seen as an essential and "given" relatedness to one's human world, creatively constituted, as a total context of meaning.[117] The openness or contingency of this, its "precariousness" in Merleau-Ponty's phrase, as a project towards the world, would deny neither an underlying original ontic "givenness" of its own, nor the fact that the relatedness in question ultimately regards other persons in their givenness to me.

The analogical transposition of this to God would mean the elimination of all imperfection and a concept of the Trinity as Three Inter-Personal, Subsistent Relations. This, of course, is a conceptualization of what the Three in God are in common; the concrete identity of each of these, singularly, demands distinct concepts, and here it must be recalled that the reality who is the person cannot be grasped in a concept of its own. The concepts involved rather represent characteristics of nature which the person assumes (both metaphysically and — if human — psychologically) in his personal appropriation of the common nature, and in his self-communicative activity through that nature. So conceived, the Pure Activity of God is then precisely a dynamism of infinite and really identical knowledge and love, marking a coalescence in God of what we understand distinctly as necessity and freedom; constituting God as an Unoriginate Father eternally generating His Son with and through whom he spirates forth their Spirit; and establishing him as a Transcendent in whom are reconciled the realities of Absolute and Relative, of One and Many.

*　*　*

Obviously, much of the problem in reworking our concepts of God lies in the vast remove of Divine Reality from an intelligence that knows discursively. Or it may be better to put the problem in opposite terms and say that it is due to the very proximity of the Three who are God to what is deepest and most mysterious in ourselves, to the fact that They are closer to us, in a sense, than we are to our very selves. The dark orientation of our mind to the Reality here by way of notional

216

theology may have to give way to mystical theology, in the non-esoteric sense of that word. At least, contemporary speculation points that way in calling for a dialectical inter-play in our knowing between an objective, reflective element and one of pre-reflective religious experience, both personal and communal, under the guidance of the Spirit.

# NOTES TO INTRODUCTION

1. Schubert Ogden: *The Reality of God* (New York: Harper and Row, 1966), p. 1.

2. Paul Tillich: *Systematic Theology*, I, (U. of Chicago Press, 1951), p. 220.

3. The basic explanation of the need for the concept in all human intellection is the very nature of the latter as an assimilative act wherein the knower "becomes" the known in its own order of intention. Such necessity rests upon: a) the materiality of the object proper and immediate to such knowing, demanding the abstractive process, b) the potential state of the knowing faculty bespeaking a corresponding need for information and actualization, and c) the "otherness" of the known from the knower necessitating that it be rendered present intentionally in a *species*. The revealed truth that within the depths of God's uncreated intelligence there is uttered a Divine Word *(Logos)* "ex abundantia" suggests to faith that the inner word is essential and intrinsic to intellection as such.

4. This should be obvious on the basis of ordinary introspection and reflection as long as one understands that it is a question of a proper or quidditative idea representing God as he is in himself. It is St. Thomas' clear teaching that even in the Beatific Vision there is no possibility of a created *species* mediating the Uncreated Object to the intellect of the Blessed. Of the three reasons he presents for this, the second is perhaps the most cogent: God's essence is his very act of existing, and since for a concept to be is for it to represent precisely as a formal sign, then a quidditative concept of God would have to be uncreated. *(Summa Theologiae,* Ia. q. 12, a. 2). It should be noted that what is being denied in the intuitive vision of God is only a created *species;* the Divine Essence, purely intelligible in and of itself, in uniting itself to the finite intellect assumes thereby the role of the intelligible *species:* " . . . ita, divina essentia unitur intellectui creato ut intellectum in actu, per seipsam faciens intellectum in actu." *(loc. cit.,* ad 3um).

5. St. Thomas' own introduction to his tract on God beginning with Question 3 of the *Prima Pars* reads: "Now, we cannot know what God

**219**

is, but only what he is not; we must therefore consider the ways in which God does not exist, rather than the ways in which he does."

6. "Rester fidèle à ce qu'on fut, tout reprendre par le début . . .", Maurice Merleau-Ponty: *Signes* (Paris: Gallimard, 1960), p. 12.

7. Cf. William J. Richardson: *Heidegger: Through Phenomenology to Thought,* (The Hague: Martinus Nijhoff, 1963), p. 641.

# NOTES TO CHAPTER ONE

1. "Subjectivists are made, they are not born. The non-professional . . . is an extreme realist; he is so deeply impressed with the objectivity of thought, and so naturally certain that thought attains an *other* than thought, that he is inclined to overlook almost entirely the immanence of thought and scarcely adverts to the fact that thought is in the thinker and that things are known only in so far as they are in some way *in* the knower." J. F. Peifer: *The Mystery of Knowledge* (Albany, N. Y.: Magi Books, 1964) pp. 11-12.

2. Cf. E. Gilson: *Being and Some Philosophers* (Toronto, 1952), p. 109; J. Collins: *History of Modern Philosophy* (Milwaukee, 1956) p. 456.

3. In this way the Scholastic teaching is a careful avoidance of any "reifying" of the idea. By contrast, Karl Rahner's exposition of his own views on cognition do not seem to preclude this; Cf. "Scholastic Concept of Uncreated Grace", *Theological Investigations,* I, (Baltimore: Helicon Press, and London: Darton, Longman & Todd, 1961) pp. 327-328. Entitatively, of course, the "species" is something, i.e. as an accidental qualification or an informing form of the intellect, but this is in the order of being, not that of knowing. Simultaneously, and not subsequently, it is the formal principle constituting one a knower, a knower not of self but of an object which is the *res,* not however as existing but as intelligibly attained.

4. *In De Ente et Essentia D. Thomae Acquinatis Comm.,* (Taurini: 1820), q. 2, n. 14. (Available in an English transl. by L. H. Kendzierski and F. C. Wades, S. J. as *Cajetan: Commentary on Being and Essence* Milwaukee: Marquette U. Press, 1964; cf. p. 67). Cajetan is speaking here of the concept or expressed species as it is of the cognitive or intentional order — not, that is, entitatively as a mere informing form of the intellect.

5. The term "real" is used here in its most obvious sense as convertible with the exercise of extra-mental *esse.* The idea, as an immanent being, is also properly possessed of reality; is also itself an

220

instance of real being. There is no term in English to express the distinct orders or modes of being, i.e. trans-subjective and immanent, similar to the terms in German philosophy (notably in the thought of Hüsserl) *reale* and *reelle*. W. Norris Clarke tends to over-stress somewhat the distinctness of mode involved here when he writes that the realness of the idea conceived by an actual person is real *only* by an analogy of attribution, not proper proportionality, to the reality of an extra-mental thing; Cf. "What is Really Real", *Progress in Philosophy*, edited by J. A. McWilliams, S.J. (Milwaukee: Bruce, 1955) pp. 61-90. Entitatively considered, as an accidental form of the intellect, the being of the idea bears an analogical similitude of proper proportionality to the things of nature; intentionally considered, its being does depend upon an analogy of attribution from the latter.

There is still a third mode of existence over and above the *esse natural* and *esse intentionale;* this is the *esse cognitum* which is entirely ideal. It is the existence of something known precisely as it is known. It implies no newness of being at all to either the thing known or the knower. It is not the existence of the thing known in itself *(esse naturale)*, nor the existence of the selfsame thing in thought and for thought *(esse intentionale)* but an existence of the thing known under the precise formality of its being known.

6. Joannes a Sancto Thoma: *Cursus Philosophicus*, (Reiser Edition; Turin: Marietti, 1937) T. III, Pars IV, q. 11, a. 1, p. 349.

7. As in the Beatific Vision; there is a "word" here, it is true, but not one uttered by the Blessed themselves, rather the Divine Essence itself terminates the act of vision, *in ratione speciei*, i.e. in fulfilling the role that belongs to the mental word in finite intellection. As Cajètan notes there are also other secondary concepts formed by the Blessed for the sake of communication *(In I.*, q. 27, a. 1). The concept should not be confused with the imagination of the spoken word, a sort of interior language immediately preceding external speech. St. Thomas does advert to connatural intellective activity without a mental word (e.g. *I Sent.*, d. 27, q. 2, a. 1) but the intellection here is incomplete, a kind of inventive thinking, that is really the process of groping towards the concept.

8. Lonergan's "insight" is a dynamic process prior to and originative of conceptualization; the latter is described in ways that suggest it is a distinct act and that its term (the concept) is never equal to the intelligibility glimpsed in the "click" of insight. Schillebeeckx rather differently sees the entire process of conceptualization as subsequent to an implicit intuition of the totally real, a gradual thematic explication of a primal intuition of being as undifferentiated.

9. This negative, partial, ever deficient nature of the concept is forcibly expressed by Jacques Maritain in *The Degrees of Knowledge*

221

(transl. by Gerald Phelan from the fourth French edition; New York: Scribner's, 1959), p. 127.

10. Both of these authors understand that man's knowledge of God encompasses two elements — one conceptual, the other nonconceptual — in a complementary way. Some of Schillebeeckx's expressions, however, suggest that the conceptual element is purely functional, i.e. it gives a formal direction to our knowing but the cognitive affirmation of the real is itself non-conceptual. Cf. Edward Schillebeeckx: *Revelation and Theology,* II, transl. by N. D. Smith, (N. Y. Sheed & Ward), 1968, pp. 18-20 (French edition: *Révélation et Théologie,* Approches Théologiques I, Bruxelles: Editions du Cep, 1965, p. 234); Dominic M. De Petter: "Impliciete intuitie", *Tijdschrift v. Philosophie,* I, 1939, pp. 84-105.

11. *In De Ente et Essentia,* q.1, no. 4; Kendzierski and Wade translation, pp. 45-46.

12. J. H. Nicolas: *Dieu Connu comme Inconnu* (Paris: Desclee de Brouwer, 1966), pp. 36-37.

13. One example is E. Gilson; Cf. "Cajetan et l'Existence", *Tijdschrift v. Philosophie,* June, 1953; *Elements of Christian Philosophy* (New York: Doubleday, 1960), p. 214.

14. D. Scotus: *Opera Omnia* (Paris: 1894) *III Sent.,* d. 6, q. 1, v. 15; F. Suarez: *Disputationes Metaphysicae* (Paris: 1861) d. XXXI, sec. 1, 11, v. 26.

15. Cf. respectively: *In De Ente et Essentia,* c. 5, q. 10, n. 99-101; Bañez *(Comm. in Iam,* q. 4, a. 3) understands Cajetan to be distinguishing between essence and existence as between one thing and another *(res et res):* however Cajetan himself explicitly rejects this in his refutation to the third of Trombetta's ten arguments since it would demand giving one "esse" to essence and another to existence. A more accurate explanation of how Cajetan understood the real distinction can be found in his Commentary on the Summa; *In Iam,* q. 3, a. 3. n. 6&7. The authenticity of this as being St. Thomas' own understanding of the distinction is strengthened somewhat by the fact that Capreolus *(Defensiones* I, dist. 8, q. 1) presents it in almost identical terms. *In Iam,* q. 4, a. 1, n. 5: ". . . esse secundum suam formalem rationem, est perfectissima omnium perfectionum . . .". *In Iam,* q. 8, a. 1, n. 5: ". . . in omni re est aliquid productum et conservatum a solo Deo proxime et immediate . . .".

16. *In De Ente et Essentia,* c. 5, q. 12, esp. n. 101.

17. *Comm. in Iam Partem Angelici Doctoris* (Madrid & Valencia, 1934), q. 3, a. 4: "Cum enim esse sive existentia sit prima actualitas non solum in intentione generantis, sed etiam in ratione formalitatis, cum nihil intelligatur, nisi ut habet esse, vel cum intrinseco ordine ad esse. . . . Et idcirco non placet mihi explicatio Cajetani ubi supra, videlicet, quod propterea dicatur existentia ultima actualitas rei quia est

222

ultimum in generatione. Certe hic modus loquendi, quod ipsum esse sit ultima actualitas rei, raro invenitur apud D. Thoman".

18. Cf. B. S. Llamzon: *The Primacy of Existence in Thomas Aquinas* (Chicago: Regnery, 1966), Introduction: "It is interesting to see contemporary thinkers who draw inspiration from Aquinas probe the realities of person, freedom, responsibility, knowledge, etc. in continuity with a metaphysics first thought out in the 1200's then gradually lost, then briefly and unsuccessfully upheld at a critical moment in the history of metaphysical thought in the late 1500's." For an interpretation defending Cajetan against the charge of essentialism see J. P. Reilly: "Cajetan: Essentialist or Existentialist?". *The New Scholasticism*, Spring, 1967.

19. *In De Ente et Essentia*, q. 1, n.5 (Kendzierski and Wade translation, p. 44).

20. *Cursus Philosophicus*, T. II, q. 1, a. 3 (Reiser Edition, p. 24).

21. The abstraction involved here is unique in kind; Cajetan writes: "Also what we intended to show is now clear, namely, how being is embodied in an essence able to be sensed, namely, when it is supported by neither of these abstractions, but is seen in a sensible essence abstracted from singulars but with no separation." *(In De Ente et Essentia*, q. 1, n. 5 (Kendzierski and Wade translation, p. 47).

22. St. Thomas explains this in terms of the two ways in which knowledge can be said to be abstract: "Uno modo ex parte rei cognitae . . . et sic cognoscere aliquid in universali est imperfectius . . . Alio modo ex parte modo cognoscendi; et sic perfectius est cognoscere aliquid in universali . . ." *(In Post. Anal. Arist.*, Lib. 1, lect. I, n. 37-38).

23. *Summa Theol.*, II - II, q. 173, a. 2: "Judicium est completivum cognitionis".

24. *Degrees of Knowledge*, Chap. 3; *Existence and the Existent*, translated by Lewis Galantiere and Gerald Phelan, (Garden City, New York: Doubleday, 1956) pp. 25-28.

25. *Dieu Connu Comme Inconnu*, pp. 29-55.

26. *L'Être et l'Essence* (Paris: J. Vrin, 1948), p. 258 ff.; *Being and Some Philosophers* (Toronto: Pontifical Institute of Mediaeval Studies, 1949), p. 190 ff.

27. *In De Trinitate Boetii*, q. 5, a. 3. Of considerable value here is the study of L. B. Geiger: "Abstraction et separation d'après Saint Thomas", *Rev. des sciences phil. et theol.*, 31, 1947, pp. 3-40, especially in its pointing out that the above article was rewritten several times by St. Thomas in a gradual progression beyond the position of Aristotle. On this same general point, cf. E. D. Simmons: "The Thomistic Doctrine of the Three Degrees of Formal Abstraction", *Thomist*, Jan., 1959.

28. Cf. J. Maritain: *Existence and the Existent*, pp. 32-39; Maritain here emphasizes that the concept of essence and the judgment of

existence make up "one and the same concept"; there is "a mutual involution of causes, a reciprocal priority of this concept and this judgment, each preceding the other in a different order", pp. 34-35.

29. Important here is a correct understanding of truth as realized in the judgment *(Summa Theol.,* I, q. 16, a. 2) and as achieving the full perfection of intellectual knowing. The act is not one of comparing the idea in the mind to the reality and judging that the former corresponds to the latter — this would be impossible simply because there would be no way of attaining the real as a norm except in another idea. Rather, the mind affirms that the thing is, in an exercise of real existence, as it (the intellect) has perceived it; this is the judgmental intuition instinctive to intelligence. The former view would, as Maritain has vividly shown *(Degrees of Knowledge,* p. 97, note 2), involve one in a Cartesian impasse. In this very act, the intellect also affirms itself, i.e. it knows itself as conforming to reality and thus as attaining truth. St. Thomas says all this somewhat succinctly in *Q.D., De Veritate,* q. 1, a. 3, ad 3um: "Veritas quae in animo causatur a rebus non sequitur aestimationem animae, sed existentiam rerum . . .".

30. *In Iam,* q. 2, a. 1, n. 7; q. 82, a.3, n. 13.

31. *I Sent.,* d. 3, q. 4, a. 4.

32. Cf. "Faith and Self-Understanding", *The Word in History,* edited by T. Patrick Burke (New York: Sheed and Ward, 1966), p. 43. See also Chap. III of this present study.

33. "Cognitional Structure", *Collection* (New York: Herder and Herder, 1967), p. 226: "There is intentional presence, in which knowing is involved, and it is of two quite distinct kinds. There is the presence of the object to the subject . . .; there is also the presence of the subject to himself . . .; it is presence in, as it were, another dimension, concomitant and correlative, and opposite to the presence of the object." See also Chap. III of this present study.

34. Cf. "The Concept of *Verbum* in the Writings of St. Thomas", *Theological Studies,* VII, 1946, p. 392. Lonergan is one of those who differentiate sharply between the actual work of St. Thomas and the tradition which consolidated around him; the shift within that tradition he attributes in large measure to the influence of Scotus (cf. *Insight,* p. 406) as Schillebeeckx does also (cf. *Revelation and Theology,* II, p. 157).

35. Completed in 1498, the most recent edition available is that of P. N. Zammit, O. P., which was published in a revised edition at Rome in 1952 by P. H. Hering, O.P.: *De Nominum Analogia; De Conceptu Entis.*

36. Santiago Ramirez: "De Analogia secundum doctrinam Aristotelico-Thomisticam", *La Ciencia Tomista,* Julio, 1921; Enero, 1922.

37. T.-L. Penido: *Le Rôle de l'Analogie en Théologie Dogmatique,* Bibliothèque Thomiste, XV, (Paris: 1931).

38. *In Iam,* q. 13, a. 2, n. 7: "id quod boni nomine formaliter importatur, est in Deo formaliter."

39. A detailed exploration into Cajetan's doctrine of analogy will be attempted in Chapter Four of this study. For now it will suffice to note that he distinguishes four modes of analogical speech; 1) Analogy of Inequality (individuals of the same species participating in an identical formal perfection of their nature to greater and lesser degrees), Chap. 1; 2) Analogy of Attribution, Chap. 2; 3) Analogy of Proper Proportionality, Chap. 3, n. 26; 4) Analogy of Improper Proportionality (when a perfection formally in one reality is attributed metaphorically to another on the basis of a similarity in effect, e.g. the actor is a "star" because he sheds lustre upon the stage, suggesting imaginatively the manner in which the astral body lights up the sky, Chap. 3, n. 25. In the first mode, the concept is really univocal, i.e. having the same meaning in all its applications, and so Cajetan calls it analogy *abusive dicta*; the analogy in this case is one employed by the physicist; Chap. 1, n. 6 and 7. Attribution involves an analogical concept thanks to the intellect's own comparative consideration; the analogy here is *secundum intentionem tantum,* and the proper tool of the logician; Chap. 2, n. 21. Only in proper proportionality is there a concept that is fully analogical, thus here the analogy is *secundum intentionem et secundum rem,* and this is the domain of the metaphysician; Chap. 3, n. 30.

For Cajetan, analogy is something of the real and ontological order that the mind comes to recognize and upon which it bases its predication. Between uncreated and created being then there is a relation not only of proportion but of proportionality. The former, which he prefers to call attribution, is a proportion in terms of a reference of one thing to another or others, and is based ultimately upon some causal relationship; there is but one concept which is univocal and so properly signifies one thing and is merely extended to others to indicate the pure reference so that nothing intrinsic is said about the secondary analogates — to speak of a book as "sad", for instance, is not to make it the subject of an emotion but is to say that it is such as to occasion that emotive response in the reader. In analogy of proportionality, by contrast, the concept is not univocal but truly analogical; it signifies not one thing but all the objects of which it is predicated, so that the perfection is to be found intrinsically and formally in them all, yet in widely diverse modes. The verb "sees" expresses the reaction of the corporeal eye to color and of the human mind to truth; obviously, a different meaning is intended in either case but there is a proportionate unity to the concept "seeing" which embraces both cases and so

225

requires but a single word (even if, in the above example, the *original* application of "sight" to intellection was metaphorical). When Cajetan asserts that the principal analogy between God and the world is proportionality, he understands this as always including virtually an underlying analogy of attribution.

40. *In Iam,* q. 13, a. 12, n. 9.

41. *In De Ente et Essentia,* Chap. VI, q. 15 (Kendzierski and Wade translation, p. 270): "Aliud est cognoscere quidditatem, seu cognitio quidditatis, et alius est cognitio quidditativa, seu cognoscere quidditative"; Cajetan is here arguing against any such quidditative knowledge of immaterial substances.

42. *In Iam,* q. 13, a. 2, n. 7: ". . . ly ét hoc altiori modo' non est accipiendum ut pars significati. Non enim, cum dicimus 'Deus est bonus', significatur bonitas Dei et eminentia eius, sed bonitas tantum: eminenter vero ex modo significandi innuitur...".

43. Cf. e.g. Schillebeeckx: *Revelation and Theology,* II, p. 157 f. The express reference here is not to Cajetan but to Scholasticism in general and especially to T. L. Penido: *Le Rôle de Analogie en Théologie Dogmatique;* nonetheless Schillebeeckx does implicate not only Cajetan but St. Thomas himself in a qualified essentialism: "I am of the opinion, however, that the abandonment of essentialism was not a definitive achievement in the historical Thomism, since it is always possible to detect essentialist echoes even in Aquinas's later works, even though these generally occur under the pressure of current philosophical formulae.", p. 165, Note 18.

44. T.-L. Penido: *Le Rôle de Analogie en Théologie Dogmatique;* A. Malet: *Personne et Amour dans La Théologie Trinitaire de S. Thomas d'Acquin,* Bibliothèque Thomiste, 32 (Paris: Vrin, 1956); C. Vagaggini: "La hantise des 'rationes necessariae' de Saint Anselme dans la théologie des processiones trinitaires de saint Thomas"; *Spicilegium Beccense* (Paris: 1959).

45. It is questionable whether other writers do not in fact imply this; cf. e.g. T.-L. Penido, *op. cit.,* who writes of the transcendental idea as formally signifying not created reality alone, but, in a proportionate way, both finite and the infinite: "Nous avons là, en réalité, un concept transcendant qui *domine* l'un et l'autre rapport, et abstrait inadéquatement de l'un comme de l'autre: il y a un principe 'unum proportione' ni exclusivement divin, ni exclusivement créé, mais qui vise tous les deux, qui *est* tous les deux, proportionnellement.", p. 190.

46. *In Iam,* q. 12, a. 2, n. 9: "...species domus in mente oportet quod sit forma domus...";  Maritain in developing the role of the concept qualifies considerably the limited intelligibility it can represent apropos of the thing, cf. *Degrees of Knowledge,* p. 127.

47. Cf. M. Daffara: *De Deo Uno et Trino* (Taurini: Marietti, 1945):

"*Fundamentum* autem huius distinctionis in Deo est duplex: primum quidem, et veluti remotum, ex parte ipsius rei conceptae, quod est divini esse eminentia et virtualis multiplicitas...", p. 94.

48. The balance to St. Thomas' treatment on God can be perceived only when that teaching is viewed in an integral way, e.g. it is necessary to attend to the close interrelationship between Divine Being and Divine Intellection as the eternal speaking of the Word which is by intrinsic necessity shown to be the generation of a Son, and to the spontaneous origin of love from knowledge and thus of the procession of Divine Spirit from Father speaking and Word spoken; cf. *Summa Theol.*, I. qq. 14, 19, and 27. A balanced judgment on what St. Thomas actually achieved can be found in C. Strater: "Le point de départ du traité thomiste sur la Trinité", *Sciences Ecclesiastiques*, 14, 1962.

49. *Cursus Theol.*, I, Disp. 34, a. 3, n. 7.

50. *Theological Investigations*, IV, pp. 77-102.

51. Cf. A. Malet, *op. cit.*, and the criticism of this study by F. Von Gunten: "La primauté de la personne et amour dans la théologie trinitaire de S. Thomas d'Aquin", *Angelicum*, 35, 1958; also C. Vagaggini, *op. cit.*, the latter believes that the theological reasons of St. Thomas taken from St. Anselm are necessary reasons "demonstrating" the real distinction of Persons.

52. Notable among the former: A. Gardeil: *La structure de l'âme et l'experience mystique* (Paris: 1927); R. Garrigou Lagrange: "L'Habitation de la Sainte Trinité et l'Experience mystique", *Revue Thomiste*, XI, 1928; J. H. Nicolas: "Présence Trinitaire et Présence de la Trinité", *Revue Thomiste*, I, 1950. For the latter position, see among others: K. Rahner: "Some Implications of the Scholastic Concept of Uncreated Grace", *Theological Investigations*, I, pp. 319-346; M. Donnelly: "The Inhabitation of the Holy Spirit", *Proceedings C.T.S.A.*, (New York: 1949). For a discussion of appropriation, cf. W. J. Hill: *Proper Relations to the Indwelling Divine Persons* (Washington: Thomist Press, 1954), pp. 43-53.

53. "Theologie und Heilsökonomie in der Christologie der 'Tertia'", *Gott in Welt*, II (Freiburg im Breisgau: Verlag Herder, 1964).

54. *Summa Theol.*, III, q. 3; St. Thomas is here attempting to illuminate the character of the Union as hypostatic, and in so doing considers, in terms of God's absolute power, and abstractly, all purely logical possibilities. He does not expressly advert to the perspective of God's willed economy until Article Eight and then only to seek arguments of convenience.

55. This latter is somewhat a pseudo-problem, perhaps best conveyed in the remark of Yves Congar that eventually one has to find within the *Deus-in-Se* the ultimate explanation of what God is as the *Deus-pro-nobis:* "Is there not in the mystery of this *en Soi*, a presence, a call for the *pour nous*...?"; "Christ in the Economy of Salvation and in our

Dogmatic Tracts", *Concilium*, Vol. II, (New York: Paulist Press, 1965), p. 23.

56. St. Thomas, citing Aristotle in the *De Anima*, writes: ". . . sensibile in actu est sensus in actu, et intelligibile in actu est intellectus in actu.", *Summa Theol.* I, q. 14, a. 2. The intellect's abstractive conceiving, as overcoming the density of the thing and rendering it transparent, is thus a process whereby it "becomes" the object.

57. St. Thomas' own expression of this is: "Essentiam Dei in hac vita cognoscere non possumus secundum quod in se est; sed cognoscimus Eam secundum quod representatur in perfectionibus creaturarum.", *Summa Theol.*, I, q. 13, a. 2, ad 3um.

58. *Summa Theol.*, II-II, q. 1, a. 2, ad 2um: "Actus autem credentis non terminatur ad enuntiabile, sed ad rem."

59. Such objectivity safeguards the historical character of Revelation, wherein salvific truth is conveyed by means of actual events and words interpretative of those events spoken by the prophets and Christ; St. Thomas expresses this in terms of the twofold source of faith: ". . . fides principaliter est ex infusione, . . . sed quantum ad determinationem suam est ex auditu. . .", *IV Sent.*, d. 4, q. 2, a. 2, sol. 3, ad 1um.

60. "A Believer's Look at the World", an essay in *The Christian and the World*, Readings in Theology (New York: P. J. Kennedy, 1965), pp. 68-100.

# NOTES TO CHAPTER TWO

1. Rabbi Moshe ben Maimon (Moses Maimonides) 1135-1204; his major work *Guide for the Perplexed*, is available in a recent translation by Shlomo Pines (U. of Chicago, 1963).

2. Maimonides himself refers to this many times throughout Part I of the *Guide*, e.g., in Chapters 1, 26, 35 and 36.

3. *Op. cit.* I, Chap. 59. p. 138.

4. Op. cit. I, Chap. 57 and 58. pp. 132-137.

5. *De Nominum Analogia*, cap. 3. n. 25. pp. 25-26.

6. *Op. cit.* I, Chap. 51. pp. 112-114.

7. A. D. Sertillanges, O.P. (1863-1948): *Agnosticisme ou Anthropomorphisme* (Paris: Bloud, 1908), p. 60. The above book originally appeared in the form of two articles in the *Revue de Philosophie*, vols. I and II, 1906; a review published irregularly and superceded by *Recherches de Philosophie* in 1955.

8. For example T. L. Penido, *Op. cit.*, pp. 170-175; J. Maritain: *Degrees of Knowledge*, Appendix III, pp. 425-429.

9. A. J. Kelly: "To Know the Mystery: The Theologian in the Presence of the Revealed God", *Thomist*. Jan., 1968, p. 34.

10. *De Trinitate Boetii*, II. q. 2, a. 4.

11. Sertillanges: "Agnosticisme ou Anthropomorphisme", *Revue de Philosophie*, 1906, II, p. 158.

12. Cf. "Reseignments téchniques" in Sertillanges' French translation of St. Thomas' *Summa Theol.*, Editions de la Revue des Jeunes, t. II (Paris, Tournai, Rome: Desclée et Cie, 1926), p. 383.

13. *Ibid.*

14. See Roger Aubert: "Recent Literature on the Modernist Movement," *Concilium* (New York: Paulist Press, 1966), Vol. 17, for a survey of the more significant recent studies. Especially noteworthy is Emile Poulat: "Histoire, dogme et critique dans la crise moderniste", in *Religions et sociétés* (Paris, Tournai: Casterman, 1962).

15. Denzinger-Schonmetzer, n. 3475-3500.

16. L'Evangile et l'Eglise (Paris: 1902), transl. as *The Gospel and the Church* by Christopher Home (New York: Charles Scribner's Sons, 1904); also *Autour d'un petit livre* (Paris: 1903).

17. *Through Scylla and Charybdis* (New York: Longmans Green, 1907).

18. *Op. cit.*, Chapter XI, esp. pp. 280-307.

19. Bultmann has himself minimized his indebtedness to Heidegger's early Existentialism, realizing that such a dependence opens him to the charge of subordinating Revelation to philosophical system, and moreover one that is avowedly atheistic or at least non-theistic. Apart from such a disavowal, he does acknowledge at least a commonness of view: "Some critics have objected that I am borrowing Heidegger's categories and forcing them upon the New Testament. I am afraid this only shows that they are blinding their eyes to the real problem, which is that the philosophers are saying the same thing as the New Testament and saying it quite independently."; "New Testament and Mythology" in *Kerygma and Myth*, edited by Hans Werner Bartsch, transl. by Reginald H. Fuller (New York: Harper and Row, 1961) pp. 24-25. Hans Jonas, in the keynote address delivered at Drew University, Madison, N. J., April, 1964 in a symposium entitled "The Problem of Non-Objectifying Thinking and Speaking in Contemporary Theology", has taken the opposite tack and vehemently disclaimed any relevance of Heidegger for theology. The most critical and balanced judgment on this question yet to appear in English is to be found in *The Later Heidegger and Theology*, New Frontiers in Theology, edited by J. M. Robinson and J. B. Cobb, Jr. (New York, Evanston, and London: Harper and Row, 1963).

20. *Church Dogmatics*, edited by G. W. Bromilery and T. F. Torrance, Vol. I, Part I, transl. by G. T. Thomson (Edinburgh: T. and T. Clark, 1936). p. x: "I regard the *analogia entis* as the invention of Antichrist and think that because of it one cannot become Catholic". Cf. also Vol.

II, Part I, transl. by T. H. L. Parker, W. B. Johnston, H. Knight, and J. L. M. Haire, 1957, p. 79; "...the accessibility of the nature and being of God as Lord, Creator, Reconciler, and Redeemer is not constituted by any analogy which we contribute but only by God himself....the lordship of God evades all the analogies that we can bring . . . the creation of God also evades all the analogies that we can bring. . . ."

21. This typical Barthian principle was qualified by Barth himself not long before his death in an address to the Swiss Reformed Ministers' Association in 1956 in which he spoke of the humanity of God as a sort of divine attribute on which basis human existence gains a correspondence with the divine; cf. K. Barth: *The Humanity of God* (Richmond: John Knox Press), 1960, pp. 37-65.

22. The only authors Barth is explicitly taking exception to on analogy are P. Daniel Feuling and J. Fehr. This is done in the context of his reaction against "natural theology" which he ascribes to Liberal Protestantism as much as to Catholicism; and what he actually understands by natural theology is illustrated by his accusing such a theology of deducing the doctrine of the Trinity from a prior knowledge of the One God; "from the premises of formal logic"; cf. *Op. cit.*, Vol. II, Part I, p. 261.

23. *Loc. cit.*, p. 80: "...and although the knowability of this construct can rightly be affirmed without revelation, do we not have to ask what authority we have from the basis and essence of the Church to call it 'God'?"

24. *Loc. cit.*, p. 81. Here Barth's objections to the analogy of being reveal that he tends to construe it as a *tertium quid* in which God and man share; he rejects ".. the *analogia entis,* the idea of being in which God and man are always comprehended together, even if their relationship to being is quite different, and even if they have a quite different part in being . . . the analogy of being which comprehends both Him and us." This is precisely the understanding of analogy that St. Thomas is at pains to reject in *Summa Theol.*, I, q. 13, a. 5., i.e., an analogy between creature and God as if "multa habent proportionum ad unum".

25. *Op. cit.*, Vol. I, Part I, p. 260: "...knowledge of the Word of God is nothing else than the grace of God meeting the reality of man, the mode of which as a reality is as hidden from us as God himself..."; Vol. II, Part I, p. 261: "Who or what is 'God'? If we want to answer this question legitimately and thoughtfully, we cannot for a moment turn our thoughts anywhere else than to God's act in his revelation."; *Ibid.*, p. 79: "God can be known only through God, namely in the event of the divine encroachment of his self-revelation."

26. Some interpreters of Barth have not hesitated to say that the disparity between the intrinsic meaning of the word God requisitions in Revelation and its actual signifying of the Divine is one of contradiction;

cf. J. Rilliet's article in *Revue de Théologie et Philosophie*, XXXII, 1944, p. 129.

27. *Op. cit.*, Vol. II, Part I, pp. 264-66.

28. J. Hamer, O.P.: *Karl Barth*, transl. by D. Marucca, S.J. (Westminster, Md.: Newman, 1962), cf. pp. 69-77.

29. God's Word is not word in the ordinary linguistic sense: Barth sees it as fundamentally *personal*, i.e., Christ himself; in a derivative sense as *written*, the word of Scripture; and lastly as *proclaimed*, the word of the Church. In the latter two forms, especially that of the preaching of the Church, the unitary word as God's revealing speech is given some objectivity.

30. *Op. cit.*, Vol. II, Part I, pp. 224-243; see especially p. 228: "Indeed it is not the case that when He authorizes and commands us in His revelation to make use of our views, concepts, and words, God is doing something, so to speak, inappropriate, because, if they are to be applied to Him, our views, concepts, and words have to be alienated from their proper and original sense and usage . . . (thus it follows that) . . . we do not attribute to our views, concepts, and words a purely fictional capacity, so that the use we make of them is always hedged in by the reservation of an 'as if'."

31. J. Hamer: *Op. cit.*, p. 71.

32. Indeed it is not at all clear in what sense faith is truly of the human subject at all; in what sense it is the latter who takes hold of the Word of God under the divine initiative; cf. *Op. cit.*, Vol. I, Part I, p. 250: ". . .it is literally not the human act as such, the experienceable and the experienced as such, the thing really put into our hands, the thing man can achieve and fix as such, which absolutely distinguishes, characterizes, and qualifies this act among and from man's other possibilities as the act in which determination of man by the Word of God takes place." Barth goes on in this same passage to say that once determined by the Word man does fulfill an act, but in what sense it can be man's he does not say. The emphasis upon the divine activity is so total that there seems no room for allowing that there is a response elicited by man.

33. *God-Talk* (New York and Evanston: Harper and Row, 1967), p. 50.

34. *Language, Logic, and God* (New York, Evanston and London: Harper and Row), p. 78: "A second major theological tradition is concerned less about anthropomorphism than about pride and afraid less of agnosticism than of faithlessness. Only in the obedience of faith, this tradition insists, can man's language convey meaning and truth about God. This approach to justifying language in its theological application we shall call, therefore, the logic of obedience; it is held to be a higher rationality than any known to philosophy."

35. See *Natur und Gnade* (Tubingen, 1935) pp. v and 50.

36. *Offenbarung und Vernunft* (Zurich, 1941), p. 66; Available in an English transl. by Olive Wyon as *Revelation and Reason* (Philadelphia: Westminster Press, 1946).

37. *Dogmatics*, Vol. I, *The Christian Doctrine of God*, transl. by Olive Wyon (Philadelphia: Westminster Press, 1950), p. 136: "The God who is 'conceived' by thought is not the one who discloses himself; from this point of view He is an intellectual idol."

38. *Op. cit.*, p. 289.

39. *Op. cit.*, p. 246: "If, however, this speculative rationalistic process of the *viae* in the sphere of a Christian doctrine of the Divine Attributes is forbidden to us once for all, on the other hand a purely realistic Bible statement is also insufficient."

40. *Der Mensch im Widerspruch* (Zurich; 1937) p. 246; available in an English transl. by Olive Wyon as *Man in Revolt* (Philadelphia: Westminster Press, 1947): "The Word of God is *logos*, meaning, that is to be understood by us, i.e., to be received as an object of thought, and therefore not produced by our thinking but received."

41. *Dogmatics*, Vol. I, *The Christian Doctrine of God*, p. 282.

42. *Loc. cit.*, p. 247.

43. *The Divine-Human, Encounter*. transl. by Amandus W. Loos, (Philadelphia: Westminster, 1943), p. 41: "The Bible is as little concerned with objective as with subjective truth. The objective-subjective antithesis cannot be applied to the Word of God and to faith. It is a category of thought wholly foreign, not only to the way of expression in the Bible, but also to the entire content." Also, *Dogmatics*, Vol. III, *Christian Doctrine of the Church, Faith, and the Consummation*, transl. by D. Cairns, (Philadelphia, Westminster, 1962), p. 260: "Faith arises where all knowledge is at an end, both objective knowledge 'explanation', and also the subjective knowledge that we call understanding."

44. See *Dogmatics*, Vol. 1, *The Christian Doctrine of God*, p. 284.

45. *Loc. cit.*, p. 279.

46. *Loc. cit.*, p. 270.

47. For a discussion of Bonhoeffer's indebtedness to Barth, see Eberhard Bethge (Bonhoeffer's personal friend and editor): "The Challenge of Dietrich Bonhoeffer's Life and Theology" in *World Come of Age*, edited by R. Gregor Smith (Philadelphia: Fortress Press, 1967); also John A. Phillips: *Christ For Us in the Theology of Dietrich Bonhoeffer* (New York: Harper and Row, 1967).

48. Dietrich Bonhoeffer: *Christ the Center*, transl. by J. Bowden (New York: Harper and Row, 1966), p. 104.

49. *Op. cit.*, pp. 91-92: "What did the formula of Chalcedon say? It stated the *a priori* impossibility and impermissibility of taking the divinity and the humanity in Jesus Christ side by side or together or as

a relationship of objectifiable entities. Simple negation remains. . . . All thought forms are cut short. . . . It (the Chalcedonian Definition) speaks of 'natures,' but it expresses the facts in a way which demonstrates the concept of 'natures' to be an inappropriate one. It works with concepts which it declares to be heretical formulas unless they are used paradoxically and in contradiction. It brings the concept of substance which underlies the relationship of the natures to a climax and does away with it."; cf. also p. 101.

50.  Cf. *Letters and Papers from Prison,* Revised Edition by E. Bethge of transl. by R. Fuller, (London: S.C.M. Press; New York: Macmillan, 1967), p. 154.

51.  John A. Phillips: *Op. cit.*

52.  R. Gregor Smith in his Introduction to *World Come of Age,* cited above, p. 19.

53.  Dietrich Bonhoeffer: *Letters and Papers from Prison,* p. 188.

54.  *Existence and Faith,* edited and transl. by Schubert Ogden (London: Hodder and Stoughton, 1961), p. 98. "Every theology is dependent for the clarification of its concepts upon a pre-theological understanding of man, that, as a rule, is determined by some philosophical tradition."

55.  Cf. *Kerygma and Myth,* Vol. 2, (London: S. P. C. K., 1962), pp. 83 f.

56.  For a development of this meaning of myth, see H. P. Owen: "Revelation," *The Theology of Rudolf Bultmann,* edited by Charles W. Kegley (New York: Harper and Row, 1966), p. 41; also, in the same volume, Schubert Ogden: "The Significance of Rudolph Bultmann for Contemporary Theology", pp. 111-112.

57.  ". . . so . . . would the fact of salvation be misunderstood if it were thought of as an isolated fact that happened in some place and at some time and that requires to be mediated to the present through a communication. (It is not) . . . some cosmic process that has occurred in a certain place and at a certain time. Rather everything that is decisive for him (the hearer of preaching) takes place in his present; *'now* is the day of salvation'"; *Existence and Faith,* p. 79; quoted in C. W. Kegley: *The Theology of Rudolph Bultmann,* p. 44.

58.  *Essays, Philosophical and Theological* (London: S.C.M. Press, 1955), p. 280. Here Bultmann makes this idea concrete in the case of Christ, asking to what extent the Scriptural titles and names ". . . describe him, so to speak, objectifying him in his being in himself, or whether and how far they speak of him in his significance for man, for faith? Do they speak — I can formulate it this way too — of his *physis* or of the *Christus pro me?*"

59.  Heidegger himself readily admits such a "reversal" in his thought, and in an unpublished letter of October, 1966 to a "Symposium on the

Philosophy of Martin Heidegger" held at Duquesne University, Pittsburgh, Pa., he reiterated a plea that his thought no longer be looked upon as *Existenz Philosophie.*

60. See John MacQuarrie: *God-Talk,* p. 201, note: "Bultmann does in fact speak of a 'desymbolizing' as well as a 'demythologizing'."

61. *God-Talk,* p. 41.

62. *Kerygma and Myth,* Vol. 1, p. 197: "Such language is therefore neither symbolical nor pictorial, though it is certainly analogical, for it assumes an analogy between the activity of God and that of man and between the fellowship of God and that of man with man." In this passage he refers the reader to Erich Frank: *Philosophical Language and Religious Truth,* (London and New York: Oxford U. Press, 1945).

63. Bultmann has similar things to say about Christ, noting that a Christological pronouncement is "also a pronouncement about me"; Christ is the Son of God because he helps me, not vice versa; cf. *Essays, Philosophical and Theological* (London: SCM Press, 1955) p. 280, H. P. Owen observes this is true in the *ordo cognoscendi* not in the *ordo essendi;* cf. "Revelation": *The Theology of Rudolf Bultmann,* ed. by C. W. Kegley, p. 48, Note 12.

64. Tillich's major theological enterprise is: *Systematic Theology,* 3 vols. (University of Chicago Press, 1951-1963).

65. *Dynamics of Faith* (New York: Harper, 1957), p. 42; cf. also "Existential Analyses and Religious Symbols" in *Contemporary Problems in Religion,* ed. by H. A. Basilius (Wayne State U. Press, 1956-1965) reprinted in *Four Existential Theologians,* ed. by W. Herbeng (New York: Doubleday, 1958), p. 291: "Symbols are not signs. They participate in the power of what they symbolize."

66. *Systematic Theology,* I. pp. 240-241: "Religious symbols are double-edged. They are directed towards the infinite which they symbolize *and* towards the finite through which they symbolize it."

67. *Ibid.,* I, p. 177.

68. *Theology of Culture* (New York: Oxford U. Press, 1959), p. 58.

69. *Systematic Theology.* I, p. 239: "The symbol grows and dies according to the correlation between that which is symbolized and the persons who receive it as a symbol."

70. "Existential Analyses and Religious Symbols," p. 290.

71. *Systematic Theology,* I, p. 240.

72. *Dynamics of Faith,* p. 75: "Reason is identical with the humanity of man in contrast to all other beings." Earlier in this work Tillich has distinguished "technical reason" from "ontological reason", it is the latter that is meant here. Cf. also *Systematic Theology,* Vol. I, p. 176: "Man participates in the universe through the rational structure of mind and reality."; *Ibid.,* p. 75: "From the time of Parmenides it has been the common assumption of all philosophers that the *logos,* the word which

grasps and shapes reality, can do so only because reality itself has a *logos* character." Involved in the understanding of this is Tillich's further distinction between ontological reason as subjective and objective; cf. T. Schick: "Reason and knowledge in Paul Tillich," *The Thomist*, Jan. 1966, pp. 66-79.

73. *Systematic Theology*, I, p. 237: "(Man) uses the two categories of relation — causality and substance — to express the relation of being-itself to finite beings. The 'ground' can be interpreted in both ways, as the cause of finite beings and as their substance. The former has been elaborated by Leibnitz in the line of the Thomistic tradition and the latter has been elaborated by Spinoza in the line of the mystical tradition. Both ways are impossible."

74. This ontological participation which antecedes and founds the conscious participation is a sort of pre-conscious knowing; it apparently reduces to the *logos* structure of reality as intelligible (objective) and intelligent (subjective). It is not, as in traditional Christian theism, the possession by the whole order of finite beings of an *esse* causally derived from God yet had by the creature in an intrinsic though deficient way.

75. *Systematic Theology*, I. p. 241. Here Tillich observes that the tendency to restrict the symbol to the unreal owes something in Protestantism to Hegelianism and in Catholicism to Modernism.

76. *Op. cit.*, p. 244: "The divine life participates in every life as its ground and aim. God participates in everything that is; he has community with it; he shares in its destiny."

77. *Op. cit.*, p. 245.

78. *Op. cit.*, p. 239.

79. *Op. cit.*, p. 242: "Anthropomorphic symbols are adequate for speaking of God religiously."

80. "Existential Analyses and Religious Symbols," p. 291: "They are not true or false in the sense of cognitive judgments. But they are authentic or inauthentic with respect to their rise; they are adequate or inadequate with respect to their expressive power...". In his *Systematic Theology*, I, p. 240, Tillich nuances this in a very different way: "The judgment that a religious symbol is true is identical with the judgment that the revelation of which it is the adequate expression is true . . . a symbol *has* truth: it is adequate to the revelation it expresses. A symbol *is* true: it is the expression of a true revelation."

81. *Systematic Theology*, I, p. 273.

82. *Op. cit.*, p. 238: "The statement that God is being-itself is a nonsymbolic statement."; p. 239: ". . . other assertions about God can be made theologically only on this basis. . . . However, after this has been said nothing else can be said about God as God which is not symbolic. . . . If anything beyond this bare assertion is said about God, it no longer is a direct and proper statement, no longer a concept. It is indirect and it

235

points to something beyond itself. In a word, it is symbolic."

83. W. L. Rowe: *Religious Symbols and God* ( U. of Chicago Press, 1968), p. 189.

84. *God-Talk.* p. 51.

85. Tillich's failure to do this means that the symbol he most commonly employs for God, namely "Ultimate Concern", can mean almost anything one wishes it to.

86. Cf. esp. *Patterns in Comparative Religion* (New York: Meridian Books, 1963).

87. Cf. *The Symbolism of Evil.* transl. by E. Buchanan (New York: Harper and Row, 1967)

88. Cf. *Theology of Hope,* transl. by J. W. Leitch (New York: Harper and Row, 1967).

89. Cf. *God, the Future of Man,* transl. by N. D. Smith (New York: Sheed & Ward, 1968); see especially the Epilogue.

90. Cf. *Theology of the World,* transl. by W. Glen-Dopel (New York: Herder & Herder, 1969).

91. Cf. *Naming the Whirlwind: The Renewal of God-Language* (Indianapolis: Bobbs-Merrill, 1969).

92. "There is no saving ontology, but the ontological question is a necessary task. *Against* Pascal I say: The God of Abraham, Isaac, and Jacob and the God of the philosophers is the same God.": Paul Tillich, *Biblical Religion and the Search for Ultimate Reality* ( U. of Chicago Press, 1952), p. 85.

93. On this point Henrich Fries observes: "If *everything* were a matter of belief, then there would be no faith at all"; *Faith Under Challenge,* transl. by W. D. Seidensticker (New York: Herder & Herder, 1969), p. 36.

94. St. Thomas: *Summa Theol.,* I. p. 3, a. 5: "one cannot assign either genus or difference to God, nor define him, nor demonstrate anything of him except by means of his effects..." see also q. 12, a. 2. where he points out that even in the Beatific Vision of Glory God cannot be seen by any created likeness.

95. If this were not so, the theologian's task in this matter at least would have come to an end long ago; one is reminded of Ludwig Wittgenstein's caution: "whereof one cannot speak, thereon one must be silent"; *Tractatus Logico-Philosophicus,* transl. by C. K. Ogden (London: Kegan Paul, 1922), p. 189.

# NOTES TO CHAPTER THREE

1. Joseph Maréchal, S. J.: *Le point de départ de la Métaphysique,* Leçons sur le Développement Historique et Théorique du problème de la

Connaissance. Cahier V. deuxième édition, (Bruxelles et Paris, 1949). An instructive introduction to Maréchal can be found in *A Maréchal Reader*, ed. Joseph Donceel (New York: Herder & Herder, 1970).

2. *Ibid.*, p. 351: "Décidément l'intelligence humaine n'est pas intuitive." In spite of this denial, because he is driven to find something beyond conceptualization to explain the validity of our knowledge of God, and because what he searches for is itself a "dynamic substitute for intellectual intuition" (*Ibid.*, p. 346), his basic position can be examined under the rubric of "theological intuitionalism."

3. *Ibid.*, p. 311: ". . . l'assension ou l'affirmation est un acte de la faculté intellectuelle, et non de la volonté."

4. *Ibid.*, p. 346.

5. *Ibid.*, p. 307: "L'affirmation 'objectivante' apparaît donc comme à michemin entre une activité exclusivement synthétique, s'arrêtant à l'aspect formel de l'*être*, et une intuition intellectuelle saisissant l'*être* en plein, sans intermédiaire."

6. *Ibid.*, p. 520.

7. *Ibid.*, p. 519: "Avant l'affirmation judicative, rien, dans les représentations immanents au sujet connaissant, n'exprime encore une opposition entitative à sa propre subjectivité, un 'quelque chose,' un être."

8. *Ibid.*, p. 459.

9. *Ibid.*, p. 306.

10. *Ibid.*, p. 547: 6e Proposition, no. 1.

11. *Ibid.*, p. 547: 6e Proposition, no. 2.

12. *Ibid.*, p. 458.

13. *Ibid.*, p. 459: ". . . les représentations immanentes à notre pensée n'y ont valeur d'objet qu'en vertu d'une *affirmation implicite*; et non d'une affirmation quelconque, mais d'une *affirmation métaphysique, c'est-à-dire* d'une affirmation rattachant l'objet à l'absolu de l'*être*."

14. *Ibid.*, p. 554: "Dans tout objet de pensée, quel qu'il soit, nous affirmons implicitement l'*Être absolu* et explicitement l'*être contingent*. En dehors de cette double affirmation simultanée, il n'y a pas, pour nous, de pensée objective possible."

15. *Ibid.*, p. 526: ". . . ce sont . . . dans la synthèse objective (ou l'affirmation), la position absolu du rapport d'analogie, c'est-à-dire, en ordre de raison: premièrement, la position (implicite) absolu de l'*Être* infini, comme terme supérieur, unique et necessaire, de toute relation d'analogie; et secondement, la position absolu de la donnée, ou du contenu de la representation, comme terme inférieur, multiple et contingent, de la relation d'analogie: en d'autres terms, l'existence nécessaire de Dieu et l'essentielle contingence des choses directment représentées." p. 554, 8e Proposition: "Si la relation des données à la fin dernière de l'intelligence est une condition a priori intrinsèquement 'constitutive' de tout objet de

notre pensée, la connaissance analogique de *l'Être* absolu, comme terme supérieur et ineffable de cette relation, entre 'implicitement' dans notre conscience immédiate de tout objet en tant qu'objet."

16. *Summa Theol.*, I. q. 85, a. 2.

17. *Ibid.*, p. 311: ". . . *l'ascensio* ou *l'affirmatio* est determinée par une finalité antécédente."

18. *Ibid.*, p. 311: "La 'finalité naturelle' interne, ou l'appetit naturel d'un *être* rationnel, peut s'appeler 'volonté naturelle,' par opposition à 'volonté élicite' ou à 'volonté' tout court." p. 312 (note) ". . . S. Thomas admet, dants tout esprit créé, un 'amour naturel,' et par conséquent un 'appetit naturel,' logiquement antérieur à l'intelligence et à la volonté élicités, et (que) cet appétit naturel, dans les êtres intellectuels, est rapporté par lui à la volonté . . . si . . . l'on considére seulement les puissances intellectuelles, alors l'appétit naturel (intellectuel) est veritablement une volonté naturelle."

19. Cf. E. Schillebeeckx: *Revelation and Theology*, II, pp. 17-18; J. H. Nicolas, *Dieu connu comme inconnu*, p. 32.

20. *Ibid.*, p. 232: ". . . la signification (c'est-à-dire *ce qui* est objectivement convert par l'affirmation) est indépendante, jusqu'à un certain point, du mode particulier que la nature de notre intelligence introduit dans la représentation conceptuelle." p. 324: ". . . mais en devenant (sous l'affirmation) forme transcendante (p. ex. Dieu est *vivant, agissant*), la forme abstraite n'en demeure pas moins 'représentée,' dans notre esprit, comme numériquement multipliable;" p. 325: "Nous ne découvrons donc pas, dans la représentation comme telle, la loi ou la mesure objective de l'affirmation vraie."

21. *Summa Theol.*, I, q. 13, a. 2: ". . . significant substantiam divinam et praedicantur de Deo substantialiter, sed deficiunt a representatione ipsius."

22. *Ibid.*, I, p. 13, a. 3, ad 3[um]: "Ista nomina, quae proprie dicuntur de Deo important conditiones corporales, non in ipso significanto nominis, sed quantum ad modum significandi."

23. *Ibid.*, p. 323: "Le 'modus rei in essendo,' c'est la signification objective imposée par l'affirmation vraie."

24. *Ibid.*, p. 258.

25. *Ibid.*, p. 258.

26. L. Dewart: *The Future of Belief*, (New York, Herder & Herder, 1966.)

27. "Notions conciliares et analogie de la vérité," *Rech. Sc. Rel.*, 35 (1948), p. 255 f.

28. Rahner, of course, does not deny the activity of sensation, abstraction, conversion to phantasm, etc., but only that such empirical activity of itself yields the concept of being; cf. *Spirit in the World*, Part II, Chapters 2-4, (N.Y.: Herder and Herder, 1968 transl. by W. Dych, S. J.,

of *Geist in Welt*, 2nd edition, Kosel-Verlag, Munich, 1957).

29. *Spirit in the World*, pp. 142-146; *Hearers of the Word* (N.Y.: Herder and Herder, 1969), p. 65 (transl. by M. Richards of *Hörer des Wortes*, revised ed., of J. B. Metz, Kosel-Verlag, Munich, 1963).

30. This prehension of the Absolute is explained by Lotz with an emphasis upon the role of judgment and in terms of exemplar causality; Rahner, in a direction followed by Coreth, prefers to emphasize the role of questioning and to stress final causality.

31. Cf. *Spirit in the World*, pp. 179-183.

32. *Hearers of the Word*, p. 44.

33. *Ibid.*, p. 43.

34. "Scholastic Concept of Uncreated Grace," *Theological Investigations*, Vol. I, (Baltimore: Helicon Press; London: Darton, Longman & Todd, 1961), p. 327; transl. by Cornelius Ernst of *Schriften zur Theologie*, I (Benziger: Verlag Einsiedeln-Zurich-Koln, 1954).

35. *Ibid.*, p. 328.

36. Cf. Etienne Gilson, *Réalisme thomiste et critique de la connaissance* (Paris: 1939), pp. 131-155; Jacques Maritain: "Note à propos des 'Cahiers' du R. P. Maréchal," *Revue Thomiste*, Vol. 7, (1924), pp. 416-425; M. Casula, *Maréchal e Kant*, (Rome, 1955).

37. *The Transcendental Method*, transl. by W. D. Seidensticker, (New York: Herder & Herder, 1968), p. 215.

38. "The Transcendental Method and the Psychogenesis of Being," *The Thomist*, Oct., (1968), p. 497.

39. This at any rate, is the impression Rahner gives in *Spirit in the World*, cf., pp. 180-181; 400-401.

40. It is on the basis of this very distinction that Rahner bases his whole theory of an unthematic prehension of being. What can hardly be denied is that his understanding of this interrelationship is a rather radical departure from that of Aquinas who clearly states that the human intellect as a faculty of a bodily being is "in potentia respectu intelligibilium" and a "vis passiva respectu totius entis universalis," (*Summa Theol.*, I, q. 79, a.2, corp. & ad 3um). Moreover, the latter sees the actuality of the agent intellect as totally illuminative in kind and not at all cognitive (cf. *Q.D., De Ver.*, q. 10, a 8, ad 11 in contrarium where it is shown that the nature of the agent intellect precludes its being receptive of any intelligible form), and declares that the actuality in question here is not operative with reference to the entire range of being but only the being of the material existent (cf. *Quaest. Unica, De Anima*, a. 5, ad 3um: ".. intellectus possibilis est in potentia respectu intelligibilium, secundum esse quod habent in phantasmatibus. Et secundum illud idem intellectus agens est actus respectu eorum . . .").

41. "But in the pre-apprehension as the necessary and always actually realised condition of knowledge . . . the existence of an Absolute Being is

also affirmed simultaneously (*mitbejaht*)"; *Spirit in the World,* p. 181.

42. "This Absolute Being is not apprehended as a represented (*Vorgestellter*) object," *Ibid.,* p. 180.

43. Charles N. Bent, S.J., *Interpreting the Doctrine of God,* (Glen Rock, New York, Amsterdam, Toronto, London: Paulist Press, 1969), p. 157.

44. *Hearers of the Word,* p. 83.

45. *Ibid.,* p. 88.

46. *Ibid.,* pp. 89 and 91.

47. A full understanding of this involves Rahner's teaching on what he calls the "supernatural existential" (cf. "Relationship between Nature and Grace," *Theological Investigations,* I, pp. 297-317; "Nature & Grace", *op. cit.,* IV, pp. 165-188; *Nature and Grace* (New York: Sheed and Ward, 1964, transl. by D. Wharton, chap. 5, pp. 114-143). This amounts to a kind of "sur-forming" of man's natural spiritual being by God, as that nature is a "potentia obedientialis" for grace, which latter Rahner understands as more than a mere non-repugnance; as a positive but conditional orientation to God. The "supernatural existential" is the actual fulfilling of this capacity and is itself no denial of its universality though not itself intrinsically and formally justifying. Revelation, in the sense Rahner uses it above, then, is not simply something natural, though some thematization of historical revelation is required to recognize it as more than such.

48. Cf. "The Development of Dogma," *Theological Investigations,* I, pp. 39-77; "Considerations of the Development of Dogma," *op. cit.,* IV, pp. 3-35; Robert L. Richard: "Rahner's Theory of Doctrinal Development," *Proceedings, C.T.S.A.,* vol. 18, New York, 1964; Charles Bent, *op. cit.,* pp. 196-224.

49. "Considerations on the Development of Dogma," pp. 9, 12, 13.

50. "The Development of Dogma," p. 61.

51. See *Summa Theol.,* I, q. 93, esp. aa. 6 & 7.

52. Cf. "Theos in the New Testament," *Theological Investigations,* I, esp. pp. 104-117. Rahner here, of course, is not denying that there can be an ontology of God's attributes but only emphasizing that the New Testament is less concerned with *what* God is than with the question "as whom he wishes freely to show himself with regard to the world," *Loc. cit.,* p. 112.

53. Cf. "On the Theology of the Incarnation," *Theological Investigations,* IV, pp. 113-114. A critical analysis of this and other observations of Rahner on the concept of God is attempted in Chapter 5.

54. "Theos in the New Testament," p. 147.

55. "On the Theology of the Incarnation," p. 106.

56. *Insight. A Study of Human Understanding* (New York: Philosophical Library, 1965). To date this is Lonergan's major work upon

which this study relies in the main; the original edition published by Longmans appeared in 1957. Two earlier sources that cannot be neglected are the series of articles dealing with St. Thomas' teaching on *Gratia Operans* (*Theological Studies*: Sept. 1941, Feb. 1942, Sept. 1942, and Dec. 1942) and another series on "The Concept of *Verbum* in the Writings of St. Thomas" (*Theological Studies*: Sept. 1946, March 1947, Sept. 1947, March 1949, and Sept. 1949); this latter series has been issued in one volume under the editorship of D. B. Burrell as *Verbum: Word and Idea in Aquinas* (New York: Herder and Herder, 1967). Mention should be made too of *Collection*, ed. by F.E. Crowe (New York: Herder and Herder, 1967); as well as the Latin text *De Deo Trino*, 2 vols., (Rome: Gregorium U., 1964), the 2d volume of which was originally published as *Divinarum Personarum Conceptio Analogica* (Rome: Gregorian U., 1957).

57. Cf. "The Concept of *Verbum* in the Writings of St. Thomas," *Theological Studies*, March (1947), p. 35.

58. Edward MacKinnon, "Understanding According to Bernard J. F. Lonergan," *The Thomist*, July (1964), p. 342.

59. As is true of both Rahner and Schillebeeckx, Lonergan explicitly denies the possibility of intellectual intuition in the proper sense of the term, i.e., the direct and immediate grasp of extra-mental reality without dependence upon prior sense activity and recourse to abstractive processes. All three likewise insist upon the necessity of the concept. The theological "intuitionalism" ascribed to them in this study is a somewhat extended use of the term to indicate their common tendency to separate *conceptualization* from *understanding* as a distinct act, the latter preceding the formation of the concept and being thus itself preconceptual. "Intuitionalism" in this sense differentiates these thinkers from those whose systems lend themselves rather to what might be called by contrast "Conceptualism" or "Representational Realism."

60. *Op. cit.*, p. 373, note 125. Here, Lonergan identifies Scotus as the major influence among those who conceive of intellection in this fashion.

61. *Insight*, p. x: "Thirdly, in a sense somewhat different from Kant's, every insight is both 'a priori' and synthetic. It is 'a priori,' for it goes beyond what is merely given to sense or to empirical consciousness."

62. This distinction is roughly equivalent to that which St. Thomas draws between the first and second acts of the mind, i.e., simple apprehension and judgment.

63. *Insight*, p. 308. "Prior to concepts there are insights. A simple insight is expressed only by uttering several concepts."; p. 422: "Hegel endeavors to pour everything into the concept; we regard concepts as byproducts of the development of understanding . . ."; p. 695: "The root of this confusion is conceptualism, which places conception before understanding. . . ." It should be noted that Lonergan's insistence on this

distinction is not to be found generally in the Thomistic tradition, e.g., in Maritain's *Degrees of Knowledge*.

64. In a textual examination of St. Thomas, Lonergan points out the frequency (32 times) with which the latter designates the quiddity of the material thing as proper object of the human intellect, but then points out that many times (16 all told) he rather identifies this object as the phantasm itself. What is important here is Lonergan's own nuances, i.e., he speaks of the quiddity *in* the phantasm, or the phantasm in which somehow the quiddity is reflected; it is clear too that he has a marked preference for the second phraseology; cf. "Verbum and Abstraction," *Theological Studies,* March, (1949), p. 23.

65. Lonergan ascribes to the influence of the "De Natura Verbi Intellectus" (whose authenticity he is inclined to doubt, following Mandonnet) the teaching that the *verbum* is formed prior to understanding and that the intellect knows first the quiddity in the *verbum* and then by conversion to the phantasm knows it again as existing in corporal matter; cf. "Verbum and Abstraction," *Theological Studies,* March (1949), p. 22.

66. Lonergan further characterizes insight as that which "pivots between image and concept" (*Insight,* p. 10), which though itself one "has many concepts" (*Ibid.,* p. 14); it is "a release to the tension of inquiry . . . comes suddenly and unexpectedly . . . is a function not of outer circumstances, but of inner conditions . . . pivots between the concrete and the abstract . . . and passes into the habitual texture of one's mind." (*Ibid.,* pp. 3-4).

67. "Verbum and Abstraction," *Theological Studies,* March (1949), p. 30: " . . . intellect no more glances than sight smells . . . "

68. Put in terms of the abstractive processes involved, this is what Lonergan calls *apprehensive* abstraction, which is understanding in second act; something subsequent to *objective* abstraction by the agent intellect, which is understanding only in first act, but prior to *formative* abstraction exercised in the production of the concept.

69. Edward MacKinnon, S.J., *Op. cit.,* p. 129.

70. This could occur, in any case, only by conversion to the phantasm. Lonergan, however, wishes to locate the attainment of the trans-subjectively real in a subsequent act of intelligence, i.e., in the affirmation achieved by way of insights on the level of reflective understanding.

71. *Insight,* p. 322.

72. This fact is nothing more than the recognition of the self as an intelligent subject and of being as pure intelligibility. The former is the realization of man's transcendence, radicated in "his detached, disinherited, unrestricted desire to know;" the latter, the realization that "Being is the objective of the unrestricted desire to know. Therefore, the idea of being

is the content of an unrestricted act of understanding" (*Insight,* p. 644). Thus, "the idea of being is the idea of the total range of intelligibility." (*Ibid.,* p. 645). What Lonergan means here is perhaps clarified in the following text: "For if an act of understanding is unrestricted, it understands understanding; it understands not only restricted acts but also the unrestricted act; understanding the unrestricted act it must understand its content, otherwise the understanding of the unrestricted act is the idea of being, and so if the unrestricted act understands itself, it thereby also understands everything else." (*Ibid.,* p. 648.)

73. *Insight,* p. 672.

74. *Insight,* p. 675.

75. *Insight,* p. 709.

76. As in all complete knowledge, the act of faith includes necessarily a self-affirmation as well as an affirmation of God: " . . . the act of faith, as specified by its object will include an affirmation of man's spiritual nature, of his freedom, responsibility, and sinfulness, of God's existence and nature, and of the transcendent solution God provides for man's problem of evil." (*Insight,* p. 721).

77. *Insight,* p. 725: "For the supernatural solution not only meets a human need, but also goes beyond it to transform it into the point of insertion into human life of truths beyond human comprehension, of values beyond human estimation . . . " *Ibid.,* p. 726.

78. Cf. the Epilogue to *Insight;* also the Introduction to *Divinarum Personarum Conceptio Analogica,* Pontificia Universitas Gregoriana, Roma, 1957.

79. Cf. "Theology and Understanding." *Collection,* pp. 134-135; "The basic relation, then, of speculative theology to the teaching authority of the church is the subordination of both understanding and science to wisdom. It is a supernatural subordination that runs parallel to the natural subordination of *Quid sit to An sit,* of speculation to judgment."

80. The analytic approach not only precedes the synthetic and is its point of departure, it also confers a new formal intelligibility on the self-same objects. Lonergan notes the dominance of the first in the Patristic era, of the second in the Scholastic period, and a confusion of the two in the Manualists. His own solution to the tension is "the historical mode of understanding, which grasps the development of dogma as a dialectic of the two processes . . . "; cf. E. MacKinnon, *Loc. Cit.,* p. 372.

81. Cf. *De Deo Trino,* vol. I, *Pars Dogmatica,* esp. pp. 75-87.

82. *Insight,* pp. 739-740.

83. *Insight,* p. 734.

84. *Insight,* p. 736.

85. Lonergan certainly does not mean that St. Thomas actually taught any such theory of development himself, or that the construction of such

a theory is merely making explicit what is implicit in St. Thomas' thought. The most that he means is that the latter's epistemology is a tool that opens the way to Lonergan's own theory.

86. Schillebeeckx's cognitional theory and its implications for theology are developed primarily in the collection of various essays entitled *Revelation and Theology,* 2 vols., transl. by N. D. Smith (New York: Sheed and Ward, 1967-1968); French edition, *Révélation et Théologie,* (Bruxelles: Editions du Cep, 1965); and in "Faith and Self-Understanding," *The Word in History,* ed. T. Patrick Burke (New York: Sheed and Ward, 1966).

87. Schillebeeckx's thought here marks a departure from a more traditional Thomistic epistemology wherein the concept of and by itself (i.e., without recourse to a prior pre-conceptual "intuition," of which the conceptualization is a subsequent and deficient "formal" representation) mediates a contact of intellect with the extra-mental order of reality. Jacques Maritain offers the best explanation of this process seeing it as reflexive in nature, involving conversion to the phantasm, and necessarily including a judgment of actual existence — a judgment however that arises necessarily and spontaneously from the very apprehension of the singular existent as "something" or as "a being." Cf., *Existence and the Existent* (Image Books edition, New York, 1956): " . . . the concept of existence cannot be detached from the concept of essence . . . At the instant when the finger points to that which the eye sees, at the instant when sense perceives, in its blind fashion, without intellection or mental word, that *this exists;* at that instant the intellect says (in a judgment) *this being is* or *exists* and at the same time (in a concept) *being.*" (p. 34); "At the moment when sense apprehends an existent sensible, the concept of being and the judgment, 'this being exists,' which condition each other, arise simultaneously in the intellect. . . . The extramental existence of things was given to it from the very start in the intuition and concept of being." (pp. 35-36, note 13).

88. A Dominican philosopher from Louvain to whom Schillebeeckx's own thought is much indebted. His writings with few exceptions are available only in Flemish; noteworthy among them on this present point is "impliciete intuitie," *Tijdschrift v. Philosophie,* I (1939), p. 84 f.

89. The object of this intuition, precisely because it is an intuition preceding all conceptualization, is "being" as actual and concrete and not at all as abstract. Schillebeeckx emphasizes the real conjunction of essence and existence, seeing the latter ("actus essendi") as intrinsically constitutive of the content of essence, so that essence possesses no intelligible value of itself apart from its act of existing. Cf. *Revelation and Theology,* II, p. 165, also note no. 18.

90. An instance of reciprocal causality is involved here, i.e., a primal intuition of all reality, that is implicit and undifferentiated and achieved

as consciousness, precedes and renders possible the subsequent explicitation of this in concepts; but equally, the objective contents of such concepts orientate the intelligence back to ultimate reality so that man "rejoins" in an ever deepening and more explicit way what he has initially but vaguely intuited.

91. "Faith and Self-Understanding," pp. 43-44: "The self's being-in-the-world through self-revelation in matter is inescapably bound up with directing oneself to one's fellowmen, and man becomes present to himself in confrontation with this double orientation. . . . This self-awareness is present first and foremost in the manner of a pre-reflexive or unthematic self-understanding. . . ."

92. *I Sent.*, d. 3, q. 4, a. 4.

93. *Revelation and Theology*, II, p. 18: " . . . concepts as such cannot reach reality or truth . . . they can do so only as elements of a greater whole . . . a non-conceptual aspect is the basis of the validity of our conceptual knowledge," (p. 234 in French edition).

94. *Ibid.*, Schillebeeckx is here citing from DePetter's articles in the *Tijdschrift v. Philosophie*, 1939-1959.

95. "Faith and Self-Understanding," p. 47.

96. *Ibid.*, pp. 48 and 51; for an integral presentation of Schillebeeckx's theology of Revelation, cf. *Revelation and Theology*, I, esp. Chap. 3 "Revelation-in-Reality and Revelation-in-Word."

97. Formal object is meant here in the sense of formal *terminative* object rather than formal motive object; the supernaturality of faith requires, of course, an interior motion of God, an anointing of the Holy Spirit, called by St. Thomas the "instinctus fidei." That the events and words of Revelation are not themselves the formal terminative object of faith St. Thomas explains in *II-II*, q. 1, a 4, ad 4[um]: " . . . auditus est verborum significantium ea quae sunt fidei: non auten est ipsarum rerum de quibus est fides."

98. *Revelation and Theology*, I, chap. 6, "The Bible and Theology," esp. p. 181.

99. *Ibid.*, pp. 23-29, esp. p. 28; "Faith and Self-Understanding," p. 58.

100. Over and above the disproportion of any concept to the reality it represents, there is in this case the further difficulty of our concepts of God deriving from creatures and primarily representing them; cf. St. Thomas, *Summa Theol.*, I, q. 13, a. 4.

101. *Revelation and Theology*, II, p. 162 f.

102. *Q.D., De Potentia*, q. 7, a. 5, ad 9.

103. *Revelation and Theology*, II, p. 26; "Faith and Self-Understanding," p. 56.

104. The detailed textual study that Schillebeeckx enters upon here indicates that St. Thomas does expressly mention proportionality, but only during a brief middle period of his writing career, extending from 1256

to 1257 and covering the composition of the 3rd and 4th Books of the *Commentary on the Sentences* as well as the opening questions of the *De Veritate*. In the earlier writing there is no mention of proportionality, and in those subsequent to this brief interlude he abandons the phrase. Further, it is Schillebeeckx's interpretation that when St. Thomas does employ the term he only wishes to indicate that the "distance" between God and creature is an infinite or un-measurable one, a notion that the simpler term "proportion" does not convey since it implies a determined distance between the prime and secondary analogates. Cf. *Revelation and Theology,* pp. 181-193.

105. *Revelation and Theology,* II, p. 198: "What we have here is not a conceptual unity, a *ratio communis abstracta,* but an 'unum numero.' "; there follows a reference to St. Thomas' *Commentary on the Fourth Book of the Metaphysics,* lect. 1; cf. also, p. 183.

106. The intrinsicality here is accidental to attribution as such, but not to this particular instance of it. Any attribution is not fully intelligible unless seen not merely formally but materially, i.e., in terms of what is attributed. Though the goodness e.g., of God is other than that expressed in the transcendental concept (not only quantitatively but qualitatively) still God is indeed good and intrinsically so.

107. *Revelation and Theology,* II, p. 175.

108. *Ibid.,* p. 278, pp. 199-200.

109. It also appears that Schillebeeckx sees this initial intuition as of the self, i.e., one's own human existence as in-a-world, rather than of being itself.

110. This is Scholasticism's virtual minor distinction, something totally the work of human reason and not really in God Himself. The infiniteness, however, of God's being offers a foundation for making this distinction in a human effort at understanding; He is really all of these perfections in His utter oneness.

111. This represents Schillebeeckx's own understanding, flowing from his teaching on how, naturally or supernaturally, we know God; cf. *Revelation and Theology,* II, p. 187.

112. Dewart's thought is developed in two main books: *The Future of Belief, Theism in a World Come of Age* (New York: Herder and Herder, 1966), and *The Foundations of Belief* (New York: Herder and Herder, 1969); a significant article for the present study is "Truth, Error and Dialogue," *Concurrence,* 2, Spring, 1969.

113. Dewart's philosophical assumptions are entirely modern but somewhat eclectic: Wittgenstein, Etienne Borne, Freud, Marx, Sartre, Richard Hinners, Teilhard de Chardin, Dietrich Bonhoeffer, Rudolf Bultmann, etc. If any one thinker dominates his over-all thought, it is perhaps Gabriel Marcel.

114. *The Future of Belief*, p. 104.

115. *Ibid.*, p. 80, also pp. 83, 90-91.

116. *Ibid.*, p. 116, note: "Concepts are not the *subjective* expression of an *objective* reality . . . (but) . . . the self-expression of consciousness and, therefore, the means by which we objectify (the world and self), and the means whereby we self-communicate with another self (*including God*), that is, the means by which we objectify ourselves for another self, and by which we objectify ourselves for ourselves."

117. *Ibid.*, p. 102.

118. *Ibid.*, p. 8: "Christianity is not a message but a mission."

119. Dewart's view is that the concepts of Greek philosophy do not only resist alteration themselves, they convey the conviction that Christianity cannot develop; cf. *Ibid.*, p. 134, and *The Foundations of Belief*, pp. 104-114.

120. *The Future of Belief*, p. 49.

121. David Balas: "Christian Transformation of Greek Philosophy Illustrated by Gregory of Nyssa's Use of the Notion of Participation," *Scholasticism in the Modern World*, Proceedings of the American Catholic Philosophical Association, 1966 (Washington, D. C.), pp. 152-158.

122. *Ibid.*, pp. 90, 22, and 96; cf. also "Truth, Error and Dialogue."

123. Such enterprises are encouraged in Dewart's thinking for he sees even error not as the contrary of truth but as a less perfect approximation to what fidelity demands; a groping towards the truth that even when deficient serves, in the long run, the cause of truth. Where his positions differ with past doctrinal statements, Dewart does not intend to deny the truth value that such formulae gave expression to in their own historical moment, but to surpass them in this new historical moment.

124. Dewart takes notes of the flaw and ambiguity in Etienne Gilson's insistence that God has no essence but only an existence with which He is identical, and is right in acknowledging that Jacques Maritain more accurately renders the thought of St. Thomas, scil., that God does have an essence but none other than that which is pure existence. Cf. *Ibid.*, p. 183, and *The Foundations of Belief*, pp. 175-180.

125. *The Future of Belief*, p. 177.

126. *Ibid.*, p. 160. Here Dewart even denies a validity to the *Quinque Viae* in their own logical order, believing that they necessarily presuppose "what" God is; what they demonstrate is the real existence of a being answering to the concept that is presupposed. The misunderstanding is an ancient one, but ignores completely St. Thomas' own explanation in the *Prima Pars*, q. 3, a. 4, ad 2um: ". . . esse dupliciter dicitur: uno modo significat actum essendi, alio modo significat compositionem propositionis quam anima adinvenit conjungens praedicatum subjecto. Primo igitur modo accipiendo esse non possumus scire esse Dei sicut nec eius

essentiam, sed solum secundo modo. Scimus enim quod haec propositio quam formamus de Deo cum dicimus Deus est vera est. Et hoc scimus ex eius effectibus, ut supra dictum est."

127. *Ibid.*, p. 179.

128. *Ibid.*, p. 214. Here Dewart suggests "devising new ways to speak about God without naming Him at all."

129. *Ibid.*, p. 179, note 7.

130. Cf. St. Thomas, *Q. D., De Potentia*, q. 7, a. 5, ad 14$^{um}$ *. . . illud est ultimum cognitionis humanae de Deo quod sciat se Deum nescire, in quantum cognoscit, illud quod Deus est, omne ipsum quod de eo intelligimus, excedere."; *Ibid.*, ad 9$^{um}$: " . . . ratio illa procedit de eo quod significat substantiam definitive vel circumscriptive. Sic autem nullam istorum nominum substantium Dei significat . . . ;" *Q. D., De Veritate,* q. 2, a 11: "Nulla creatura habet talem habitudinem ad Deum per quam possit divina perfectio determinari;" *Ia Pars,* q. 13, a. 2: "Huiusmodi quidem nomina significant substantiam divinam et praedicantur de Deo substantialiter, sed .deficiunt a repraesentatione ipsius."

131. It might be noted that St. Thomas does not pose the question at all of God's *existence;* he rather asks whether God is (*"Utrum Deus sit?"*). It is the linking of subject and predicate in the proposition "God is" rather than its contrary "God is not" that St. Thomas affirms. Thus the word "is" does not attribute to God any of the quidditative notes of finite being, Cf. *Ia Pars,* q. 3, a. 4 ad 2$^{um}$; *III C.G.,* 49.

132. *The Ecumenist,* Jan-Feb., 1967.

133. *The Future of Belief,* p. 185, where Dewart is quoting Gabriel Marcel.

134. *Ibid.*, pp. 190-191.

135. *Ibid.*, p. 193.

136. *Ibid.*, p. 195.

137. *Ibid.*, p. 197.

138. *Ibid.*, p. 197.

139. The "sensu composito, sensu diviso" distinction of classical Scholasticism at least avoided so facile a solution as this.

140. *Ibid.*, p. 210.

141. *Ibid.*, pp. 210-211.

142. Max Seckler: *Instinkt und Glaubenswille nach Thomas von Aquin,* Matthias Grünewald Vlg., Mainz, 1962.

143. The gratuity here regards God's introduction of man into his own uncreated life, so that what is bestowed lies beyond anything created or creatable, thus the unexactedness is an absolute one. St. Thomas, basing himself on man's creation as in the image of God, writes of the soul as "naturaliter capax gratiae." (*Ia IIae,* q. 113, a. 10). He also teaches a natural desire for the vision of God (*Ia,* q, 12, a. 1; *Ia IIae,* q. 3, a. 8; *III C. C.,* 50). But this desire betraying an aptitude for elevation

248

to the supernatural, remains inefficacious and conditional. Man's nature is thus not merely a negative non-repugnance towards grace, but a *positive* aptitude for such, yet one that remains passive in the sense that nature is powerless to bring it to actualization.

144. *The Future of Belief,* 141.
145. *Ibid.,* p. 142.
146. *Ibid.,* p. 147.
147. *Ibid.,* p. 148.
148. The efficient causality here is something common to the Persons but does not exclude discerning within the grace-effect various modes of grace which constitute distinct affinities to each of the Divine Personalities.
149. *The Future of Belief,* p. 149 f.
150. "Truth, Error and Dialogue," p. 102.
151. *Ibid.,* p. 106.


# NOTES TO CHAPTER FOUR


1. This "return" to St. Thomas is not intended as simply one more textual study, a plethora of which already exist on this focal question of analogy, offering a broad spectrum of varied interpretations. Rather, the effort here is hermeneutical in a more speculative sense. It is a return to the masterworks of a thinker of genius from the precise vantage-point afforded by those very interpretations over a long historical perspective to see if there does not come to the fore a certain sustained directedness. What is sought is less an eclectic consensus than the reoccurrence of certain tendencies that appear to survive the test of time and criticism. What is assumed is that the vitality of the original thought is such that when re-thought by others certain virtualities implicit within it assert themselves and develop within a process of history. Readers of Heidegger will recognize this as akin to his methodology of *Wiederholung* or "Re-trieve", i.e. the coming of the future of thought into the present by a re-thinking of its past. Obviously, there is a weakness in such a theory, the unavoidable one of somewhere along the line having to make options. But such a limitation and inherent weakness does not leave it entirely bereft of all illuminative power as a methodology.

2. See Chapter III.

3. This *a priori* presence of being to the intellect, prior to all activity is not realized by way of an innate idea, but as a dynamic "disposition". Maréchal appears to conceive of it as the very nature or form of the

intellect preceding all contact with the material singular by way of sensation; by reason of it man knows everything *as being.* The *élan* does not pertain to the intellect apart from the will; thus the drive is radicated in spirit as subjectivity or self-awareness and issues spontaneously into exercise and specification by will and intellect respectively. Cf. Maréchal: *Le point de départ de la métaphysique,* Cahier V, (Paris: 1920), esp. pp. 223-298.

4. James B. Reichmann, S.J.: "The Transcendental Method and the Psychogenesis of Being", *The Thomist,* Oct., 1968, pp. 506-507: "Consequently any claim to have reached an actual awareness of the unlimited and unrestricted horizon of Being by a transcendental reflection or inner intuition of the knowing subject is inescapably self-refuting, if one is speaking of the human intellect, which, having as its proper object the quiddities of material things, must advance to the metaphysical domain of Being through the painstaking path of affirmation and negation, both of which constitute the radical modes of self-alienation and self-fulfillment."

5. It was apparently the realization of this that led Merleau-Ponty in some of his later writings to explain man's situation "within-a-world", (not as a place but as a total context of meaning) as achieved in and by his very *bodiliness.* He is generally regarded, and rightly so, as far less susceptible to the pitfall of subjectivism than many other Phenomenologists, e.g. Edmund Hüsserl in the later phase of his work.

6. Cf. as one of the latest and best argued defenses of this position, B. Montagnes, O. P.: *La Doctrine de l'Analogie de l'Être D'Après Saint Thomas D'Aquin,* (Louvain: Publications Universitaires and Paris: Béatrice - Nauwelaerts, 1963). Somewhat similar is the position adopted by L. B. Geiger, O.P.: *La Participation dans la Philosophie de S. Thomas d'Aquin* (Paris: J. Vrin, 1953). Both of the above authors oppose thinking of essence as pure potency in an order to existence as the sole source of actuality; following Ferrariensis *(Comm. in Contra Gentes* I, 25, no. VI-XII) they look upon "ens" as being grammatically a noun rather than a participle as Cajetan in his *Commentary* on the *De Ente et Essentia* is inclined to view it.

7. Cf. the review of Montagnes' book by J. H. Nicolas, O.P. entitled "L'Analogie de l'être d'après S. Thomas" in *Revue Thomiste,* 1963, 63, pp. 425-431. Nicolas takes exception to the suggestion that there can be two such Thomistic metaphysics.

8. B. Montagnes, *Op. cit.,* p. 160, note 3: "Nous proposons d'appeler induction de l'être la démarche nécessaire pour fonder le jugement négatif de séparation, afin de la bien distinguer de l'intuition." L.-B. Geiger develops a somewhat similar doctrine on "separation", Cf. "Abstraction et Separation d'après S. Thomas," *Revue Des Sciences Phil. et Theol.,* 31, 1947, pp. 3-40.

9. *In De Trinitate,* c. 5., a. 3: "Sciendum igitur, secundum Philos-

ophum 3 *De Anima,* quod duplex est operatio intellectus. Una quae dicitur intelligentia indivisibilium, qua cognoscitur de unaquaque re quid est. Alio vero est qua componit et dividit, scilicet enuntiationem negativam vel affirmativam formando: et haec quidem duae operationes duobus quae sunt in rebus respondent. Prima quidem operatio respicit ipsam naturam rei. . . . Secunda operatio respicit ipsam esse rei. . . . patet quod secundum hanc secundam operationem intellectus abstrahere non potest vere quod secundum rem coniunctum est, quia in abstrahendo significatur esse separatio secundum ipsum esse rei . . ." (transl. as *The Trinity* by Sr. Rose E. Brennan S.H.N., St. Louis and London: B. Herder, 1946, pp. 150-151.)

10. Cajetan's teaching is developed in his *In De Ente et Essentia,* prooem.; an application of the doctrine worked out there can be found in his *Commentary* on the *Summa Theologie,* Ia Pars, q. 1, a. 3. For John of St. Thomas, see *Cursus Phil.,* I, *Ars Logica,* II, q. 27, a. 1.

11. Among the other places where St. Thomas adverts to the mind's attainment of being are: *In Metaphy.,* prooem.; In I *Post. Analytica,* 41, nn. 361-371; *De Sensu et Sensato,* c. 1, a. 1.; more important than any of these however, because it is subsequent in time to the composition of the *De Trinitate,* is the text from the *Summa Theol.,* I, q. 85, a. 1, ad 1am and ad 2am. In the ad 2am he writes: "Quaedam vero sunt quae possunt abstrahi etiam a materia intelligibili communi, sicut ens, unum, potentia et actus, et alia huiusmodi, quae etiam esse possunt absque omni materia, ut patet in substantiis immaterialibus." Cf. on this point, Edward D. Simmons: "The Thomistic Doctrine of the Three Degrees of Formal Abstraction", *The Thomist,* Jan., 1959, pp. 37-67. For one of the better attempts to establish the contrary, see L. B. Geiger O.P.: "Abstraction et Séparation d'après S. Thomas", *Revue des Sciences Phil. et Theol.,* XXXI, 1947, pp. 3-40.

12. The causal dependences here are of the efficient order but at the same time involve exemplarity, explaining not only the having of "esse" but also the formal hierarchy of perfections attributable to essence. Both Geiger and Montagnes see in St. Thomas' thought not only an Aristotelian influence but another that derives from Platonic participationism.

13. Cf. L.-B. Geiger: *Loc. cit.,* p. 22.

14. St. Thomas: *De Trinitate,* q. 5, a. 3. It needs to be noted here that the achievement of the judgment is also "conceived" within the intellect and brought forth as itself a kind of concept. But this is not the real existence encountered outside the mind; it is *esse ut concepta,* not *esse ut exercita.* The concept in simple apprehension, on the other hand, expresses only simple intelligibility and leaves aside the deeper question of existence.

15. J. Maritain: *Existence and the Existent,* p. 28.

16. St. Thomas clearly indicates that the role of essence within the structure of real being is one of positive, perfective determination, e.g. *De Ente et Essentia,* c. 1: "essentia dicitur secundum quod per eam et in ea ens habet esse" (p. 28 in transl. by A. Maurer, Toronto, 1949); at the same time, he elsewhere supplies a nuance that indicates that existence is the sole source of all actuality, e.g. *Summa Theol.,* I, q. 4, a. 1, ad. 3[um]: "Ipsum esse est perfectissimum omnium; comparatur autem ad omnia ut actus . . . est actualitas omnium rerum et etiam ipsarum formarum. Unde non comparatur ad alia sicut recipiens ad receptum, sed magis sicut receptum ad recipiens. Cum enim disco esse hominis vel equi, vel cuiuscumque alterius, ipsum esse consideratur ut formale et receptum, non autem ut illud cui competit esse." See also *Ibid.,* q. 7, a. 1: "esse est formalissimum omnium," and *De Pot,* q. 7, ad 2, ad 9[um] where *esse* is the "actualitas omnium actuum, et propter hoc perfectio omnium perfectionum."

17. Cajetan clearly understands St. Thomas' explicit teaching that the knower is made aware of the extra-mental reality *directly,* even if by way of the concept, so that the concept itself (i.e. the formal concept) is only known secondarily and reflexively. What is meant here is that the objective concept (i.e. the extra-mental reality as conceived) is taken for the integral existent, its "esse" being neglected.

18. Joannis Duns Scotus: *Opera Omnia* (Studio et Cura Commissionis Scotisticae, Civitas Vaticana, 1954), Lib. I, Dist. III, Pars Prima, *De Cognoscibilitate Dei,* Quest. 1-4, pp. 3-123; cf. E. Gilson: *Jean Duns Scotus* (Paris: 1952); Cyril L. Shircel: *The Univocity of the Concept of Being in the Philosophy of John Duns Scotus,* Doctorate Dissertation, Catholic University of America, Washington, D.C. 1942.

19. Since it is a question of proportionality here, the oneness of the concept is such only proportionately; the abstractness here is unique in kind and embraces *actually* all of the differences so that there is an underlying multiplicity of concepts. The conceptual unity in analogy of proportionality is not, for Cajetan, like that in analogy of attribution where the concept is really univocal but when predicated analogically expresses distinct proportions to one "ratio".

20. Here Cajetan is basing himself on St Thomas' clear teaching; *Summa Theol.,* I, q. 13, a. 3: "Quantum igitur ad id quod significant huiusmodi nomina, proprie competunt Deo . . . . Quantum vero ad modum significandi, non proprie dicuntur de Deo . . . ."

21. Here there should be noted a major divergence from those theories inspired by Joseph Maréchal; the dynamism which Schillebeeckx envisions is objective in kind and strictly cognitive, unlike Maréchal's which is subjective and ultimately arising from non-cognitive resources within the human spirit. For a fuller treatment of Schillebeeckx's epistemology and by contrast that of Maréchal, Rahner, and Lonergan, see Chapter IV.

252

22. *Op. cit.*, pp. 255-256.

23. This, of course (as was noted above in the exception taken to the explanations by Lonergan and Rahner), is a common objection to all the theories that emphasize, under the influence of Phenomenology, the transcendental subjectivity of man. A corrective to this, at least in some degree, is being attempted by those newer philosophies which have assumed the common name of Structuralism, represented for example by the work of Claude Levi-Strauss.

24. *Op. cit.*, p. 249.

25. Cf. *Summa Theol.*, I, q. 13, a. 12: "Intellectus noster secundum diversas *conceptiones* ipsum cognoscat Deum ex creaturis, format ad intelligendum Deum conceptiones proportionatas perfectionibus procedentibus a Deo in creaturas." Underlying this entire treatise on the Divine Names is St. Thomas' clear teaching that names, as linguistic symbols for the "rationes" conceived by the mind from creatures, designate God (in some cases) absolutely and affirmatively; see especially art. 2.

26. M. V. Leroy: "Le Savoir Spéculatif", *Revue Thomiste*, 48, 1948, p. 286.

27. Cf. Cajetan *In De Ente et Essentia*, q. 1: "Conceptus entis est forma generalissima ipsius intellectus, sicut forma corporeitas est forma generalissima ipsius materiae ... Est enim conceptus entis quasi naturalis ipsi intellectui, sicut et cognitio primi principii"; (p. 51 in Kendzierski and Wade transl.).

28. *Summa Theol.*, I, q. 4, a. 3: "Omne agens agit sibi simile inquantum est agens, agit autem unumquodque secundum suam formam, necesse est quod in effectu sit similitude formae agentis"; this text goes on to establish that the "form" of God is "esse", and that the similitude between God and creature while formal is only such analogically. *Ibid.*, q. 13, a. 2: Here St. Thomas observes that goodness convenes to God not "... inquantum causat bonitatem; sed potius e converso, quia est bonus, bonitatem rebus diffundit", i.e. to apply the idea of goodness to God is not merely to say that He can cause it but rather that He is good, formally and intrinsically.

29. *Q. D., De Pot.*, q. 7, a. 5, ad 2$^{um}$; *Summa Theol.*, I, q. 13, a. 3: "Quantum igitur ad id quod significant huiusmodi nomina, proprie competunt Deo, et magis proprie quam ipsis creaturis, et per prius dicuntur de Deo. Quantum vero ad modum significandi, non proprie dicuntur de Deo: habent enim modum significandi qui creaturis competit." Here as well as in *C. Gentes*, I, 30 and *I Sent.*, d. 22, q. 1, a. 2: St. Thomas makes abundantly clear the necessity of this distinction. Schillebeeckx would appear to *not* allow this distinction; for him to project the *ratio significata* onto God is to enclose the Divine within the creaturely *modus significandi*.

30. Cajetan in his *Commentary* on the *De Ente et Essentia* relied

primarily on St. Thomas' development of analogy in the early questions of the *De Veritate* where the latter does expressly write of "proportionality", and this textual influence remained dominant in Cajetan's original work, the *De Nominum Analogia.*

31. H. A. Wolfson: "The Amphibolous Terms in Aristotle, Arabic Philosophy and Maimonides", *Harvard Theological Review*, 31 (1938), pp. 151-173.

32. Cf. *Topics*, I. 15, 106 a 9; II, 3, 110 b 16. Similar references can be found in the *Metaphysics*, IV, 2, 1003 a 33; VII, 4, 1030 a 34.

33. Cf. *De Malo*, q. 7, a. 1, ad 1um; *Summa Theol.*, I, q. 5, a. 6, ad 3um; I-II, q. 88, a. 8, ad 1um; II-II, q. 120, a. 2.

34. An invaluable and nearly exhaustive collection of St. Thomas' texts referring to analogy can be found in two appendices to *St. Thomas Aquinas on Analogy* by G. P. Klubertanz, S.J. (Chicago: Loyola University Press, 1960). The first cites the texts numbering 436 all told, and in order following the chronology of I. Eschmann, O.P.; the second is an analytical index to the texts.

35. St. Thomas reacts strongly against this temptation in *Summa Theol.*, I, q. 3, a. 5.

36. *Summa Theol.* I, q. 13, a. 5: "Dicendum est igitur quod huiusmodi nomina dicuntur de Deo et creaturis secundum analogian, idest proportionem. Quod quidem dupliciter contingit in nominibus: vel quia multa habent proportionem ad unum . . . . vel ex eo quod unum habet proportionem ad alterum . . ."; I *C. Gentes*, 34: "Quod quidem dupliciter contingit. Uno modo, secundum quod multa habent respectum ad aliquid unum . . . . Alio modo, secundum quod duorum attenditur ordo vel respectus, non ad aliquid alterum, sed ad unum ipsorum . . ."; *De Potentia*, q. 7, a. 7: "Huius autem praedicatur de duobus per respectum ad aliquod tertium . . . Alius modus est quo aliquid praedicatur de duobus per respectum unius ad alterum . . . ."

37. One very clear example: *Summa Theol.*, I, q. 13, a 5. What he is refusing to allow, in rejecting the first type of analogy, is any proportion between God and creature in virtue of their respective proportions to some third common factor, most obviously to a common concept of being somehow including both.

38. Cajetan does seem to keep this distinction clearly in mind in his *De Nominum Analogia.* Somewhat surprisingly Ralph McInerny (*The Logic of Analogy*, The Hague; M. Nijhoff, 1961) accuses him of being too metaphysical while Bernard Montagnes, O.P. (*La Doctrine de l'Analogie de l'être d'aprés S. Thomas d'Aquin,* Louvain: Publications Universitaires, Paris: Beatrice-Nauwelaerts, 1963) considers his failing to have been the restriction of his doctrine to the logical order. In a sense both are right. Cajetan's divisions are logical and formal, scil. attribution as solely extrinsic predication and proportionality as intrinsic predication; and are

more considerations of the concept of being. However, he thought of his notional divisions as exactly reflective of the real order and so moves easily from one to the other.

39. It is not without significance that one of St. Thomas' more mature and developed treatments of transcendental analogy is not worked out within the immediate context of God's *being* and relationship to the world (*Summa Theol.*, I. qq. 2-11, and 14-26), nor that of our *knowledge* of him (*Ibid.*, q. 12), but within the distinct problematic of how we go about *naming* God (*Ibid.*, q. 13). Cf. I *C. Gentes*, 33, where analogy is termed a matter of community of name founded upon causality (i.e. participation).

40. The most explicit option for this view of analogy is to be found in Ralph McInerny, *Op. cit.*, where it is argued for in convincing fashion. He suggests that St. Thomas has no formal treatise on analogy for the simple reason that he never did a commentary on Aristotle's *Topics*. Much earlier this doctrine on analogy was developed in a qualified way by Mannes Matthijs, O.P. in *dispensae* (class notes) for his courses on analogy at the *Angelicum* in Rome, especially in an insistence upon the improper abstractive process involved in arriving at the analogical concept. Schillebeeckx, *Op. cit.*, II, p. 181 writes: "Aquinas too regarded *analogia* in the first place as an objective or ontological relationship. . . . In addition, however, he also called the unity of predication, on the basis of this objective *analogia,* an *analogical predication. . . .*" Other studies, without explicitly identifying analogy as a being of logic, make out a strong case for considering it as attribution rather than proportionality, following in this the understanding of Ferrariensis in his *Commentary* on the I *C. Gentes*; cf. Klubertanz, *Op. cit.*, also F. A. Blanche: "Une théorie de l'analogie", *Rev. de Phil.*, 32 (1932). A major but overlooked study taking exception to Cajetan's view but cautioning against an understanding of attribution in a Suarezian sense is S. Ramírez O.P.: "En torno a un famoso texto de Santo Tomás sobre la analogía", *Sapientia* (Buenos Aires), 8, (1953), pp. 166-192.

41. The very first situation, of course, is one of real being in its participationist or analogical structure, but only potentially known as such. Next is the abstractive intuition of being; being is actually known but only implicitly as analogical. This is followed by a gradually expanding knowledge of beings in their intrinsic relatedness, i.e. by analogical knowledge and its reflection in analogy of names. This ever-deepening process of understanding finally culminates in the explicit grasp of being as itself analogical, i.e. as really characterized by its unity of order, its real rapport to First Being.

42. I *C.* Gentes, 34; *Summa Theol.*, I, q. 13, a. 5; *In Lib. Periher-meneias*, I, 8, no. 20; *Summa Theol.*, II-II, q. 120, a. 2.

43. *Q.D., De Veritate*, q. 2, a 11, ad 6um: "Dicendum quod ratio illa

procedit de communitate analogiae quae accipitur secundum determinatam habitudinem unius ad alterum...."

44. Other instances of this division of analogy: *Q.D. De Pot.*, q. 7, a. 7; *I C. Gentes*, 34.

45. Founding such a transfer of a name is a relatedness that may be causal (in which case it can mean either giving the name of the cause to the effect in a diminished way or the name of the effect to the cause in an eminent way) or solely a similitude or formal convenience either real or (as in metaphor) imagined. In all cases, one thing is known in virtue of its partial likeness to another and because of this is denominated from that other.

46. *I Sent.*, d. 19, q. 5, a. 2, ad 1^um.

47. Schillebeeckx, *Op. cit.*, II, has worked out in detail how these two groups of texts offering different divisions of analogy can be subordinated one to the other, in the manner suggested above; cf. pp. 202-203.

48. Actuality, whether as form or as existence, bespeaks only perfection and thus cannot be understood as limiting itself. Limitation must then originate in a principle really distinct from act and yet commensurate to it. This limiting principle cannot, of course, be "extrinsic" to being; thus it answers to St. Thomas' understanding of Aristotelian potency. It has been suggested that potency for Aristotle is solely a principle of change and nowise of limitation; cf. W. Norris Clarke, S.J.: "The Limitation of Act by Potency", *New Scholasticism* XXVI, April, 1952. This is no denial of a richer use of the concept by St. Thomas, of course; apart from that, while it does reflect what Aristotle says in Book V, Chapter 12 of the *Metaphysics*, a somewhat less narrow interpretation is suggested by what he says a bit later on in Book IX, Chapter 1: "For potency and actuality extend beyond the cases that involve a reference to motion." (1046 a 1; W. D. Ross transl.)

49. *Summa Theol.*, I, q. 4, a. 2: "Omnium autem perfectiones pertinent ad perfectionem essendi: secundum hoc enim aliqua perfecta sunt, quod aliquo modo esse habent."; *Ibid.*, a. 1, ad 3: "... ipsum esse consideratur ut formale et receptum, non autem ut illud cui competit esse." *Ibid.*, q. 7, a. 1: "Illud autem quod est maxime formale omnium, est ipsum esse...."; *De Pot.*, q. 7, a. 2, ad 9: "... *esse* est inter omnia perfectissimum: quod ex hoc patet quia actus est semper perfectio potentia. Quaelibet autem forma signata non intelligitur in actu nisi per hoc quod esse ponitur ... *esse* est actualitas omnium actuum, et propter hoc est perfectio omnium perfectionum ... Unde non sic determinatur *esse* per aliud sicut potentia per actum, sed magis sicut actus per potentiam." (italics supplied).

50. For an explanation as to *how* this occurs see the section immediately following on analogical knowledge.

51. Participation is formally distinct from causality which is a prerequisite to the former however — efficient causality in a remote way;

exemplarity in a more proximate sense. Cf. *Summa Theol.*, I, q. 44, a. 1: "Si enim aliquid invenitur in aliquo per participationem, necesse est quod causetur in ipso ab eo cui essentialiter convenit . . .;" *Ibid.*, ad 1: ". . . ex hoc quod aliquid per participationem est ens, sequitur quod sit causatum ab eo." The most detailed study to date of this relationship is to be found in C. Fabro: *Participation et Causalité selon S. Thomas d'Aquin.* St. Thomas clearly indicates the metaphysical inter-changeability of participation with the potency-act composition (some modern authors give logical priority to participation; others insist the real distinction logically grounds the participationist structure); *Quaest. Quodlib.*, III, q. 8, a. 20: "Omne autem participans se habet ad participatum sicut potentia ad actum . . ."; *Summa Theol.*, I, q. 75, a. 5, ad 4: ". . . Omne participatum comparatur ad participans ut actus eius . . ."; *Comm. in Lib. Physicorum*: VIII, 10, lectio XXI, no. 13: "Omne autem participans componitur ex participante et participato, et participans est in potentia ad participatum."; II *C. Gentes*, 53: "Omne participans aliquid comparatur ad ipsum quod participatur ut potentia ad actum: per id enim quod participatur fit participans actu tale."

52. Not all would agree that participation is the irreducible ontological category. Cf. on this L.-B. Geiger's study *La Participation dans la Philosophie de St. Thomas d'Aquin* where he contrasts two systems of participation, one by imitation, the other by composition and limitation; and the objections to his conclusions favoring the first of these by C. Fabro (*Op. cit.*, note 51). What is at issue here is the question as to whether the potency-act structure of finite being is prior to and explanatory of its participationist character, or vice versa. It is helpful to remember, at any rate, that to participate is to share *in a partial way (partem capere)*, and thus does not signify pure imitation. The causality of God as pure actuality is, of course, primary but this means not mere efficiency but exemplarity as well. Seemingly then, the possibility of things imitating God's perfections enjoys a logical priority over the necessity that such imitation be limited and thus involve composition (ultimately the real distinction) as the causal explanation of the deficiency of the resemblance. Perhaps this is only to acknowledge that in an absolute and ultimate sense act has priority over potency.

53. At the opposite extreme to merely *virtual* participation, which posits something intrinsic in the effect derived from the cause but not convening formally with it, is *formal* participation that is *univocal* in kind. This, however, is participation in the intentional order, consequent upon a mental abstraction, and its ontological counterpart would be the many unique realizations existentially of a common categorical perfection. As real, then, this latter instance of participation is analogical, though as Cajetan notes, it is termed analogical in a somewhat abusive sense; St. Thomas labels it analogy *secundum esse tantum* (*I Sent.*, d. 19, q. 5,

a. 2, ad 1). All of this serves to show the irreducibility of participation as an ontological scheme.

54. *Summa Theol.*, I, q. 4, a 3.

55. *Rom.* 1:20, Vulgate transl.; St. Thomas writes: "... cognoscimus Deum in via, per similitudinem eius in creaturis resultantem, secundum illud *Rom.* 1:20: 'Invisibilia Dei ea quae facta sunt intellecta conspiciuntur'."

56. There is of course but one God; the God of the philosophers is the God of Abraham, Isaac, and Jacob. The identity here is a material one, that is, there remains a formal distinction between the cognitive object of the act of reason and the act of faith. "Eaedem res, sub diversis rationibus cognoscendi acceptae, diversitatem cognoscibilium inducunt"; Cajetan: *Comment.* in I^am, q. 1, a. 1, no. xix.

57. Reason can never know the essence of God but only his existence and certain of his essential attributes. Faith does attain even to the former; it knows what is the very quiddity of God, but obviously in a nonquidditative way.

58. Both, however, are instances of analogical knowing, i.e. of knowing what is otherwise unknown from its rapport to what is known — an extrinsic purely causal relation in one case, a negative relation in the other. For St. Thomas these constitute the "via causalitatis" and the "via negationis".

59. *Summa Theol.*, I, q. 13, A. 2. "... Huiusmodi quidem nomina significant substantiam divinam, et praedicantur de Deo substantialiter, sed deficiunt a repraesentatione ipsius".

60. *Revelation and Theology*, II, p. 18 and p. 177.

61. For one of the better known instances of this, cf. T.-L. Penido: *Le rôle de l'analogie en théologie dogmatique*, cited in Chap. 4.

62. Here, too, analogy is a matter of attribution, of proportion to another rather than what Cajetan calls proportionality. However what is being said of the secondary analogue, i.e. of that which is designated in a metaphorical way, is intrinsic to it and not merely a causal relationship. Also it is characteristic of that subject improperly, i.e. only in its appearances or its operations so that the analogy can be expressed *in the form of* an analogy of proportionality. But it is still an instance of attributing the appearances of one thing to another, of denominating one from the other as the prime analogue.

63. St. Thomas also employs the term "proportionality" in his attempt to explain metaphor; cf. *Summa Theol.* I, q. 3, a. 1, ad 33; *I Sent.*, d. 45, q. 1, a. 4. In the *Supplement of the Summa*, q. 69, a. 1, ad 2, (taken from *I Sent*, d. 34, q. 3, a. 1, ad 2) metaphor is called "similitude of proportionality" in contrast to "similitude of analogy."

64. The characteristic note of these metaphysical properties of being is that the objective concept, while it includes all the limited ways in

which the perfection can be actualized, does so *indeterminately* so that the idea does not necessarily include reference to any given limitation and thus admits of a further analogous transformation when the mind distinguishes between the perfection signified and the mode of signifying; cf. *Summa Theol.*, I, q. 13, a. 3.

65.  *Summa Theol.* I, q. 13, a. 3: "In nominibus igitur quae Deo attribuimus, est duo considerare: scilicet, perfectiones ipsas significatas, ut bonitatem, et huiusmodi; et modum significandi."

66.  Q.D., *De Pot.*, q. 7; wisdom e.g. is generically an accident like other human virtues and is also unique as its own kind of quality; in attributing such names to God the generic element is eliminated and the specific ratio no longer tied to the generic has actually been expanded into a common idea that can be used to designate a perfection of God. This is the analogical concept — not that it includes *representationally* the divine "difference" but that it can be used to designate the latter. "Sapientia et justitia . . . . veniunt in divinam praedicationem secundum rationem differentiae et non secundum rationem generis"; *Ibid.*, ad 2.

67.  If the common and proper meanings of the term are not distinguished then its application to anything other than what it primarily signifies can only be an instance of metaphorical speech, as in the transferral of the phrase "to see" to the order of intellective activity. The proper notion by itself signifies first of all the one reality of which it is primarily said (the prime analogue), and secondarily other realities in their order of approximation to this first meaning (secondary analogues). In the latter case, the attribution to other realities is an expanding of the proper meaning into the analogical idea. By way of illustration, the proper meaning of "to see" would appear to be one kind of direct perception, signifying initially the operation of the eye, but expanding to where it can equally mean the mind's seizure of a principle, because of an intrinsic similitude that is a proportion between the activity of the eye and that of the intellect. St. Thomas does not appear to deny analogy of proportionality entirely, but only between God and the world.

68.  *Degrees of Knowledge*, p. 478.

69.  The original concept is grasped in an improper abstractive process (improper, because it cannot positively prescind from all its differences, otherwise the resulting idea would be univocal not analogical) involving judgments that amount to a spontaneous reasoning process. Thus from the very beginning the idea is of the real; its imperfection and contingency as really existing demands postulating the perfection in a pure state, this is in effect to discern in spontaneous intellectual insight the underlying participationist structure to reality, and so the existence of what is participated. At this point: (1) the analogical concept which includes indifferently all finite modes of actualization is denuded of all of them; (2) what remains leaves the divine mode (or complete lack thereof) unex-

pressed, because not humanly knowable; and (3) then is projected in a dynamic of judgment onto God — not that God *is* what the idea represents but that his hidden being lies in the direction afforded by that idea.

70. No created concept, that is; the sole perfect concept of God is an uncreated one, the eternal *Logos* of the Father; cf. *I Sent.* d. 2, q. 1, a. 3.

# NOTES TO CHAPTER FIVE

1. Langdon Gilkey: *Naming the Whirlwind, The Renewal of God-Language* (Indianapolis: Bobbs-Merrill, 1969). Gilkey's basic assumption is that contemporary man's actual secular existence "is saturated with religious elements, impoverished, because they are inarticulated and so unexamined", p. 411; the symbols of so-called "secular" man then in fact neglect significant areas of actual existence.

2. Mircea Eliade: *Patterns in Comparative Religion* (New York: Meridian Books, 1963), p. 429 f.

3. If it be a question of acknowledging God's identity precisely as God, this is absolutely unobtainable from any efforts that are exclusively man's. To affirm the God of the philosophers, as e.g., Absolute Being, remains possible, but historically and factually problematic apart from religious presuppositions.

4. All revelation is personal in the sense of being ultimately a disclosure of the self as subject; thus Divine Revelation is in fine encounter with the very personhood of God. This bespeaks a certain resistance to objectification since the other is disclosed as subject, as meta-conceptual. But this has to be mediated objectively; I encounter my friend in hearing *what* he says, in seeing *what* he does, etc. There is no speech without a word mediating between speaker and listener. Personal awareness is thus conceptual not in the sense that the person as such is grasped within a concept, but that concepts provide an objective focus within which I can encounter his very personhood.

5. Thus when metaphysics utters the name of "God", the practitioner has, in fact and existentially, exceeded the limits of his science, a condition that is spontaneous and normal. St. Thomas' natural theology was entirely developed within the theological perspective of a believer (indeed much of the misinterpretation of the *Prima Pars* is made inevitable by the tendency to read it as formally philosophy). What is absolutely necessary is that the intelligible grasp of a concept, proposition or argument retain its own autonomy within its own proper sphere; i.e., that the "use" of metaphysics by theology not violate the intrinsic

demands and limitations of reason within its own proper ambit.

6. The sole possibility of a knowledge of God as he is in himself is that of the Beatific Vision which as vision or intellectual intuition is not conceptual knowledge at all. Such a vision, whose very possibility is known only by faith, is reserved for the life that is to come — "No man has at any time seen God" (St. John 1:18); it is achieved only by way of God's supernatural elevation of the intellect in the infusion of the consummating gift of grace that is the *lumen gloriae,* enabling the finite intelligence to receive the very essence of God in *ratione speciei;* and even here the intellect of the blessed is enabled to intuit God only in a partial, non-exhaustive way; it is the Infinite God that is "seen" and immediately but in a finite way; the intuition is still intentional, i.e., tending towards the inexhaustible intelligibilities of its object.

7. This is the point of a study by J. B. Metz: "A Believer's Look at the World" in *The Christian in the World,* compiled at the Canisianum, Innsbruck (New York: P. J. Kenedy, 1965).

8. *Proslogion,* VIII, transl. by S. N. Deane (LaSalle, Ill.: Open Court Publishing Co., 1903), p. 13.

9. *Christ the Center,* transl. by J. Bowden (New York: Harper and Row, 1966), p. 101.

10. *The Future of Belief.* (New York: Herder and Herder. 1966); *The Foundations of Belief* (New York: Herder and Herder).

11. *The Future of Belief.* p. 114: "Consequently, the Christian faith is never found in the state of a 'pure' religious experience . . . . In reality the Christian experience of faith can be found only as conceptualized and, therefore, under one cultural form or another".

12. *Ibid.* p. 91: " . . . it (man's psychic life) is the mind's self-*differentiation* of its-self out of a reality with which it was originally continuous and united in un-differentiation." (italics are the author's own); cf. also Note on p. 116.

13. *Ibid.,* p. 179, Note.

14. *Ibid.,* p. 114.

15. *Ibid.,* p. 168.

16. *Ibid.,* p. 168, Note.

17. Since faith is a theological virtue its formal object is uncreated — God himself, but still God as known, otherwise one is not talking about an object (objectum) as distinct from an entity (res). God is known however only within the knower and his conception — but since the concept whereby God is known is not a proper concept representing him it cannot be said that God has an intentional existence in the knowing creature as does a finite object of cognition. Thus the formal object of faith is God himself, signified but not represented by an analogical concept. Needless to say the term "concept" here refers not to the formal concept (as a product of the intellect) but to the objective concept,

(i.e., to the reality known as it is intentionally within the knower).

18. Cf. Franz Mussner: "The Paraclete and Apostolic Tradition", *Theology Digest*, Summer, 1964, transl. from *Biblische Zeitschrift*, 1961.

19. Revelation should be conceived of as continuing, as the perduring personal address of God to man in terms of the offer of salvation. This is Revelation in an authentic sense, but obviously there is a prior unique meaning to the word limiting it to the definitive manifestation of God in the Incarnation and Redemption. God is not to do more than he did then, and in this sense Revelation has been consummated or is closed. It continues in the sustained offer now to men of every generation and world-situation of what God unveiled then in the events of salvation-history.

20. For example, H. Bouillard: *Conversion et Grâce chez Saint Thomas d'Aquin* (Paris: 1944).

21. *L'Evolution homogène du Dogme catholique*, 2 vols. (Fribourg: Libraire de l'oeuvre de Saint Paul, 1924), transl. from the Spanish.

22. This is how St. Thomas appears to understand dogmatic development i.e., as a quantitative increase in the "articles of faith"; cf. *Summa Theol.*, II-II, q. 1, a. 7. The word "article" here derives from the verb "articulate" signifying the dismembering of a complex organism at its joints.

23. "Exegesis, Dogmatics and the Development of Dogma" in *Dogmatic vs. Biblical Theology*, edited by H. Vorgrimler (Baltimore-Dublin: Helicon, 1964); also to be found in the collection *Revelation and Theology*, Vol. I, (N.Y.: Sheed and Ward, 1967) pp. 167-195.


# NOTES TO CHAPTER SIX


1. In *Jesus Christ and Mythology* (N. Y.: Scribners, 1958) p. 53, Bultmann writes "The question of God and the question of myself are identical." It is important to note that Bultmann distinguishes (in a way Barth will not allow) between the pure experience of faith and theological reflection upon the latter. In the second case our language does apparently have some objectivity, not however the misleading objectivity of myth nor that of metaphysics, but an objectivity residing in a language of analogy, the analogy being only that of personal encounter. It does not allow us to speak of God as obscurely hinted at by nature or as manifesting himself in Revelatory events of history and prophetic utterance.

2. After writing "The statement that God is Being-itself is a non-symbolic statement" in *Systematic Theol.*, Vol. I (London: Nisbet,

1953), p. 264, Tillich goes on to say in Vol. II, p. 10 that the sole non-symbolic statement is "the statement that everything we say about God is symbolic." The ambiguity is further compounded by his recourse to the expression "Ground of Being" which he explicitly calls a metaphor (*Ultimate Concern* - N.Y.: 1965, p. 46); in this same passage he writes "If I were able to go back to the scholastic term *esse ipsum*, I would prefer that." Elsewhere, for example in *The Courage to Be*, God is not presented as answering to Subsistent Being.

3. *God-Talk* (N.Y. and Evanston: Harper & Row, 1967), p. 51.

4. *Op. cit.*, p. 175: "What the religious experience of God discloses is a reality *beyond* being . . . We do *experience* God, but . . . we do not experience him as *being.*" (Italics are the author's own.)

5. *Ibid.*, p. 176; Dewart surprisingly does not suggest any limitations to this category of "presence," and in one place (p. 180) writes of a term of this type as "not intrinsically inadequate" for speaking of God. God's presence is simply disclosed to us, experientially, in the empirical intuition of objects. It is the experience of an inevident reality and thus amounts to belief, but one which is "neither supra-rational nor infra-rational nor infra-empirical" (p. 179, note).

6. *Ibid.*, p. 180: "To attribute existence to God is the most extreme form of anthropomorphism."

7. *Ibid.*, p. 158.

8. *The Foundations of Belief*, p. 443.

9. *Ibid.*, p. 178.

10. *Ibid.*, p. 178.

11. This is St. Thomas' rather clear teaching in article 3: "Is God to be identified with his own essence or nature?" and article 4: "Can one distinguish in God nature and existence?" cf. *Summa Theol.*, I$^a$, q. 3.

12. *Ibid.*, p. 158.

13. The real distinction of essence and existence in the creature, grasped in the realization that essence is intelligible apart from actual existence (cf. *De Ente et Essentia*, IV; p. 46 in Maurer transl.) culminates in both spontaneous and reflexive thinking in the perception of the contingency of creatures. Yet these are intuited as *really* existing, though in a way that is not self-explanatory, which is to establish for understanding the *real* existence of their Source whatever that be. The existence of a First Cause (and this means only in the precise formal line of its very causation) is not a concealed premise but a conclusion in the *Quinque Viae;* the nominal definition of God is not assumed but sought as a term. Dewart's contention is that the *concept* of a God with identity of essence and existence underlies the real distinction in creatures so that "every argument for the existence of God which would appear based on the contingent existence of creatures would surreptitiously introduce that identity into the argument." This is, of course, the ontological

argument. But only in the *ontological* order is the simplicity of God presupposed to the complexity of creatures; in the *gnoseological* order it is the inverse, and here our ideas attain the reality of God but only from within the creaturely.

14. Logically prior to the existential judgment is the mere enunciation in which subject and object are mentally joined and in which the verb "is" functions only as the copula. But this is not the judgment of being in which intellection naturally terminates; this latter is the mind's conformity with the real, a consciously lived conformity however, and not the mind's declaration of conformity after a comparison of idea and thing. Cf. St. Thomas: *Comment. in Metaphysics*, Lib. IV, lectio 4; on the basis of this, Cajetan understands the judgment as "illa cognitio quae sui ipsius conformitatem cum re cognoscit" (*In Ia*, q. 16, a. 2, n. 5).

15. Even God's creative word summoning things into being is not spoken into the Void, for it is not something that pre-exists the entities (though it can be metaphorically spoken of in this way). Also, we can humanly speak of the Void but even here only in terms of being which it negates.

16. In *The Foundations of Belief*, Dewart wishes to explain this givenness as sheer contingency. But the mere non-necessity of things, that they need not be as they in fact are, implies some sort of factual beingness. Dewart himself speaks of "being-found-ness" but means by this that reality is found or given to empirical experience as indeterminate and awaiting man's determination. In effect, this is to obfuscate the distinction between essence and existence and to make quiddity contingent, in exactly the same way as is existence; cf. Chapter 3, esp. pp. 139-195. Dewart's argument here rests upon his contention that the distinction between "is" as a copula and as conveying an existential judgment is due to Arabic translations of Aristotle, notably those of Al-Farabi and Avicenna, and "is not included by Aristotle in the *Metaphysics*" (p. 148). The distinction that Aristotle does make in the *Posterior Analytics* between that a thing is and what it is, is interpreted by Dewart as a distinction "between the objectivity or in-itself-ness of the objects of demonstration, and that which is demonstrated about the objects of demonstration" (p. 147).

17. Finite existence, intelligibly laid hold of in the judgment, is expressed not in a concept of its own but in the concept of being. In a later reflexive act the mind can isolate the formality of existence from that of essence as actuality of the latter, but this is what Cajetan understands as the *notion* of being that the mind forms for itself to signify to itself existence that it grasps (and thereby participates in) rather as *act;* it is *"existentia ut signato"* rather than *"existentia ut exercito;"* cf. Chapter 1, p. 23.

18. Towards the end of article 2 (in *Summa Theol.*, I, q. 2) the word

"praeexistere" does occur, but St. Thomas is there speaking of created causes in relation to their effects.

19. *Summa Theol.*, I, q. 3, a. 4, ad 2ᵘᵐ: " . . . esse dupliciter dicitur: uno modo significat actum essendi, alio modo significat compositionem propositionis quan anima adinvenit conjugens praedicatum subjecto. Primo igitur modo accipiendo esse non possumus scire esse Dei sicut nec eius essentiam, sed solum secundo modo. Scimus enim quod haec propositio quam formamus de Deo cum dicimus Deus est vera est."

20. *Summa Theol.*, I, q. 3, a. 5, ad 1ᵘᵐ where St. Thomas explicitly states that God is not a substance.

21. *Principles of Christian Theology* (N.Y.: Scribners, 1966), p. 99.

22. *Ibid.*, p. 103.

23. *Ibid.*, p. 109.

24. *Ibid.*

25. *Ibid.*, p. 105.

26. In *Summa Theol.*, I, q. 14, a. 6, St. Thomas writes: "Non solum autem id in quo creaturae communicant, scilicet ipsum esse, ad perfectionen pertinet; sed etiam ea per quae creaturae ad invicem distinguuntur. . . . Et omnis forma, per quam quaelibet res in propria specie constituitur, perfectio quaedam est." The reference here, of course, is to specific determination, but the principle holds true as well regarding individuality, since the species as such (even in the angelic order) cannot exist. Rahner, in the somewhat distinct framework of his own philosophy, has underscored with clarity the positive perfection of the individual as far more than a mere repetition of the universal; Cf. "On the Question of a Formal Existential Ethics," *Theological Investigations,* II, p. 226.

27. *Comment. in 1 ᵐ*, q. 39, a. 1, no. VII: "Ad evidentiam horum, scito quod, sicut in Deo, secundum rem sive in ordine reali, est una res non pure absoluta nec pure respectiva, nec mixta aut composita aut resultans ex utraque; sed eminentissime et formaliter habens quod est respectivi (imo multarum rerum respectivarum) et quod est absoluti: ita in ordine formali seu rationum formalium, secundum se, non quoad nos loquendo, est in Deo unica ratio formalis, non pure absoluta nec pure respectiva, non pure communicabilis nec pure incommunicabilis; sed eminentissime ac formaliter continens et quidquid absolutae perfectionis est, et quidquid trinitas respectiva exigit."

28. Merleau-Ponty himself repeatedly disavowed both theism and atheism. In what follows he is repudiating the two schools of thought against which he stood irrevocably, what he called somewhat narrowly empiricism and intellectualism.

29. *Le visible et l'invisible* (Paris: Gallimard, 1964), p. 247.

30. "The Problem of God in the Philosophy of Merleau-Ponty," *International Philosophical Quarterly,* March 1967, p. 59.

31. Originally Merleau-Ponty thought of meaning as arising somewhat mysteriously out of the meeting between man, the co-constitutor of the world, and the preworld (pré-monde), but in the latter phase of his thinking there is an inexhaustible plenitude of meaning that does not arise with consciousness but is "given" to man as he "inhabits Being."

32. *Le visible et l'invisible,* p. 280.

33. *Ibid.,* p. 275.

34. Vandenbussche, in the article cited, in his sympathy for Merleau-Ponty's project, writes: "We should not look for God in the line of a spurious infinity," p. 59.

35. *Ibid.,* p. 55.

36. *Summa Theol.,* I, q. 8, a. 1. Cajetan expands upon this explaining that it means God is the *Causa per se primo entis ut sic,* i.e., a *per se* cause in the first of Aristotle's four modes of saying *per se.* This does not mean only that God is the exclusive cause of being but that it belongs to him to create somewhat as, analogously, a property belongs to an essence. St. Thomas' own phrase here is that "created being is a proper effect of God much as to burn is a proper effect of fire."

37. Necessary, of course, solely on the assumption that God freely chose to call a world into existence in the first place.

38. If it be objected at this point that there is no real dependence in God on the side of nature as well (e.g. immutability explains eternity, it does not cause it), it can be pointed out the reason here is the real identity of the attributes. The significance in the case of the Trinity is that there is no dependence among really distinct Persons. Personalist categories then may well open the way to transcending questions of causal dependence. Man remains totally dependent upon God because he is not an autonomous person but a personified nature; created personality is neither identical with nor autonomous of its nature.

39. For a fuller treatment of some of the implications of this, cf. Walter E. Stokes, "Is God Really Related to this World?" in *Proceedings* of the American Catholic Philosophical Association (1965), pp. 145-151.

40. There is no question, of course, of such distinctions being real in God; they are entirely the work of human rational discourse. But obviously they cannot be introduced arbitrarily, otherwise the resulting distinctions would be merely verbal or semantic in kind (called by the Scholastics distinctions *"rationis ratiocinantis"* or of reason reasoning). Some justifying foundation has to be sought for this activity of reason in order for it to be a true distinction of formalities (a distinction *"rationis ratiocinatae",* or of reason reasoned), and since God is known from creatures the basis can be either external, i.e., the creaturely perfections which are the point of departure, or internal, i.e., the very eminence of God who as *Ipsum Esse* must precontain all the perfections of being. In the latter case, the distinction is said to be *virtually* in the thing

distinguished. Nearly all the Commentators on St. Thomas adopted the above position, and even strove for more precision by further differentiating virtual distinctions into major and minor according as the formalities excluded or included one another. Concerning the divine attributes, the distinction was understood as a virtual minor distinction of reason.

41. The fact that faith in a revealed mystery illumines an analogy otherwise unavailable — as in the example of the Trinity given above where even if reason could establish the natural and necessary origin of a word within divine intellection it could not even surmise that such a word is distinct and personal within the Godhead — does not alter the basic noetic possibility.

42. See *Spirit in the World*, pp. 400-405.

43. St. Thomas: *C. Gentiles*, I, 30.

44. St. Thomas: *Summa Theol.*, I, q. 32, a. 2.

45. Cf. St. Thomas: *Summa Theol.*, I, q. 2, a. 2, ad 3.

46. Cf. *Summa Theol.*, I, q. 13, a. 5.

47. This is best illustrated in quantitative terms: 2 to 4, as 50 to 100, as 1,000 to 2,000 — where the proportion in each case is double, but nothing is said of the relationships between the three orders of doubleness.

48. In the real or entitative order, analogy is concerned with what is primarily a divine quality and only derivatively a creaturely one, thus the being of a creature is defined in terms of its greater or lesser approximation to (or better, remove from) the Absolute Being of God. In the cognitive order, the direction is inverse; here God is known and named in terms of the created perfections expressed in our ideas.

49. *Revelation and Theology*, Vol. 2, p. 195.

50. Schillebeeckx is indebted for this epistemological theory to Dominic DePetter, O.P.; cf. the latter's "Begrip en werkelijheid aan de overzijde vean het conceptualisme: Impliciete Intuitie," *Tidjschrift voor Philosophie*, 1, 1939, pp. 25-43; for a presentation in French, cf. "L'Intuitif implicite dans l'acte de connaissance," *Actes du Xième Congrès international de philosophie*, Amsterdam, 1948.

51. *I Sent.*, d. 35, q. 1, a. 4, ad 6.

52. Those perfections of the created order that imply a potency-act relationship lack any fundament in God for being predicated distinctly of him and so are excluded here. Such distinctions, as e.g., between intellect and intellection, will and volition, and essence and existence, when they enter our speech about God represent only an extrinsic virtual distinction, one whose foundation is outside of the thing distinguished. Seemingly in this category is to be included the distinction between being and knowing in God, thus the formal constitutive of the divine nature would appear to be Being as Subsisting Knowing.

53. Cf. B. M. Lemaigre, O.P.: "Perfection de Dieu et Multiplicité

des Attributs Divins," *Revue des Sciences Phil. et Theol.*, (50), 1966, pp. 198-225. The chronology noted above is that of I.T. Eschmann, O.P., which can be found as an appendix in E. Gilson: *The Christian Philosophy of St. Thomas Aquinas* (New York: Random House, 1956), pp. 379-439; Lemaigre, however, follows the opinion of Glorieux and Dondaine and places at least Q. 10 of the *De Potentia* between 1262 - 1264 (cf. p. 210), seeing even in this work some influence of Peter of Tarantasia. St. Thomas' response to the request of the Master General of the Order that he examine the work of Peter of Tarantasia is edited as one of his smaller opuscula, usually entitled *Declaratio CVII Dubiorum*.

54. A laudable theological effort to explain how we must balance this conceptual aspect to our knowledge of the divine attributes with an existential faith-awareness of God as he discloses himself in salvation-history can be found in Anthony J. Kelly, C. SS. R.: "To know the Mystery: The Theologian in the Presence of the Revealed God," *The Thomist*, Jan. and April, 1968.

55. *Process and Reality* (New York: Macmillan, 1929), p. 524 f.

56. *Theological Investigations*, Vol. IV, p. 113: "God can become something, he who is unchangeable in himself can *himself* become subject to change *in something else*" (italics are author's own). Rahner develops his position here within the context of the Incarnation; the article was originally given at a symposium in 1961 whose Proceedings were edited by H. Bouesse, O.P. and J. J. Latour under the title *Problèmes Actuels de Christologie* (Desclee de Brouwer, 1965). This latter article was subject to a critical review by Dom Illtyd Trethowan in *Downside Review*, July, 1967.

57. Cf. the article cited earlier in *Downside Review*, July, 1967.

58. The concept is, of course, a negative one but when said of God in the proposition "God is immutable," it is the very Divine Reality itself that is designated so that what is meant is not simply that God lacks the motion and change that characterizes in some fashion all creatures, but that positive prerogative of God by which he necessarily transcends the universe of contingency. What is apt to be forgotten is that "immutability" is only a negative designation of a perfection that lies beyond our positive conceptualizing powers.

59. *Proslogion*, VIII, transl. by S.N. Deane (LaSalle, Illinois: Open Court Publ. Co., 1903), p. 13.

60. *Man and Sin* (U. of Notre Dame, 1965), p. 50, note.

61. *Ibid.*, p. 114, note.

62. This is the clear teaching of St. Thomas, e.g., *Summa Theol.*, I, q. 6, a. 4 (in the explicit context of goodness): "all things are said to be good by the divine goodness as the first exemplar, efficient, and final principle of all goodness — yet each thing is said to be good by a similitude of the divine goodness inherent within itself, which is formally

its own goodness whereby it is denominated;" *I Sent.*, d. 8, q. 1, a. 2, Contra: "Ergo constant quod esse creaturae, quo est formaliter, non est divinum esse." When Rahner speaks of God "positing the other as his reality" (*Ibid.*, p. 114) it is not clear how, within the categories of nature, this can allow *logically* for understanding that God communicates to the creature a distinct existential act; which is in effect to deny that God is a true efficient cause and to do away with the analogy of being.

63. For a critique of De La Taille's teaching, cf. T.U. Mullaney, O.P.: "The Incarnation: De La Taille vs. Thomistic Tradition", *The Thomist*, Jan., 1954; and two articles published as a "Reply" (William F. Macomber, S. J.) and a "Rejoinder" (T. U. Mullaney) in *The Thomist*, April, 1959. For a critique of Rahner's "quasi-formal causality," see W. J. Hill, O.P.: "Uncreated Grace: A Critique of Karl Rahner," *Vatican II, The Theological Dimension*, edited by A.D. Lee (this latter appeared as the entire 1963 volume of *The Thomist*).

64. "The Immutability of God," *Proceedings of the American Catholic Philosophical Association*, Washington, 1967.

65. *Comment. in Iam*, q. 13, a. 7, no. XVIII.

66. *Ibid.*, p. 114.

67. Cf. *God-Talk* and *Principles of Christian Theology*.

68. "Immortality and the Modern Temper," *Harvard Theological Review*, 55, 1962, pp. 1-20.

69. "On the Theology of the Incarnation," *Theological Investigations*, Vol. IV, p. 114.

70. Whitehead's concept of God is usually presented as bipolar, but he frequently speaks of a *superjective* nature in addition to the *primordial* and *consequent* natures: cf. *Process and Reality*, pp. 46-47; 134-135; 521-533. Noteworthy among studies of Whitehead on God are Charles Hartshorne: "Whitehead's Idea of God," *The Philosophy of Alfred North Whitehead*, edited by P.A. Schilpp (New York: Tudor Press, 1951); A.H. Johnson: *Whitehead's Theory of Reality* (Boston: Beacon Press, 1952); also James Collins: *God in Modern Philosophy* (Chicago: Regnery, 1959), pp. 315-324.

71. *God in Modern Philosophy*, p. 321: "Indeed, although there is becoming in His consequent nature, the latter is not temporal but a transmutation of time."

72. *Being and Time*, transl. by MacQuarrie and Robinson (New York: Harper and Brothers, 1962), p. 499, note no. xiii.

73. Schubert Ogden: *The Reality of God* (New York: Harper and Row, 1963), p. 151.

74. *Ibid.*, p. 152.

75. *Summa Theol.*, I, q, 10, a. 2, ad 1um; the text from Boetius' *De Trinitate* is from Chapter 4.

76. Cf, Cajetan's commentary on art. 2, no. VI: " . . . sicut punc-

tum . . . non est causa lineae in esse reali, sed est causa eius in esse cognito, quia facit cognitione illius in nobis; ita *nunc stans* dicitur, causare aeternitatem, non in esse reali, sed in esse cognito, quia causat rationem illius in nobis."

77. *Loc. cit.*, a. 1, ad 5um.

78. *Loc. cit.*, a. 4 and 5; "Sic ergo tempus habet prius et posterius: aevum autem non habet in se prius et posterius, sed ei coniungi possunt: aeternitas autem non habet prius nec posterius, neque ea compatitur." (a. 5, corp.).

79. S. Ogden, *op. cit.*, p. 152.

80. This statement is to be found in Dietrich Bonhoeffer's *Letters and Papers from Prison* (New York: Macmillan, 1967), p. 199; the exact phrase reads: "the transcendent is not the infinitely remote, but the nearest at hand."

81. This is the meaning of the words "tota simul et perfecta" occurring in Boetius' definition of eternity as "interminabilis vitae tota simul et perfecta possessio;" cf. St. Thomas' adoption of this in *Summa Theol.*, I, q. 10, a. 1. Elsewhere, in Ia-IIae, q. 32, a. 2, in observing that motion and its apprehension are a cause of delight, he explains that this is because of an inclination to grasp reality in an integral way; there is some faint experience of the wholeness of things in contemplating with delight the ever changing face of reality.

82. Cf. e.g. Jürgen Moltmann: "The Future as a New Paradigm of Transcendence," *Concurrence*, 4, Fall, 1969.

83. Cf. esp. the Epilogue to *God: The Future of Man*.

84. *Naming the Whirlwind*, p. 339, note 21; p. 346, note 24.

85. Bodiliness here is not an extrinsic and tangible symbol or vehicle used in a subject's contact or communicating with another object or object-subject, something which contains and hides meaning beneath appearances, which functions as instrument of communication; on the contrary, it is the very reality itself as it appears, as its meaning emerges into consciousness. Each body-person thus "participates" through his bodiliness in all other bodies; this is the objective pre-given world for men.

86. See B. Lonergan, "Christ as Subject: A Reply," in *Collection*, ed. F.E. Crowe, S. J. (New York: Herder and Herder, 1967), pp. 164-197; and K. Rahner, "Dogmatic Reflections on the Knowledge and Self-Consciousness of Christ," *Theological Investigations*, V, pp. 193-215.

87. B. Lonergan, *Insight*, p. 320.

88. B. Lonergan, *Collection*, p. 178, N. Leslie Dewart observes that Lonergan has "a sound idea of consciousness with an unnecessary pre-commitment to the classical concept of knowledge," *The Foundations of Belief* (New York: Herder and Herder, 1969), p. 516. This is because Dewart sees the subject-object polarity as the *outcome* of knowledge

whereas for Lonergan it is an ontological precondition (see p. 515).

89. Consult on this point C. Strater: "Le Point du départ du Traité Thomiste sur la Trinité," *Sciences Ecclésiastiques*, 14, 1962, pp. 71-87. The tract in the *Summa* on God (Ia, q. 2 - 43) manifests a growing tendency to identify the *Actus Purus* and *A Seitas* of the Divine Essence precisely as a Trinity of Persons.

90. *Summa Theol.*, III, q. 3, a. 8.

91. This "order" is understood by St. Thomas in terms of Subsistent Being that as Subsistent Knowing irrupts into the Engendered Word whence proceeds in the spontaneity of Immanent Loving the Consubstantial Spirit. The self-same Word proceeds temporally in the Incarnation, and after the Ascension to the side of the Father, sends temporally the Spirit-Paraclete. As "doctrine" all of this, of course, is an explanation of what God reveals of himself. For a study of how St. Thomas' Trinitarian theology is structured as an *ordo doctrinae,* see R. Richard, S.J., *The Problem of an Apologetic Perspective in the Trinitarian Theology of St. Thomas Aquinas,* Rome: Gregorian U. Press, 1963.

92. *Op. cit.,* p. 63.

93. *Principles of Christian Theology* (New York: Charles Scribner's Sons, 1966), pp. 182-185.

94. K. Rahner and H. Vorgrimler, *Theological Dictionary* (New York: Herder & Herder, 1965), transl. by R. Strachan of *Kleines Theologisches Wörterbuch,* ed. C. Ernst, O.P.

95. *The Future of Belief,* pp. 140-141.

96. *Ibid.,* p. 142.

97. "Theos in the New Testament," *Theological Investigations,* I, pp. 125-148; " . . . when the New Testament thinks of God it is the concrete, individual, uninterchangeable Person who comes into its mind, who is in fact the Father and is called ὁ Θεός; so that inversely, when ὁ Θεός is being spoken of, it is not the single divine nature that is seen, subsisting in three hypostases, but the concrete Person who possesses the divine nature unoriginately . . . . " (p. 146).

98. "On the Theology of the Incarnation," *Theological Investigations,* IV, p. 106; Rahner's significant teaching here that *only* the Son could have become incarnate seems to me to be only in verbal disagreement with St. Thomas' speculations about abstract possibilities (cf. *Summa Theol.,* IIIa, q. 3, a. 5).

99. *The Trinity* (New York: Herder and Herder, 1970), transl. by Joseph Donceel, p. 86 (italics supplied).

100. "It would be more biblical and Greek to start from the one absolutely unoriginated God, who is still the Father, even when it is not yet known that he is the Begetter and Spirator, because he is known as the unoriginated hypostasis, who may not be thought of *positively* as 'absolute,' even when he is not yet known expressly as relative": "Remarks

on the Dogmatic Treatise 'De Trinitate,'" *Theological Investigations*, IV, p. 84.

101. "Thus the free decision is essentially a disposal of himself made by man . . . the free decision also tends essentially to shape and modify this whole essence arising from the centre of the person": "Theological Concept of Concupiscentia," *Theological Investigations*, I, p. 362.

102. Rahner obviously acknowledges that these concepts can be used to elaborate our understanding of the Trinity and the Incarnation only as they undergo alteration. As Cornelius Ernst observes in a translator's note (to the above citation), Rahner's concepts "are not wholly akin to the Scholastic tradition" and "cannot be avoided" (p. 363). They may indeed be richer than the traditional nature-person categories in which the existential dimension of personality was neglected. All that is pointed out here is that these newer concepts cannot stand by themselves, but need to be balanced off by a dialectical play with other conceptual schemas, lest they give rise to the idea of a finite God who is in process.

103. "Scholastic Concept of Uncreated Grace," *Theological Investigations*, I, pp. 343-346. For a critique of the position represented in the above article, see W. J. Hill, O.P., "Uncreated Grace: A Critique of Karl Rahner," *The Thomist*, April, July and October 1963 (also published in book form as *Vatican II: The Theological Dimension*).

104. *Ibid.*, p. 345.

105. *Summa Theol.*, I, q. 43, esp. a. 3. St. Thomas' teaching here can be presented as a quasi-formal causality but solely in the intentional order, whereas, Rahner understands such causality as operative in the entitative order.

106. *The Trinity*, p. 86. Note no. 9.

107. It should be noted here that when an appropriation is taken formally, i.e., considering not merely *what* is appropriated but the precise affinity on which basis the appropriation is made, it is proper and cannot be so used of the other two Persons.

108. *The Trinity*; this is a translation published in 1970 of *Mysterium Salutis*, vol. 2, chap. 5 (ed. by J. Feiner and M. Löhrer; Einsiedeln: Benziger Verlag) originally published in 1967.

109. John A. T. Robinson, "The Debate Continues," in *The Honest To God Debate*, ed. D. L. Edwards (Westminster Press: Philadelphia, 1963), pp. 254-256.

110. *Dieu et l'homme*, Approches Théologiques, 2, transl. P. Bourgy (Bruxelles: Editions du Cep, 1965), pp. 150-152; English transl. by E. Fitzgerald and P. Tomlinson, *God and Man* (New York: Sheed and Ward, 1969), pp. 168-169.

111. Rahner himself admits as much: "Yet the word 'person' hap-

pens to be there, it has been consecrated by the use of more than 1500 years, and there is no really better word, which can be understood by all and would give rise to fewer misunderstandings." *The Trinity,* p. 44. In spite of this he later suggests substituting "distinct manner of subsisting" for the "modern, unavoidably burdened word 'person' " *(Op. cit.,* p. 112) — but it is difficult to see in this any gain at all.

112. *Tractatus Logico-Philosophicus,* 5.631 - 5.641. Wittgenstein is not denying that the I, or person, is a center of consciousness that structures to some degree "the world," i.e., that personal consciousness is process. What he intends to say is that such process is not ultimately a psychological one but an ontological one.

113. *Summa Theol.,* I, q. 29, a. 4 and q. 28, a. 2.

114. *In Ia.,* q. 39, a. 1, no. VII.

115. *In Ia.,* q. 3, a. 3; q. 29; *In IIa,* q. 4, a. 2; *In De Ente et Essentia,* cap. V, q. 9. For an exposition of Cajetan's position and a comparison with that of Capreolus, cf. Thomas U. Mullaney, O.P., "Created Personality: The Unity of Thomistic Tradition," *New Scholasticism,* XXIX, 4, Oct. 1955, pp. 369-402.

116. *In I Sent.,* d. 4, q. II, a. 1, and *In III* Sent., d. 5, q. III, a. 3. These can be found in the Paban-Peques edition of Capreolus' *Defensiones Theologiae,* Vol. I, p. 228 ff., and vol. V, p. 100 ff., respectively.

117. This transposition to an ontology of existence is no denial of a more basic ontology of being; it rather suggests that the latter indigenously issues in the former and retains its ground there.

# INDEX OF PROPER NAMES

275

# INDEX OF SUBJECTS

279

280

116, 119, 121, 147, 186, 241

appropriation
    25, 212, 272
    theory of 211
*a priori*
    3, 55, 67, 68, 69, 71, 75, 82,
        84, 107, 113, 128, 177
Arabian thinkers
    125
Arabic
    125
Aristotelian
    6, 34, 124, 153, 251, 256
Aristotelian-Thomistic synthesis
    67
Aristotle's *Metaphysics*
    124
assent
    notional 79
    real 79
atheism
    173
atheistic
    164, 229
attributes of God, divine
    23, 33, 46, 65, 77, 187, 267,
        268
*attributio*
    124
attribution
    21, 53, 127, 130, 136, 246, 254
    intrinsic 94
*Augenblick*
    197
Augustinian ( -ism )
    1, 76, 126
authentic
    54
authenticate ( -ion )
    55
authenticity
    57
Averroism
    4

# B

175
Barthian god
Beatific Vision
    87, 183, 219, 221, 236, 261
Begetter
    271
being
    concept of 135
    degrees of 134
    *per aliud* 133
    *per se* 133
    proportionate 84
Being (*Sein*)
    69, 121, 122, 137, 170, 172, 195,
        196, 204
    Absolute 62, 64, 83, 90, 95, 115,
        181, 186
    Expressive 207
    Divine 141, 205
    First 133
    Infinite 133, 194
    *per essentiam* 176
    Plenitude of 187
    Primal 133
    Primordial 207
    Pure 180
    Subsistent ii, 115, 133, 136, 176,
        263, 271
    Supreme 166, 170
    Uncaused 184
    Unitive 207
beings (*das Seiende*)
    69, 121, 170, 172
Being-Itself
    54, 170, 172, 235
belief
    34, 35, 36, 38, 66, 85, 102, 104,
        155, 159
believer, ( -s )
    148, 164, 165
Bible, the
    39, 100, 151, 199, 232

Biblical
46, 87, 150, 208, 214, 271
commentaries 2
concepts 45
God 175
literature 41
bodiliness
72, 80, 129, 202, 203, 250, 270
body-person (-'s)
202, 270

# C

Calvinist
40
care (*Sorge*)
202
Cartesian
62
*Cartesian Meditations*
202
Catholic, Catholicism
3, 34, 35, 39, 55, 58, 59, 109,
157, 189, 196, 201, 235
Catholic School of Tübingen
160
Catholic theologians
157
Catholic tradition
ii, 176
*causae ad invicem*
117
causal
136, 139
causality, (-ties)
52, 64, 97, 133, 134, 140, 192,
211, 235, 255
efficient 126, 183, 249, 256
exemplar 183
quasi-formal 192, 211, 269, 272
causation
efficient 194
cause
63, 88
efficient 269

Chalcedon (-ian)
44, 45, 102, 151, 203, 232
Chalcedonian Definition, the
233
Christ (-'s)
26, 40, 44, 45, 46, 57, 75, 79, 97,
105, 107, 157, 176, 182, 194,
201, 203, 205, 208, 227, 228,
231, 232, 233, 234
Christ Event, the
74, 156
Christian
101, 138, 149, 150, 152, 153,
157, 173, 174, 202, 204, 209
God 165, 166
Tradition 165, 166
Christianity
150, 247
Greek 208
Latin 208
Christological
44, 45, 87, 202, 234
Christology
56, 176, 203
Church, the
44, 76, 86, 100, 148, 157, 231
teaching authority of 152
cognition, (-al)
3, 185, 204
cognitive
iii, 51, 63, 69, 72, 83, 92, 144,
158, 186
*Collection* (Lonergan's)
80
*Commentary on Sentences of Peter
Lombard*
125, 126, 127, 132
communication
85, 86, 91, 98, 177, 192, 196,
270
communion
105, 106, 114, 136
conative
63, 68, 72, 76, 89, 101, 147,

282

284

286

287

288

Nicaea, Council of
87, 101, 102, 205
Nicene Christology
176
(*das*) *Nichts*
168, 170
Nineteenth Century
160
noetic (-s) (-ally)
2, 16, 17, 20, 36, 48, 61, 67, 69,
89, 109, 115, 118, 127, 129,
131, 135, 143, 149, 164, 187,
205, 267
Nominalism
1, 33, 59, 149
non-cognitive
45, 62, 63, 65
non-conceptual (-ly)
2, 9, 17, 25, 27, 65, 89, 90, 91,
93, 94, 96, 120, 139, 152, 161,
182, 222, 245
non-objectifying thinking
229
non-representational
139
non-symbolic
54, 151
nothingness
170
notion
82
notional
27, 47, 153, 157, 205, 255
noumenal
60, 62, 68, 96, 145
*Nouvelle Théologie*
55
numinous
147

O

object (-s)
5
formal 155, 245, 261

immanent 3, 13, 27
motive 245
of affirmation 65
of representation 65
phenomenal 68, 72
terminative 245
objectification, objectifying
33, 44, 48, 61, 63, 74, 89, 91,
108, 113, 152
objectified thinking
45
objective
64
dynamism of intellect 88
objectivity
59, 62, 70, 84, 114
objectivized
55
*oikonomia*
26, 205
Old Testament
78, 204, 205
omnipotence
104
omnipotent
54
ontic (-ally), (*existenziell*)
56, 92, 121, 122, 128, 137, 140,
146, 148, 172, 194, 202, 216
ontological (-ly), (*existenzial*)
50, 51, 52, 53, 54, 55, 56, 57,
61, 62, 63, 69, 70, 98, 105,
121, 122, 124, 130, 132, 135,
137, 143, 146, 148, 150, 172,
177, 179, 182, 184, 195, 202,
225, 235, 258, 264, 271, 273
ontological argument, the
167, 263-264
ontological difference (Heidegger)
52, 55, 121, 171
ontologism
59
ontology (-gies)
53, 180, 181, 182, 202, 236

295

212
projective
63
proleptic
82
proof for God
Lonergan's 83
Rahner's 69
prophetic
35, 100
Prophets, the
32, 148, 228
*proportio*
124
proportion (-s)
125, 132, 133, 136, 140, 142,
143, 144, 183, 184, 185
*multa ad unum* 130
*unum ad alterum* 130
proportionality
94, 103, 118, 119, 122, 123, 124,
125, 126, 127, 128, 131, 132,
133, 140, 184, 185, 245, 246,
254
proper 182
proposition (-s) (-al)
36, 74, 85, 92
*prosopon*
101
Protestant
3, 35, 40, 43, 46, 157, 189
Protestantism
ii, 37, 151, 235
American 199
contemporary 31
Liberal 230
Providence, God's
77, 78
psychological
90, 124, 158
psycho-physicalism
5
Pure Act (*Actus Purus*)
172, 186, 199, 271

Pure Actuality
175, 177, 190
Purely Actual Understanding
ii

# Q

quality
124, 130
quantity
124, 130
quasi-transcendental
141
quidditative
111, 120
quiddity (-ties)
81, 82, 116, 117, 121, 183
*Quinque Viae* (St. Thomas)
90, 102, 247, 263

# R

Radical Theologians
201
*ratio, rationes*
119, 120, 123, 125, 126, 128,
129, 139, 140, 141, 142, 144,
183, 184, 187, 188, 191, 246
analogica 94
*concepta* 93, 185
*Dei* 186
generic and specific 259
*nominis* 128, 143
*significata* 21, 22, 119, 124, 183,
253
ratiocination
8, 14
rational (-istic)
33, 173
-appetite
63
rationalism
20, 35, 59, 158
realism
2, 109, 137, 145
conceptual 9

297

300